THE TREASURY OF
HUNTING
BY LARRY KOLLER

THE TREASURY OF
HUNTING
BY LARRY KOLLER

A RIDGE PRESS BOOK
——————
ODYSSEY PRESS,
NEW YORK

Editor in Chief: Jerry Mason
Editor: Adolph Suehsdorf
Art Director: Albert Squillace
Art Associate: David Namias
Associate Editor: Evelyn Hannon
Associate Editor: Moira Duggan
Associate Editor: Margaret Kane Geer
Picture Editor: Peter Lacey
Art Production: Doris Mullane

━━◄◉►━━

Prepared and produced by
The Ridge Press, Inc. Printed in
the United States of America
by Western Publishing Company, Inc.

─────────

This edition
prepared for distribution by
Crown Publishers, Inc.

CONTENTS

FOREWORD

Civilized man has lost the need but not the urge for the chase, the stalk, and the kill. The passion for hunting and its fulfillment match, and perhaps surpass, most forms of high excitement he has been able to devise for himself. Even though it has been a long time since anyone had to depend on his prowess in the field to assuage his hunger, the atavistic spirit burns brightly still. The soft, rustling sound of unseen whitetail in the offing still tickles the hunter's scalp and stirs faint reminders of the prod of necessity that underlay all hunting in the remote and forgotten past. It is not likely, as long as men are men, that hunting will diminish. ✍ Hunters, and particularly writers on hunting, seem constrained to justify the killing of animals in the name of sport. There will be no such justification in this book. Wildlife preys upon itself; the age-old law of fang and claw still prevails. The wilderness offers no Utopia to any of its inhabitants. Disease and starvation attack most of those escaping the predators. It is a rare specimen that lives long enough to die a natural death. Given these conditions, the contemporary hunter's toll is only a fraction of the total, and needs neither justification nor excuse. ✍ The philosophy of the hunter differs, of course, from that of the fisherman. Even though the hunter may be highly selective, and content with less than his legal allotment, his quest inevitably ends in the kill. The angler can choose to kill or release his catch. ✍ The traditions of hunting, and the hunter's personal code, dictate that game be taken in the spirit of fair play. Admittedly, this is a nicety of no concern to the animal pursued. But it should have meaning for the hunter; for to achieve any measure of honest satisfaction from the sport, he must meet the game on a common, relatively equal ground. This means pitting the human skills of woodcraft and of natural science, as well as marksmanship, against the animal's strong and clever instincts for survival. ✍ Theodore Roosevelt stated the case well in his *American Big Game Hunting* published in 1893. His "Credo of Fair Chase" set a pattern which is followed faithfully today by trophy hunters everywhere and is reflected in the present rulings of the Boone and Crockett Club: "The term 'Fair Chase' shall not be held to include killing bear, wolf, or cougar in traps, nor 'fire hunting,' nor 'crusting' moose, elk or deer in deep snow, nor killing game from a boat while it is swimming in the water, nor killing deer by any other method than *fair stalking* or *still hunting*." ✍ These rules, laid down some seventy years ago, are simple and succinct. They establish a level of conduct for practitioners of the sport, and no man who takes pride in being a hunter will violate them. He will honor the spirit as well as the letter—particularly in these days of unfair use of cars, airplanes, and other mechanical hunting aids not in existence when T. R. envisioned the "Fair Chase." ✍ A proper hunter has respect, and even affection, for the game he seeks. If he does not accord it dignity in life, as a trophy it becomes meaningless. Unfortunately, too many hunters still rate their results in the field by the weight of the game bag. This is a false standard that never again will be valid. It really perished with the outlawing of the market hunter. The chase is the thing. The game in hand is not much more than a reminder of the pleasurable effort expended on its taking. ✍ North America still has an abundance of game. On the whole, the supply is less than it was a century ago, but our increased knowledge of game management is providing a harvestable crop for millions of hunters. Available hunting areas have been shrinking since the turn of the century, but modern transportation is making it quick and easy for the hunter to gain access to game country where thousands of top trophy animals flourish. The amazing increase in the size of the Boone and Crockett *Big Game Records Book* during the past decade, even in the face of higher minimum standards, is a clue to the improved hunting conditions of the present time. ✍ Federal programs to increase recreational areas cannot fail to improve the hunter's lot by giving him more land to explore and, especially, more small game to shoot. The program will put the landowner in the business of being his own game manager, either in raising animals and birds for release, or in improving habitat, or both. ✍ Trophy hunters are becoming choosier. Only rarely are they guilty of promiscuous shooting. This is all to the good. It leaves fewer crippled animals. It leaves younger, more vigorous males to perpetuate their kind. This is not to say that a hunter should forego killing a legal animal, for only a relatively few men can afford the luxury of passing up a number of heads before taking the one that suits. Yet by elevating his own level of sport, the trophy hunter will inevitably improve the lot of those following him in the years to come. ✍ Beyond this, any hunter gains from the days he spends afield. His perception of wildlife becomes keener and more sensitive. He builds his knowledge of the game he seeks and immeasurably increases his chances for further success. ✍ And, finally, more than any other sportsman, he is given the opportunity to glory in the majestic forests, the high mountains, the fabulous wilderness territory that still abounds on the continent of North America. The taking of game may fulfill his passion for the chase, but the land where he seeks it is truly balm for his soul. ✍ LARRY KOLLER

The author wishes to make special acknowledgment of the co-operation of GUNS AND HUNTING *magazine, of which he is supervising editor, in acquiring certain pictures.*

AMERICAN
HUNTING
HISTORY
1

The bearded man, clad in filthy buckskins, sat in knee-deep prairie grass, his back resting against a gumbo outcropping. Before him stretched a great basin ending in grassy hills rolling up to the horizon. The basin's rich greenery was spotted, and in places almost obliterated, by the shaggy forms of great, hump-shouldered beasts, all munching busily on the high and abundant grass.

The man lifted a heavy, long-barreled Sharps rifle from the ground beside him, snicked down the finger lever, and shoved a long brass cartridge carrying a .45-caliber bullet into the chamber. He closed the lever and pulled back the huge side-hammer until it clicked into place. Slowly, quietly, he raised himself to a kneeling position, his elbow resting on his left kneecap, his left hand holding the fore-end of the gun. The barrel pointed at a dark clump of buffalo about a hundred yards away.

A bull moved a few yards away from the herd. He peered briefly and incuriously at the bearded man, then lowered his head to crop a mouthful of grama grass. Even as he munched, a puff of white smoke spurted from the big rifle. Dust flew from the buff's shoulder as 550 grains of lead plunked into his body. He humped his withers still higher, lurched, took three faltering steps, then tumbled heavily on his side. His forelegs jutted rigidly from his body. A gush of blood from his nostrils mingled with the green grass still clutched in his jaws. And so he died.

A cow detached herself from the herd to sniff at the carcass, but turned back, unperturbed, to continue feeding. The bearded man was again squinting over his Sharps. Again came the spurt of smoke and the dull plunk of a bullet hitting solid meat. The cow gave a hoarse grunt, ran a few steps toward the open prairie, then stopped, shook her head, and fell. Before she was still, the hunter had ejected the fired case from the Sharps, reloaded, and picked another target animal from the edge of the herd.

Within an hour, several dozen buffalo carcasses were strewn across the prairie basin. It was almost too easy. The lethargic buffalo were not alarmed either by the

man or his death-dealing weapon, and the slaughter stopped only when the grazing herd moved out of range. The hunter left his stand after picking up his empty brass cases, his cleaning rod, and water jug. Before he reached his saddle horse, tied out of sight in a coulee, the skinner's wagon rumbled up from the valley to begin the chore of flaying the dead buffalo. The hunter mounted his horse to look for another stand and another herd, so the slaughter and the skinning could continue.

The relentless destruction of the American bison, or buffalo, is the most spectacular example of wanton waste of a game resource in American history. Although the millions of animals that were slaughtered were ostensibly killed for reasons of profit—and a paltry profit it was—the decimation of the herds was more truly related to the politics and economics of Western expansion. As long as buffalo were still reasonably abundant, Western lands could not be claimed and farmed. Where the buffalo roamed, the Indian followed, living comfortably—by his standards—on the great herds. The carbines of the U.S. cavalry, the Henrys, Sharpses, and Remingtons of the cattlemen and homesteaders could not keep the Indian in check. But he could be starved out if the buffalo were eliminated.

At their peak, the herds of the Great Plains are estimated to have totaled not less than 60,000,000 animals. Yet it took only about fifty years to liquidate them. The killing began quietly enough with the entry of the mountain men into the Northwest, following the trail blazed by Lewis and Clark. They trapped beaver and lived off the land.

It was a land rich in game, and the most rewarding animal of all was the buffalo. The newcomers quickly learned from the Indian that a man could eat his fill of buff meat day after day and never tire of it. The fat, protein-rich flesh kept him healthy and vigorous —as it did the Indian. Best of all, powder and ball could be conserved; usually a single ball from a big-bore muzzle-loader could knock down a half ton of meat.

But the superabundance of buffalo provided by prodigal nature made the white trappers choosy. They took only the choice parts: the "bass," or hump, just in

Preceding pages: Hunters bag their deer from canoe, a favored
method of getting venison in early days.
Mounted Indian (right) gathered his buffalo meat and
hides with bow and lance. Indians usually killed game only as necessary,
had small part in extermination of herds.

front of the shoulders; the hump ribs; the "fleece," a fat portion covering the ribs; and usually the tongue—all of which could be cut off or out with a minimum of effort. The rest of the huge carcass was left for the coyotes and other carrion eaters.

Soon, as civilization moved westward, these choice parts became marketable. A trade in buff meat developed and grew, although it did not even begin to dent the supply until the 1850's. The buffalo's high replacement factor was more than equal to the demand.

The railroad drive across the plains after the Civil War, however, was the beginning of the end. The many thousands of laborers working in the railways' construction gangs were fed off the herds. Hundreds of hunters, among them Kit Carson, undertook to supply the meat.

But there was a market for more than meat. The affluent East decided that the warmest and most luxuriant carriage robes it could command were buffalo hides. Out-of-work war veterans carrying big Sharpses and Remingtons moved West to capitalize on the fad.

The Southern herd went first. Tongues, hides, and bones were funneled East by way of the Kansas-Pacific and Atchison, Topeka & Santa Fe railroads. The last-known survivor was killed west of Dodge City in 1879.

The Northern herd hung on a bit longer. The last of it was a harried band of 10,000 animals on the Cannon Ball River in North Dakota. In 1883, Cree Indians

and white hunters moved in, guarded the water holes and built fires along the riverbanks to keep the parched beasts from quenching their thirst. Hemmed in and waterless, the herd was polished off in about two months. Except for a few stragglers, these were the last of the uncounted millions of American buffalo.

Where were the sportsmen and conservationists while all this was going on? The answer is that they were aroused and active, for there was a great deal of sports shooting of buffalo, as well as utilitarian slaughter. As early as 1874 the sportsmen forced a control bill through Congress making it illegal for anyone but an Indian to kill a female bison and restricting the killing of bulls to those specifically needed for food or the market. The bill, having successfully passed both houses, went to President Ulysses S. Grant for signature.

Grant consulted his army chiefs, among whom was the redoubtable Phil Sheridan, and found them agreed

First known picture of hunting in America
(left) gave a distorted notion of the abundance of game
in colonial times. Below: Early American
wild-fowler armed with flintlock usually took his
ducks sitting, rather than on the wing.

that as long as there were buffalo the Indians would continue to inhabit the plains and impede settlement of the Great West. Grant pigeonholed the bill. The buffalo was doomed—and the Indian with it.

Sentimentalists have bemoaned the fate of the buffalo for almost a century now, but it is unlikely that the animal could have been preserved in its native habitat under any circumstances. The slower and less spectacular, but no less inexorable, transformation of the prairies to agricultural land eventually would have eradicated the buffalo even without the depredations of the market and hide hunters. The lesson to be learned from the virtual extinction of the animal is that economics, politics, avarice, and what we like to call the progress of civilization are the limiting factors in preserving wild game—whatever the species.

The Indian has been held up as a prime example of the true conservationist who took no more than he

15

Tradition of "shooting flying" began with the gentry.
Shooters hunting woodcock with pointers (top) and rail (below) are using
smoothbore flintlocks. Bottom: Hudson River long fowler.

needed, who utilized every scrap of every animal or bird he killed. This is an idealistic view. The Indian was a conservationist by circumstance, not choice. His weapons and his techniques limited his ability to destroy game. In the light of present ecological knowledge, it also is clear that in a well-preserved natural environment, such as the Plains Indian enjoyed, the enormous capability of wild life to replace itself went far beyond the Indian's ability to limit it.

Before the Spaniards brought the horse to the Western plains, the Indian hunted on foot. He stalked animals and managed to kill enough to maintain life if he used the carcass to the fullest extent—meat, hide, sinew, bone.

Horses gave the Indian mobility and power. With them he could stampede herds over cliffs or into strong corrals for close-range slaughter. As food gathering became easier and meat more plentiful, the Indian grew wasteful, and like the white man of later times picked only the choice parts. George Catlin, the noted illustrator of the West, tells of a Sioux hunting party which slaughtered fourteen hundred buffalo for their tongues alone, since the village already was stocked with meat.

It seems to be true that the Indian could be a prodigious eater of buffalo meat, as well. Colonel R. I. Dodge reported that an Indian could consume as much as fifteen pounds in the course of a long night of feasting. General Sully, after wiping out a Sioux village of four hundred lodges in September, 1863, discovered a store of about half a million pounds of dried buffalo meat—apparently the winter supply. Even so, that is a lot of meat for four hundred families, and represents a lot of killing.

Despite such waste, however, the take of the Plains Indians could not and did not surpass the replacement factor of the buffalo. It took the white man, armed with powerful rifles and the skill to use them in a sustained program of destruction to do this.

It is not his only triumph. The civilized white man has achieved the same results on many other types of wildlife by destroying their habitats. This method is far more deadly than the gun. We now know that where

game is protected by laws which permit a reasonable annual harvest by hunting, and where food and cover remain at a high level, species not only survive but steadily increase. The key factor is the preservation or improvement of habitat. If this can be done, the normal capacity of game to propagate itself will insure a harvestable crop.

There is no question that the first explorers of America found a teeming game population. In the East and South, the first white Americans found the Indians almost wholly dependent on deer and wild turkey for meat. The deer, furthermore, provided hide for garments and moccasins, antlers and bones for tools. Hides also were used for barter, and the deer symbol was paramount in many tribal rites.

Clever as the Indian might be, however, stalking with the bow and arrow did not produce deer in large quantities. Other methods had to be devised. Samuel de Champlain reported in considerable detail a deer drive by Indians in 1615. Four or five hundred savages lined up in the woods, and with great yelling and clapping pushed the deer toward a river, where other Indians waited in canoes. The deer driven into the water were at the mercy of the Indian bows and lances. Another kind of drive required a lot more labor, but was equally successful. This was constructing a triangular stockade of heavy saplings and driving the deer into it to be dispatched with lances. Snares, pits, and deadfalls also contributed to the deer take.

The colonials were quick to take advantage of the game supply, particularly deer and turkey. It is certain that many of the early settlements would have been doomed—perhaps not even started—if it had not been for the availability of game. It took years to clear land and get regular crop returns; game and fish were an immediately available harvest. In 1694, the Jamestown colony recorded that "A good woodsman will keep a house in venison, for there are an abundance of brave red deer."

Venison and deer hides assumed economic importance early in the colonies. Money was scarce and hides were a common means of exchange. Great quantities of them 17 were shipped back to England. In the twenty years prior to the Revolution, customs records show that 2,600,000 pounds of hides (from some 600,000 deer) were shipped from Savannah, Georgia, alone.

The commercial traffic in hides from New England quickly decimated the deer population. Rhode Island established the first closed season in 1646, Connecticut the second in 1698. Massachusetts followed a short time later. The New York legislature passed hunting restrictions as early as 1629. At the start of the Revolution, most colonies had restrictions of one kind or another on deer. Some of these were repealed when the colonies became states, but usually new laws were written or the previous ones re-enacted. The birth of conservation was at hand.

The deer of the West and the Midwest did not feel the pinch of commercialism until a much later date. But it did not take the market hunter long to follow the footsteps of the pioneers and take advantage of the local demand for venison and the Eastern market for hides. Hundreds of thousands of deer were killed in the Midwest for their "saddles" alone. Lumber camps springing up in the Northern states were a steady market for meat. Many camps hired professional deer hunters to

18

Antlers of elk in foreground (above) are in early stages of growth. Elk fleeing hunters in background has full headgear. Jacklighters (right) used torch to rivet deer's attention, and rifle like Kentucky flintlock (top).

assure themselves an adequate supply for the table.

The middle years of the nineteenth century drained the country of its deer. By 1900, they were at a low ebb. The numbers killed for profit were astronomical, but not to be doubted. The slaughter is a matter of record. For example, one of the first of the wealthy Texans, George Barnard by name, laid the foundation of his fortune not in oil, but in animal skins, mostly deer. In the decade between 1844 and 1853, he shipped from his trading house near Waco not less than 75,000 deerskins.

In terms of our present standards, the hunting of game prior to 1900 can hardly be viewed as sport. Deer were trailed by dog packs and driven into water for easy killings. They were shot from canoes at night while transfixed by a jacklight. They were chased through deep snow and knocked in the head with axes as they wallowed helplessly in the drifts. Every conceivable trick of mass killing was used. Even where such practices had been outlawed, it made little difference. Game wardens were few, and restrictive laws were regarded as a nuisance, if not a menace, to an honest market hunter's livelihood.

Originally, the American deer population was vast. Naturalist Ernest Thompson Seton estimated that 10,-

19

000,000 mule deer and 40,000,000 whitetails lived on the North American continent when Columbus first sighted San Salvador. By 1908, Seton felt, the population of both species was down to 500,000. By 1850 deer had been virtually exterminated in Connecticut. By 1880 they were almost unknown in Pennsylvania.

Seton's estimate of deer abundance seems generous in the light of current knowledge of deer requirements. An enormous area of the United States was covered with virgin timber in the eighteenth and nineteenth centuries, and this is by no means good whitetail habitat. The best range was in the river valleys, where low growth provided good feed. Since these valleys also were the settlers' and the Indians' choice for homesites, it can be assumed that the concentration of deer within sight of man led to exaggerated estimates of their total number throughout the region.

The improvement of deer habitat came with the clearing of land for farms, the tremendous waves of timber cutting, and the increase in forest fires—all of which created new, second-growth brush land and edge cover, the ideal deer range.

Yet the chance combination of circumstances that had improved the deer's environment, and thus their ability to reproduce, also left them vulnerable to the hunter. The improvement of habitat could not keep pace with the destructive elements threatening the deer's survival.

Rigid restrictions, relentlessly applied, were the only hope of saving the deer of America. Sportsmen, seeing their favorite big-game animal following the buffalo into oblivion, put pressure on legislatures and game commissions to save it.

The solution was not readily apparent. Management of deer is a complicated problem, because the animal is a choosy feeder and can starve in a timbered area that looks to a layman like a fertile feeding ground. In any case, the first efforts at control were to reduce the length of seasons and then to limit the take. After some years of experimentation, the heart of the problem was revealed: the females had to be protected.

Within a relatively few years the "buck law" was enacted almost universally. California was first, in 1901, then Pennsylvania in 1907, New York in 1912, Michigan in 1921, and so on. The herds began to rebuild and were bolstered by the importation of new stock to special deer-preserve areas. These deer were kept under rigid observation and complete protection until they were well established. They were then turned loose to intermingle with native stock. Within thirty years, the herds were flourishing.

Now, however, conditions in the North and East changed again. There was a reduction in the cutting of hardwoods for timber, sulphuric acid, and alcohol. Less hemlock was cut for tanbark. And improved fire control

*Search for valuable beaver fur used in 19th-century
men's hats led to opening of great Northwest Territory. Mountain
men, like hunters in Currier & Ives lithograph
(bottom), lived off the land as they traveled. Pressure by
trappers and explorers for more firepower
led to development of sixteen-shot, .44-caliber Henry rifle
(below), ancestor of the famous Winchester.*

enabled second-growth hardwood to quickly reach sapling size. In short, the hardwoods outgrew the stage at which they provided browse for deer, but were not yet mature enough to produce mast (nuts) for the autumn fattening that carries healthy deer through a hard winter. This subtle change in the deer's food supply was crucial for the now-burgeoning herds. The deer moved out to edge growth and attacked the farmer's crops. But even this was not enough. The pendulum of plenty had swung the other way.

For at least two decades now in the East, North, and Northeast, we have been suffering from an abundance of deer living in lands that can ill support them. Proof of this can be seen in the small body-size and puny antler growth which now characterize the animals taken in much of today's deer country.

Curiously, the deer problem is not now a biological one entirely. Psychology—human psychology—has entered the picture. When the buck laws were first enacted, veteran deer hunters threw up their hands in despair. Shooting bucks exclusively was no way to hunt deer, they complained. You had to take any animals you saw if you wanted to get deer. But these old-timers are now long gone, and the new crop of veterans accepts the buck laws completely. It has been brainwashed into believing that you can't have deer unless you save the does.

Well, we have saved the does and the fawns from the hunter only to have them die a lingering death in the middle of winter. No one gains from this except the scavengers.

Pennsylvania's record of deer management is a case in point. Starting with almost nothing in the early 1900's, the state began to import deer to serve as the nucleus of a herd. In the rich, second-growth areas of the state, the herds, spurred by a policy of harvesting bucks only, grew apace. Year after year, throughout the 1920's, Pennsylvania reported the biggest kill of any state in the Union.

It could not last. Brush grew into saplings and saplings into trees. No one cut new clearings and forest fires were held to a minimum. With each succeeding generation the deer grew thinner, smaller, and hungrier. The "deer line"—a complete cleaning out of vegetation as high as the deer could reach—was a common sight in

22

Above: Before cartridge arms were developed,
birdshooters were hampered by slow, tedious chore of recharging their
muzzle-loaders. Opposite page: Despite picture's
title, Southern gunner is obviously shooting bobwhite quail
from a rising covey over brace of pointing setters.

PARTRIDGE SHOOTING.

the forests and woodlands. There was a serious increase in agricultural damage as the deer left the woods and swarmed over the farmers' fields in search of food. In fourteen years the game commission spent $91,000 to build protective fences, and finally had to permit farmers to kill deer to protect their crops. Thousands were wiped out in off-seasons, but it was no more than a stopgap measure that missed the main problem.

The state took the ultimate step in 1923, when it opened the season on antler-less deer. Presumably this meant does, although there was nothing in the ordinance that distinguished between the sexes.

This was not done without resistance from sportsmen, but the state persisted. Similar seasons were declared from time to time during the next twenty-five years. Up to 150,000 animals were reported killed each of these years, with probably as many as another 50,000 killed and unreported.

Yet the taking of more than 1,000,000 deer in this period did not relieve the pressure. Each year of a heavy take of does was followed by the complaints of sportsmen that the herd had been wiped out. The buck law would be re-enacted and enforced until the herd again built up to intolerable size, and then the "antlerless deer" law would be dusted off and put into effect in a vain attempt to stem the tide.

This on-again, off-again policy is no reflection on the fine work of the state's game commission. The commission is subject to the whims of the license-buying hunter, who often is ignorant of game management and still psychologically entranced by the buck law.

The state has tried to open up new feeding areas by selling off timber-cutting rights at low prices and by bulldozing large sections to encourage new growth. But in the face of a hungry deer population eating several pounds of vegetation per animal per day, the program cannot keep up with the demand.

Pennsylvania's deer are becoming smaller each year. 23

THE LIFE OF A HUNTER.

24

*Predatory mountain lion (top) destroyed many sheep and
cattle in early ranching days, required government control. Attack
by whitetail buck (above) is highly unlikely
incident in any hunter's life. Remington rolling-block, single-shot rifle (right)
was well regarded by post-Civil War hunters.*

Legal bucks seldom scale more than 110 pounds dressed. Does weigh a scant seventy. This is tragic when you consider that under good feeding conditions a northern whitetail buck carrying his first eight-point rack will dress out to at least 150 pounds.

Meanwhile, the deer range continues to dwindle. Where new feed is to come from, no one seems to know. But the hunter who complains so bitterly about the scarcity of bucks and shootable racks also insists on giving complete protection to the does.

In critical areas—and these are far more widespread than is generally realized or acknowledged by the hunting public—deer populations that existed twenty or thirty years ago will never be seen again. If hardwood timber were to be cut on a commercial scale once more, there might be a chance, but there is no evidence that this is about to happen. Even if deer could be magically removed from the critical feeding areas, it very likely would take a decade to restore the vegetation to the level necessary to support a minimum of deer.

This, of course, becomes a problem beyond the jurisdiction of game-management officials. Once again it is the economics of civilization that is tilting the scales against the game.

Fortunately, there still is fine whitetail deer hunting in many other parts of North America. Maine, for example, has both a logical approach to the deer problem and one of the best-balanced herds in the United States. Annually it provides a harvest of some 50,000 choice whitetails. Michigan also has excellent deer hunting, as does Wisconsin. Both states have adopted realistic programs of deer reduction regardless of sex, and have made them stick.

Some of the finest heads on the continent are now being taken in the Canadian provinces of Alberta, Saskatchewan, Manitoba, and New Brunswick, where current "either-sex" laws keep the herds in balance, with an assist from nature.

The Western mule deer also suffered the depredations of the market shooter, who preceded the steamboat on the upper Missouri. The hunter killed the deer and dragged it to the shore, where it was picked up as the boat made its passage up or down river.

The traffic in hides was fully as vigorous in the West as in the East. Buffalo hunting took precedence, but with the buff gone the market shooters turned quickly to deer, antelope, and elk to keep their rifles busy. The little Arizona whitetail, now known as the Coues deer, furnished the meat for the U.S. army's Indian campaigns of the 1890's. Silver City, New Mexico, also provided a steady market for deer during the early mining days in that area.

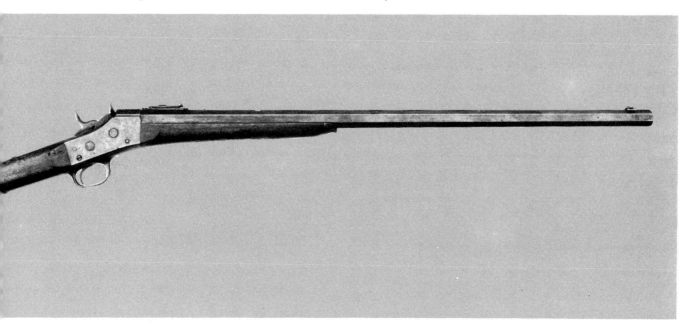

Eventually the mule deer were driven into the mountains, west of their normal plains habitat, where they may be found today. Their original terrain has been taken over by whitetails.

Increased protection of the mule deer and effective management practices of Western game commissions, fortunate enough to have a freer hand than their colleagues east of the Mississippi, have brought the big gray deer back in startling numbers. Something approaching 500,000 mulies are harvested each year in the Rocky Mountain states. More mule deer, by far, are killed each year than any other Western big-game animal. And the harvest increases every season.

Like the mule deer, the Western pronghorn did not feel excessive hunting pressure until after the passing of the buffalo. But the same reasons of land economy that made the buffalo unwelcome on grainfields and cattle ranches affected the antelope. Landowners didn't want them around eating grain or grass that could support steers. Even though the modest horns were not then considered to be in the trophy class, and their meat was less desirable for market than that of other game, the speedy little animals were hunted and killed without quarter. A conservative estimate of the pronghorn population in 1800 was 40,000,000 head. By 1908, Dr. T. S. Palmer, of the Biological Survey, calculated that the total herd had been reduced to fewer than 30,000 animals.

In the 1920's a concerted program to restore the pronghorn began. Legal hunting of the animal had been halted in 1914, but the herd continued to shrink. The Biological Survey then conducted a sustained program of predator control to cut back the number of coyotes and bobcats preying on pronghorn kids. A population increase was noted, but no significant rise occurred until 1937, when Paul Russell, of the New Mexico Game Department, conceived a plan for trapping and transplanting pronghorns to better environments.

Russell, an experienced trapper of wild horses, used cars and horses to drive the adult pronghorns into a cage similar to the bag-shaped fyke net used by fishermen. The procedure worked, and the first catches were released on historic antelope ranges where the animals had not been seen in years. By 1942, Russell was using small aircraft to herd and drive the animals into his traps, a method now widely employed in all Western states for redistribution of pronghorns.

Russell's pioneer antelope trapping made game-conservation history. Within a few years nucleus herds swelled to harvestable size. By 1941, open seasons on pronghorn were declared in some areas, and within a dozen years hunting was permitted in fourteen states. The reported continental kill (including two Canadian provinces) in 1957 was 53,987, a figure which has been topped several times subsequently. The pronghorn seems destined to provide much sport for hunters in future years throughout the West.

The buffalo, generally considered a Western animal, also populated the East in colonial days. The plains of western and central New York teemed with the great beasts, and as late as 1790 a herd of some 10,000 animals was massacred near Syracuse. Thousands lived in the forests of Pennsylvania during the Revolutionary War, but by 1800 the herds were killed off. The last stragglers survived until 1810.

The same sad tale can be told of Eastern and Northeastern moose. Once numerous in New England, New York, and as far south as central Pennsylvania, the moose

27

*Wild turkey (top) was a prolific and vulnerable game bird
for colonial hunters throughout the East, was more valued in some areas
than deer. Early wild-fowlers (above) shot their
mallards and other water birds with double-barreled hammer shotguns,
like Model 1882 Remington breechloader (top).*

gradually disappeared under the pressure of progress. Perhaps the last ones were killed in the Adirondacks in the 1860's. The moose had a refuge, however, in the wilds of Canada, where they are found in huntable numbers today.

Among big-game animals, the elk—or wapiti—has been driven farther from his native habitat than any other species. At one time elk were common in New York State, and were still recorded there in 1842, although by then they were becoming rare. They disappeared from the Adirondack area around 1847 and made their last Eastern stand in the Pennsylvania mountains. The final kill, as far as is known, was made in 1877 by one John Decker.

In the Allegheny Mountains of the South, the big deer held out longer against the hunter's rifle. The last wild herd was reported near Nashville, Tennessee, and its remnants were protected on the estate of General William H. Jackson. The last bitter stand of the Eastern elk was in Missouri, in 1898; not one specimen was preserved for posterity. Oklahoma's last was killed in 1891.

The elk of the West retreated before the onslaught of meat, hide, and tooth hunters into the remote fastnesses of the high Rockies. There they remain today, though certainly in no danger of extinction. This is one of the great trophy animals and is carefully husbanded. Elk herds are growing in most of the Western mountain states and well up into Canada. Recent estimates place the total United States crop at something over 300,000 animals, with open seasons in a dozen Western states. Wyoming and Montana actually have over-population problems as a result of too many elk crowding in on restricted winter range. The situation parallels that of the whitetail in the East, but is being combated by intelligent harvesting in critical areas.

The only limitations on elk stem from the permits granted to cattlemen and sheepmen to graze their stock in the National Forests in competition with the big

Three Winchester rifles which helped
"win the West," in order of their power and
development are (top to bottom): Model 1873 in .44
Winchester (.44/40), Model 1886 in
.45/70 Government, Model 1895 in .30/40 Krag.

Professional hunters demanded bigger rifles to
kill huge plains buffalo shown in Frederic Remington painting (below).
First of the big-bore muzzle-loaders was the
"Plains rifle" (top), an enlarged Kentucky with shorter barrel.
Big Sharps cartridge rifle (bottom) was a real killer.

game these areas theoretically were established to support. In recent years, ranchers have been complaining that elk are damaging the forage their livestock depend on. Demands are being made that elk—and deer—be killed off to make room for the stock. This has ever been the cry of the game-destroying commercial interests, but in this era of enlightened game management it seems unlikely that these threats to the game will succeed.

America's small game also has suffered depredations, although not to the extent of the big animals.

Wild turkey, for one. In the seventeenth and eighteenth centuries, the turkey was not only plentiful throughout the colonies, but relatively tame, and thus an easy target even for the inefficient firearms of the time. By the 1850's it was gone from New England, and by 1900 from all the northern states—although in all fairness it does not seem that shooting alone accounted for the bird's disappearance.

The economic factor that promoted the increase of whitetail deer—the cutting of big timber in the North and East—spelled the doom of the wild turkey. For this game bird requires a special forest habitat of mature, mast-bearing hardwood trees in an area fairly free of underbrush. These conditions are most generally found in the Southeast, although as mature, hardwood timber comes back in the North and Northeast, we are witnessing a resurgence of the turkey there. In northern Pennsylvania, where turkey had not been seen for some seventy-five years, there is now a fine harvestable crop. At least 70,000 hunters bag their single-bird season limit in Pennsylvania each year. New York State also has a short open season, and so does Montana. A conscientious

program of building up wild breeding stock and then releasing the flocks in a favorable environment is restoring the bird over much of its original range. If, in consequence, the change has switched the ecological advantage from whitetail deer to turkey, who can say that this is a bad bargain?

The depletion of native game can be blamed in large part on the market gunners; not, however, the reduction of wild fowl. It certainly is true that colonial America teemed with ducks and geese, that the migrating flocks would appear in great clouds, and that the flushing of birds from the water sounded like thunder. How many birds such a profusion represented, no one can say for sure. Probably it was somewhere in the billions.

The market gunner took his share, no doubt of that. He shot millions of birds each year, relentlessly, with shotguns, swivel guns, and punt guns, by baiting them into traps, by hitting them in both the spring and fall migrations. It was slaughter, but it is probably safe to say that it barely harvested the annual crop of birds. For with optimum nesting and feeding conditions, the broods of young were enormous.

As long as the birds were left alone on their nesting grounds, the supply of ducks was unlimited. But as early as 1849, when, with passage of the first Swamp Act, some 70,000,000 acres of northern breeding grounds were drained, the decline of the duck had begun. The cutting of hardwood timber in the North Central states decimated the tree-nesting species, among them the beautiful wood duck. The final blow came in the early years of the twentieth century with the draining of 100,000,000 acres of American wetland nesting areas to make way for

Preceding pages: North-country moose were traditionally hunted near, and often from, water—as is true today. Bighorn sheep (right) were relentlessly hunted for their delicious meat until they retired into remote country to escape extinction. Sharps-Borchardt single shot in .38 caliber (top) was favored for long-range plains shooting.

more wheat planting. Wetlands in Alberta and Saskatchewan also were converted to wheat growing. The loss in ducks and geese through these drainage programs is incalculable. Furthermore, the losses continue. Between 1943 and 1961, more than 1,000,000 acres of wetland were drained in the North Central states, most of it prime nesting area for wild fowl.

Probably the first step in wild-fowl restoration was taken in 1916, with the signing of a Migratory Bird Treaty between the United States and Canada, which established some semblance of order in the pattern of regulatory control. This also paved the way for a similar treaty with Mexico in 1936.

But laws and treaties alone cannot save waterfowl. The vast drought of the Thirties in central Canada and the United States converted once-rich areas into dust bowls barren of both grain and fowl. This natural phenomenon drove home the hard facts that North American game species are dependent for survival not merely on protection from the hunter's gun, but also on the establishment of proper habitat.

Ambitious game-management programs are under way, but the problems are tremendous. Experience has shown that, unless the habitat is suitable, measures such as restocking with native or imported birds are only wasteful. Due to natural attrition, the hoped-for results never materialize. Thus, gunners continue to be restricted to short seasons and meager bag limits.

Still, the Federal government is pushing its programs to provide proper ecological conditions for wild fowl. It continues purchasing new nesting areas and restoring others with funds acquired from various allocations and

from the sale of Duck Stamps. These measures point to improvement in the future, although probably the far distant future.

As far as small game is concerned, the situation is bright. There is suitable habitat and therefore an abundance of upland birds and small furred game. The American sportsman must simply be content with less and must be willing to travel further than his forebears to get his limited bag. Of pleasure he will get the same.

The fluctuating conditions of the game have also been affected by the course of firearms development. Both rifles and shotguns have evolved from primitive forms into reliable and highly accurate weapons of versatility and sophistication. Cartridges likewise have increased in range, firepower, and consistency.

The first settlers were burdened with smoothbore muskets, either matchlocks or one of a variety of early flintlocks. In either case, they were hopelessly inaccurate arms, effective only at short range. Something better was needed, and early Pennsylvania gunsmiths provided it.

The specifications were those of the frontiersman, who traveled west looking for greener fields and more buckskins to tote back to Eastern markets. He needed a gun that would place a ball well at ranges up to a hundred yards, that could be loaded quickly and easily, and that did not require an enormous amount of powder and lead to be effective. Furthermore, since he traveled on foot, he could not afford to be unduly encumbered.

The Pennsylvania gunmakers, all of German origin, started with the Jaeger rifle, a heavy German hunting arm, which was slow to reload because the ball had to be pounded down into the bore with a stiff iron rod, but which was accurate.

Shortly before the Revolution began, a new design had been created. Its secret was the use of a patched ball—a round bullet of bore size that was wrapped in cloth or buckskin—which could be pushed quickly down the bore with a light wooden rod. The new rifle was made with a long barrel, which gave a higher velocity to the ball, and a bore somewhat smaller than that of the big Jaeger. Thus the graceful, lightweight "Kentucky" rifle was born, the gun that would be in every frontiersman's hands as he opened the way to the settlement of the Ohio and Mississippi valleys.

Across the Mississippi and up the wide Missouri, the adventurer found bigger game than he was used to back East: elk, buffalo, and the fierce grizzly. He needed more power—and at the same time, greater long-range accuracy for the smaller animals of the open plains and prairies. The Hawken brothers of St. Louis obliged by designing

34

Late 19th-century market hunters immediately took to Model 97 Winchester pump gun (top), first of a long line of successful magazine-repeating arms designed for Winchester by John M. Browning. Currier & Ives medallions show snipe and woodcock (left), canvasback and mallard (right).

the first of the "plains" rifles. It resembled the old reliable Kentucky, but had a larger bore, a shorter barrel, and a less-than-full-length stock. Packing a heavy ball, the plains rifle could drop a buffalo with one shot through the lungs. It was short enough to be handy for a mounted man—and most significantly, it had a percussion lock rather than a flintlock. The man who carried it in bad weather did not need to worry about ignition troubles.

Still, like all muzzle-loaders, it was slow to recharge and required that the hunter carry loose powder, a pouch of balls, and a supply of caps. The market hunter wanted faster firepower, preferably a self-contained cartridge carrying all components in one small package. Christian Sharps responded in 1848 with a breechloading rifle using a linen cartridge. It still had to be primed with a separate percussion cap, but represented a considerable advance. It also could be loaded with loose powder and ball if the supply of made-up loads should run out. By the early 1870's, the Sharps fired brass cartridges, in time to hasten the demise of the buffalo.

The clamor for more firepower created the Henry rifle, the gun that could be "loaded on Sunday and fired all week." It carried sixteen short, .44-rim-fire cartridges. It fell far short of either the plains rifles or the Sharpses, yet in its design was the basic idea of the still-to-come Winchester Model 1873, the famous hunter's and Indian fighter's rifle. The Winchester '73 had a notable career, although it never packed the power of the big single shots for buffalo or other large Western game.

It remained for the genius of John M. Browning to supply power in a fast-action repeater. His first such design was the Model 1876 lever action, firing the big .45-75 Winchester cartridge. This was followed shortly by the even more powerful Model 1886, which could be had

in a wide range of big black-powder loads, from the .45-70 Government Springfield to the .50-110. This was the ultimate in big-game repeaters until the advent of smokeless powder.

The last of Browning's famous lever-action rifles for big game was the Model 1895, designed for the new, higher-velocity, smokeless-powder cartridges: the new .30 Army, the .30 Springfield, and .303 British, all military cartridges that were quickly applied to killing big game. The 1895 was made in several other sporting calibers, including the giant .405 Winchester that President Theodore Roosevelt carried on his African safari.

These, then, were the guns that helped sweep the Western praires almost clean of big-game animals. Actually, the bulk of the game was gone even before the smokeless-powder era began.

35

Fortunately, with the change to higher-velocity, smaller-bore rifles capable of making cleaner kills at far longer ranges came the awareness that unless quick and concerted action were taken there would be few targets left for the fine new rifles.

We will never again see the passenger pigeon, whose migrating billions darkened the sun and broke the branches of trees by the sheer weight of their roosting numbers. We will not again have the chance to kill fifty ruffed grouse in a day. Nor should we care to. Instead, we will get our hunting pleasure from a brace of ringnecks or a pocketful of woodcock.

It is tragic that many hunters today rate their pleasure afield in terms of bag weight or limits filled. These are the ones who decry the scarcity of game and the dwindling of available hunting grounds.

Yet, as has been said, it is economic pressures that account for the shrinking of game habitat, for otherwise the quality of the existing range for small game is steadily improving. What the complaining hunters often forget is the fact that today a hundred men take to the field where a century ago only one stood.

Game management is greatly increasing the productive capacity of our available land. And perhaps the most encouraging aspect of recent research is that ways have been found to restore native game to at least part of its original range. This, I am sure most American sportsmen will agree, is a more satisfying development than attempting to establish exotics where they may not properly belong. Wild turkey, prairie chicken, mourning doves, and the wood duck are on the upswing. Geese, antelope, Rocky Mountain goat, and moose are providing a growing harvest each season. Deer we shall have, and rabbits, even if the small-game cycle of profusion and scarcity continues, as apparently it has forever. As far as hunting sport is concerned, I, for one, will settle for deer and rabbits, if need be.

Browning's first automatic (self-loading) shotgun, which appeared in early 1900's, quickly made the grade with wild-fowl market hunters. An extension magazine made it possible to load this gun with nine shells. Above: Shooting Canada geese, by Arthur Frost.

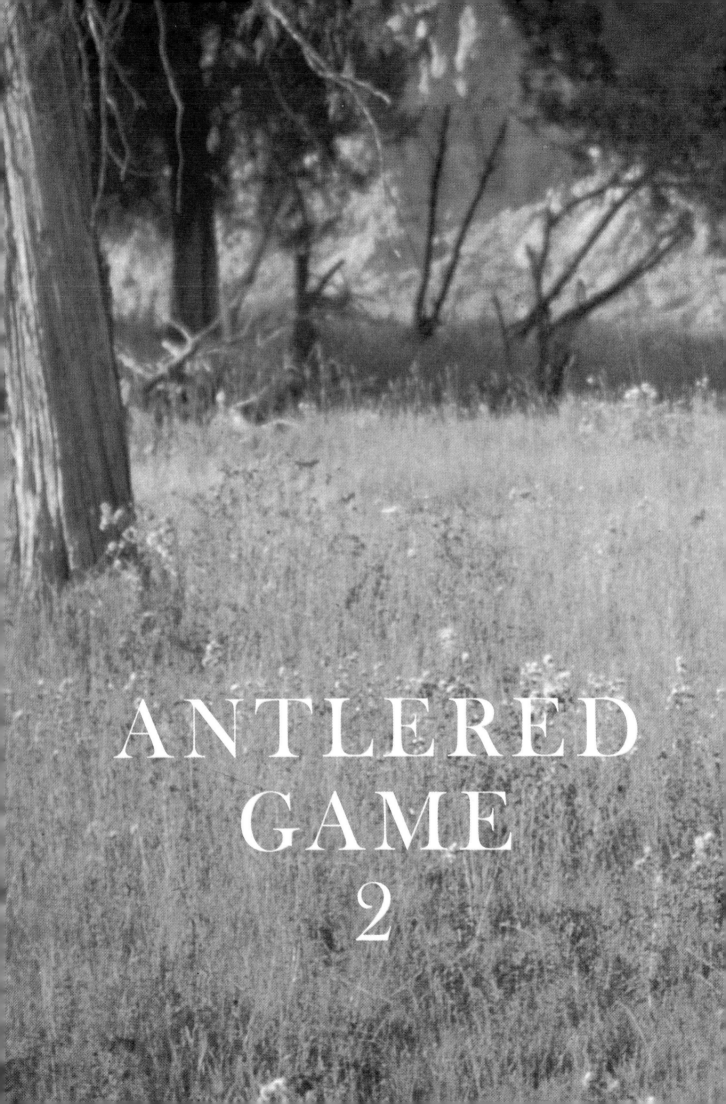

ANTLERED
GAME
2

WHITETAIL DEER

The first pink rays of a rising autumn sun bathed the tips of bare hardwoods on the crest of Beech Ridge. Below, at the foot of an unbroken slope of gaunt timber spanning a mile, the river moved briskly, almost inaudibly, in semidarkness, through its deep cleft in the forest hills. Wisps of vapor hung low over the riffles, adding to the thick coat of hoarfrost that whitened the alder brush along the banks. Slender rods of ice covered the tips of a willow branch dragging in the current; glassy ice crystals rimmed the bellies of midstream boulders. The air was sharp as only November air can be in the Catskills.

The whitetail buck had already left the valley floor with the first graying of dawn. His night had been a lusty one, spent with two fat does, one in the full heat of oestrus. He was weary enough to travel slowly up the long slope to his bedding ground near the crest of the ridge. Not that he ever moved anywhere without caution. He paused in each bit of thick cover to check the way ahead, testing the air with a moist, black muzzle and swinging his sensitive ears as though they were semaphores. He tucked them under the wide beams of his ten-point rack as his eyes swept the forest before him, then he swung them to the rear in twin arcs that could pick up flank sounds made by a whitefooted mouse rustling through the leaves fifty yards away. His eyes, he had long since learned, were untrustworthy without a confirming scent or sound. He saw his world only in tones of black, white, and gray. The still, scarlet-coated form of a hunter crouching against a tree bole might well be just another oddly shaped rock, unless a flicker of movement signaled danger.

Moving up through the massed, straight trunks of maple, oak, and yellow birch, all gray-black in the dimness of dawn, the deer's sleek tawny body brushed now and then through low laurel shrub and small winter beech. Only a faint *crush, crush,* as his polished black hoofs pierced crisp dead leaves, gave away his movements. He traveled a familiar path, indistinct to the eye of man, but one which he knew well after two years of almost daily use. It joined his bedding grounds in the scrub-oak thicket on Beech Ridge with his feeding grounds deep in the hollow of the valley.

A windless autumn dawn in the north country is steeped in stillness. The exuberant song birds are gone. The rustle of leaves, the sounds of grouse and squirrels stirring in the brush—the deer is tuned to this pitch, which would be barely audible to man. His footfalls are gentle and unhurried, furtive, cushioned with distrust, until the reality of danger destroys the pattern.

The whitetail buck, now well up the slope toward Beech Ridge, made no moves to alter the pervasive silence. He knew the sounds of danger and was forever ready to respond to them with quick, bounding action, but the season, so far, had been tranquil. Only a few minor contests with young bucks had ruffled him these past days. One thrust of his lowered ten-point head, backed by a rut-thickened neck, had been enough to send these less well-equipped invaders of his territory bouncing for cover.

But hunters had moved into his territory on this opening day of the season. A red-coated pair shuffled along the woodland road on the mountaintop in the gray of morning and had perched themselves against a big boulder on Beech Ridge. They munched breakfast doughnuts and waited for full light before separating to take their first stands near the scrub oak patches. A lone hunter moved along the river trail searching for signs of a crossing. He found a fresh hoofprint pointing down toward the river, deeply impressed in the black mud of an alder patch. Here the big buck had come off the ridge the night before on his way to the tryst with the does. The hunter decided to await his return. He picked a spot against a fallen log barely fifty yards from the crossing the buck had used, only moments before, on his way back up the ridge. The hunter settled himself, his back to the log, his eyes on the river, facing the direction from which the deer should come to him. By now the valley was light. The hunter could see the mist rise from the riffles. The kill was at hand.

40

Preceding pages: Magnificent royal bull elk, largest of
the world's round-horned deer, is rated by many hunters as top trophy
in America. Adult eight-point whitetail buck (right)
is also a trophy animal in these days of heavy hunting pressure.
Better heads than this are hard to come by.

The magic of the rising sun charged the forest with shimmering light, transforming it from a black mass to discernible, familiar patterns. Straight, smooth, gray beech trunks stood out amid the rough black boles of the oaks; loose curls of bark hanging from the yellow birches became visible and the slim gray birch trees gleamed white against the bulk of heavier hardwoods. The low outline of a deer's body could now be seen against the standing timber. The buck's pace slowed even more as he moved up the slope. He was within a hundred yards of his bedding grounds. He stopped in a small laurel clump, well screened except for the tips of

his antlers, and scanned the timber, peering through the slots of light now showing between the tree trunks.

As he watched, his ears moved slowly back, then swung quickly forward. He caught the faint rumble of deep male voices. Puzzled, he raised one forefoot in an imperious gesture and lifted his head a bit higher. His thickened neck made it impossible for him to raise it completely. As his eyes searched for the source of the low murmur, the strident squawk of a blue jay burst from the treetops about a hundred yards ahead. But he could not see the dim forms of the hunters lumped against the base of the boulder. The screen of timber

Only on rare occasions will a whitetail hunter get
such a clean shot at a mature buck. Normally, the whitetail stays
in heavy thicket and brush in daylight hours.
Watchful, waiting hunter (right), however, can count on getting
a fair shot when deer move to water or feeding grounds.

and undergrowth was too dense for his keen eye.

Alert now, the buck stood firm, ears cocked, a sculpture in brown and gray. The jay screeched again, then flew off along the ridge, his cry fading as he went. Only a nervous switch of the buck's white-fringed tail broke his stony pose, a sign that his hair-trigger reflexes were prepared for a sudden departure.

But the low rumble did not come again and the deer lowered his head to sniff the leaf-carpet at the edge of the laurel clump, searching for a clue. Again his tail flicked and he stepped forward gingerly, taking himself clear of the brush. As he moved, the Pow! Pow! of a

rifle burst from the valley wall on the other side of the river, directly behind the buck. He had withstood rifle fire twice before and made a clean escape each time, although the sharp crack of the bullets passing over his back had terrified him. That was man danger, but these distant reports were no more meaningful to him than the shattering violence of a thunderstorm in summer.

Nonetheless, the two rifle shots triggered the buck's desire to move into the shelter of his bedding ground thicket, and he moved warily through the big timber, a few steps at a time, stopping to scan the way ahead for strange objects or movement. He was within fifty yards 43 of the big boulder before danger, in the shape of a red-capped head, was suddenly visible above the profile of the rounded mass of gray stone.

One of the pair of hunters had decided to move to his stand along the ridge, spurred into action by the shots. He rose quickly to his feet, then shuffled a bit in the dead leaves before looking about. The rustle, like that of a squirrel searching for acorns, assailed the buck's ears a moment before the man's head came into view. For a few seconds in the still dim light the head might have been a fat-bellied porcupine clambering up on the boulder. And for those few seconds of security in the thick curtain of undergrowth, with only his crown of antlers showing, he paused to bring together his sharp senses of sight, hearing, and scent to choose between the inevitable enemy or the innocuous neighbor.

The hunter, momentarily foggy-eyed after looking down to check the safety of his rifle, could be forgiven for not spotting the wide spread of ivory-tipped antlers projecting above the brush, even though they gleamed in the morning light. And when his eyes could discern the familiar conformation of the whitetail's beams in the mass of bare branches, the buck had already committed himself to escape.

Before the hunter made his move, the deer's powerful hindquarters were bunched for a leap. On his slim forelegs, he pivoted to one side and crashed from the brush in a single great bound. Within two seconds he was bouncing down the slope, dipping and ducking through the timber as bullets from the rifles of both hunters rained wood chips and shreds of bark on his sleek back. They fired again and again, until they could no longer see the white beacon of his tail flashing through the trees.

The buck, unhurt but in a wild fright, drove headlong down the slope, clattering rocks and cracking dead limbs, pounding the firm earth with hoof-thumpings audible for a furlong. Yet his great terror could not completely overcome his habitual patterns. Normally, he used a different runway on his trips down to the valley. Now, in his first few moments of flight, he found himself covering his uphill route in reverse. This would not do. He swerved with a sudden violence to the right,

leaped across a tiny mountain rill, and found himself on the familiar downhill path. He would keep to it until he reached the safety of the alder thickets along the river.

Near the valley floor the lone hunter stirred into action. The wild rifle firing bouncing from the hills and rolling across the river caused the young man to rise quickly from his seat against the log. He about-faced in time to hear the clattering of rocks and dead wood on the slope above. With his heart pounding in his ears, he snapped off the safety and stood ready with his rifle for the arrival of a deer.

The buck's fright cooled somewhat as he neared the lower reaches of the slope. He had escaped unhit. He was on familiar ground. Once in the alder thickets he could hide safely, as he had done many times before when hunters prowled the ridges and shots thundered through the valley for days. He would never have achieved his size of antler spread if he had wandered around in the timber during daylight hours in those critical periods.

But now as he neared his sanctuary, the strong scent of man wafted up to him on the rising warm air of morning and filled him with new alarm. He stiffened his forelegs and dug his hind feet into the soft earth, bringing himself to a slipping, slithering halt. The man smell was powerful. The hunter had to be nearby, and the buck knew instantly he must change course along the slope, must circle to right or left to locate this new source of danger. Again he bunched his powerful leg muscles, pivoted on the slim forelegs. It was as he made his turn that the bullet took him fair in the shoulder. His body crumpled down the slope. He rolled, kicking and jerking, until he came up against a coarse-barked oak tree, with one set of antler tips buried in the leaf-mold and the long span of dead-white belly hair turned upward, toward the pink haze of the November sunrise.

———◆———

The fate of any whitetail deer in this nation is an unnatural death. In the case of bucks, violent death is

almost preordained. Does fare better at the hands of hunters, but many meet death by slow starvation. All deer, of course, are subject to nature's predations in a small way, either as young fawns or when weakened by lack of food; but death delivered by coyotes, bobcats, cougar, and the like is minimal. Man is the major cause—either directly or indirectly—of the whitetail deer's demise. His gun is one means of destruction, his colossal ignorance of game management is the other.

At birth a whitetail is endowed with the keenest set of senses that the Creator has given to any animal for purposes of self-preservation. Taken individually, the bighorn and the antelope have better eyes, the grizzly a more acute sense of smell, the elk perhaps a keener pair of ears. Yet the ability to combine these three senses and respond to danger is best seen in the whitetail.

And it is quite easy to substantiate this. We have huge numbers of whitetail deer in this nation, with the greatest percentage of them in the most heavily populated and most heavily hunted areas. In years past, these same areas also abounded with other big-game animals: elk, moose, cougar, and caribou. But only the whitetail has survived. Largely, it is knowledge we have come by concerning the habits of whitetail that has aided us in preserving other hoofed game animals in the West from annihilation.

The whitetail hates man for his long destructive arm, but loves and adapts rather easily to the numerous conveniences that civilization provides. This deer is never happier than when he is feeding in a cultivated wheat or turnip field, or an apple orchard, or when browsing on rich second growth, common to areas where wholesale logging and pulp cutting is done, and where forest fires have been carelessly started. The truth of the matter is that deer would be far less prevalent without the territorial ravages of mankind. Over the years, this animal has sharpened his senses to cope with man's ineptitude as a hunter and has lived with man long enough to grow fat on his labors and to benefit by the mistakes he so often makes with the gun.

Curiously, whitetail deer possess an alarming ability to separate the dangerous man from the man who can be a provider. I remember a tremendous buck who escaped a ten-man group of hunters, some of whom were trying to drive him from a wood lot toward the others at the far edge. The animal escaped easily by cutting out of the wood lot across an open field. This, of course, is normal whitetail strategy and would have presented no problem to the hunters had there been no farmer in the middle of that field doing his fall plowing.

And then there was the buck who had eluded local hunters for years, unscathed except for a limp, the re- 45

*Young whitetail bucks try out their newly
grown antlers as rutting season begins. These usually
are brief encounters, with little
damage suffered by either animal. Older bucks, however,
occasionally lock up and die of starvation.*

sult of a leg wound inflicted by an inept hunter. On a bright autumn Sunday, when the local hunters had organized a network of drivers and standers from which there could be no escape, the buck gimped through the village churchyard. It was said that if the proper window had been opened, the minister could have killed him from the pulpit.

Without question, the animal has learned to live in man's backyard, and he seems to have done so without relinquishing any measure of his naturally wild spirit. On the other hand, wilderness whitetails are a rarity and taking one in this modern age is almost unheard of. Few hunters have the skill, knowledge, or experience to fell a wilderness whitetail—stalking him alone and far from civilization. The animal has too keen a sense of smell, sees too well, hears too well, and knows too well how to escape in brush and timber ever to become an easy target. To pit a man's abilities and experience against those of a mature whitetail buck on his home grounds is no contest at all. Odds always favor the deer.

To begin with, the whitetail is not only crafty, but has a penchant for brush, thicket, and swamp where traveling becomes difficult for man. This deer is rarely found in open country or in big timber, and then only under special circumstances: (a) when the hunting season is closed, (b) at night under cover of darkness, (c) when winter starvation brings him to the farmer's wheat fields, and (d) when he is chasing a doe in full heat. Whitetails must be hunted in the small, second-growth hardwoods where they feed, or atop the brushy ridges where they like to bed, or in a spruce swamp where it is too wet for easy walking, or in a cottonwood river bottom where spotting the animal is literally impossible.

The truth of the matter is that more whitetails are killed by accident than intent. There are so many deer and so many hunters it becomes almost impossible for these animals to save themselves from disaster. The law of averages constantly works against the deer. A loner or a group of hunters will spook a deer, or perhaps a herd of deer, in one spot without getting off a shot, or even being aware of the game's departure. The escape route of the animal will be so riddled with other hunters,

however, that almost inevitably the deer will be taken. The human population in the deer woods when the season is open far exceeds that of the legal, harvestable deer, and for this reason the whitetail's survival as the most important American game animal seems to be truly phenomenal. To achieve ten-point status a buck must either be lucky, live in a private preserve, or inhabit a wilderness area more than three miles from the nearest highway. In hunting territory, no buck lives more than a couple of years without hearing the crack of death as a bullet passes him.

Although biologists recognize some thirty subspecies of whitetail deer, ranging from Canada down to Coiba Island in Panama, all whitetails are basically the same. Size is the only noteworthy characteristic that will vary with region and species. And success in hunting any or all of them depends on the usual amount of experience and know-how. The sportsman must be aware of what the beast likes to eat and when, where he prefers to rest and when, and where he travels between resting and feeding grounds and when. The *and when* is the kicker. The books say that whitetails feed after dawn and before dusk. To this I say, "Amen!"—but only in country where the deer are undisturbed and can live a life of normal deer routine, unharrassed by hunters. Hard-pressed deer in crowded areas do not follow this pattern, nor any easily discernible pattern, except to hide in the most impenetrable cover they can find. Then, when darkness cloaks their movements, they emerge from their hideouts, move freely into the clearings and along the highways, and into the farmers' orchards and pastures. The gray of first daylight sends them back to the thickets. To get a trophy under these conditions the hunter must be in that thicket *first*. Hence, the First Law of Deer Hunting: Be on the crossing, the runway, or whatever you choose to name it, before the deer moves to his final cover for the day.

Since whitetails are found throughout the country in a wide range of cover types and conditions, methods of driving the deer into the open where the hunter may get a shot vary. In the Deep South, the whitetails are swamp lovers and stay close to impenetrable cover. Here

46

This is an adult whitetail buck in his
natural habitat of screening saplings and evergreen
timber. Mature bucks are shy, stay well
within protective cover, and rarely give hunter time
to judge heads or get a clean shot.

the deer are run with hounds to push them out of the swamp and brush, and along runways where the hunters stand ready. The deer are usually moving swiftly by the time they reach the stands, and most of the time they are literally taken "on the fly." The best gun for these purposes is a shotgun, loaded with buckshot.

Variations on this theme are practiced in most other parts of the country by substituting men for dogs—since the use of dogs for deer is illegal in most states. In this form of group hunting, at least half of the hunting party takes its stands on known runways and crossings, and the rest of the party moves through the heavy cover where deer are believed to be, hoping to drive them past the standing shooters. This is the method universally practiced by organized hunting clubs on private grounds and is the most successful method of bringing the whitetail deer to bag. But a thorough knowledge of the territory to be hunted is essential.

Actually, the term "driving" is inaccurate, since deer cannot be forced to move in predictable directions. Once jumped or roused from their beds they seek their exits with little regard for their adversaries, or the hunters' hooting and shooting. For the standers to see the deer as they flee, they must know ahead of time where the habitual crossings and "runs" are, where the deer will eventually emerge—come what may.

Also, a mature buck, wise to the conspiracy of "drivers" and "standers," will not hesitate to run back through the drive once he has fixed the location of the moving men. Another well-used whitetail trick is to lie "doggo" in a small tight patch of cover until the drivers thrash by, then rise quietly and sneak off to safety.

The best drivers are hunters who are skilled in stalking. These men move through the cover slowly, and as quietly as possible, actually hunting, and the deer move ahead of them. There is no need for a hunter to advertise his presence by shouting, baying, ringing bells, or banging on tin pans—as is usually done on big organized drives. Any man moving through deer cover will not be there long before the deer are aware of his presence—and his location.

No matter what the method, the hunter must remem-ber that success in whitetail hunting depends upon a healthy respect for the deer's keen senses. The animal will tolerate a certain amount of leaf rustling as his adversary moves in the woods, since these are normal noises, and a deer will rarely spook until he knows for sure that man is the cause. On the other hand, the snapping of twigs or the rattling of rocks underfoot is certain to send the animal bounding for safety, and the slightest man scent carried toward the deer by gentle breeze will alert the animal to act.

The whitetail is said to have an innate curiosity which often leads to his death. I doubt that it really is curiosity; rather, the deer does not immediately assume that all strange objects, noises, and movements mean danger. Instead, he usually waits quietly, nerves and muscles tense, poised for a hair-trigger response, until the danger is fully resolved. At this point he will usually be within seconds of cover. A couple of swift bounds and he is safe in the brush.

With such a careful animal, the hunter obviously must seek out his game where the game lives. He will inevitably be shooting at deer at fairly close range, and the premium will be on a fast-handling rifle, powerful enough to deliver a killing blow at the modest range of 100 yards. More power is seldom needed except under special conditions.

The time-tried .30-30 carbine has been the deer hunter's stand-by for well over a century and is the proven firearm. Its most recent competitor is the Ruger Carbine in .44 Magnum caliber, which the manufacturer freely admits is a "brush rifle" with limited effective range. The years have not seen significant changes in the types of firearms considered suitable for taking whitetail, although dozens of different calibers and models of both rifles and shotguns have been produced and are used successfully. It does not take much to kill a big whitetail buck if the bullet is placed "where he lives," meaning in the chest cavity. I have killed many whitetail—more than a dozen, fewer than 100—but have had no problems putting them down with any standard center-fire caliber, from the little .22 Savage Hi-power to the .300 H & H Magnum.

48

Top: A good picture of the shot a still-hunter
most often gets—a jumped buck bounding away at full speed. This one
has been caught in the open, but wise old bucks,
like the one at right, grow old and wise by moving about only
after sunset, when darkness screens movements.

MULE DEER

The Western mulie is another American deer, related, of course, to the whitetail and with a remarkably similar body conformation. Standing at sundown atop a gumbo butte, and silhouetted against the Western sky, he could easily be taken for a whitetail deer were it not for his large ears—hence, his name—and his towering antlers. Aside from the similarity of build, however, he is unlike the whitetail in coloration, character, choice of homeland, and in the manner in which he breaks for safety when spooked.

A hunter dedicated to the pursuit of Eastern whitetail can be forgiven if he feels that the mulie is an easier trophy to take. Accustomed to the canny nature of the whitetail buck, most hunters are surprised to find a big mulie standing boldly on the open prairie, or bedded down on a bare outcropping along a canyon rim, with nothing to screen him from prying eyes. The mule deer likes it this way. In the wide-open range of the West he can see before being seen. His gray, tawny-tinged coat camouflages him among the drab tints of gumbo, sandstone, and sage. Bedded down, he's part of a rock ledge, a dry creek bed, or a weathered log. He'll permit you to look in his direction for a good while if he thinks you haven't found him, but when you stare too long, he leaves in a bound, bouncing away like a child on a pogo stick, all four feet touching and leaving the ground at once. This departure is the mulie's trademark. I know of no other North American animal with such a gait.

Mulie country is the land of the big sky—and it can be wide prairies or craggy mountaintops clean of cover, above timber line. This big gray deer ranges all the way from the arid desert of northern Mexico up into the high Rockies of central Alberta and British Columbia. He likes high-mountain country with big open parks among the tall evergreens, but, conversely, he seems to be just as well pleased to live in prairie country where no natural water can be found for many miles. I have seen big-racked mule bucks in eastern Montana gumbo country, where every bit of the terrain is powder dry and flat ground-cactus flourishes. And I have seen the same big, wide racks in Western mountain country, with its lush vegetation and big clear rivers sweeping down the deep valleys. The mulie is cosmopolitan in choice of habitat—as long as it's in the West.

Wherever you see the mule deer, he looks much the same. The markings are uniform: a white-gray face with a contrasting black or dark brown patch along his forehead, brown-gray coloring on his neck and body, a black brisket, and a white underbelly. Mulies of the mountain variety tend to be a bit darker than the prairie and dry-country animals, however. The latter often have a dusty look. The mule deer's tail is an insignificant bit of ropey hair, black tipped, hanging from his rump, unlike the flaring badge of the whitetail which is carried erect like a banner when he takes off in alarm. The frightened mulie clamps his tail firmly against his rump as he bounds away, although a large, off-white rump patch is readily visible as he retreats.

*Young, two-point (Western count) mulie
(above) is strictly a meat animal to trophy hunters. Big
bucks like one at right carry impressive racks
with wide beams spreading beyond outstretched ears and
tall tines towering over head.*

The most heartening aspect of the mule buck is his headgear. By Eastern whitetail standards, every run-of-the-mill four-pointer is a trophy. His rack rises almost straight up from his head, spreading wide as it breaks into paired Y's, with a span of two feet fairly common among young adults. A whitetail hunter may spend his entire life without encountering a buck carrying a twenty-four-inch spread, but many a mule-deer hunter passes up two-footers for a better trophy.

At times even the tall tines of a mule buck's antlers can be hard to see. They have a subtle way of blending into the beige tones of prairie slopes and the brown of sandstone ledges. I once watched a bedded mule buck lying at the mouth of a rock cave for at least ten minutes through a pair of nine-power binoculars before I was certain that he carried antlers, although I was reasonably sure that he was a trophy head. It was not until he rose nervously from his bed and moved out into the sunlight that I could see his five-point rack.

The problem of picking out the best head in a herd of mule deer is enormously simplified when the hunting is over snow. Then the antlers stand out like tree branches against a winter sky. Or, as so often happens, a spooked buck will trot up a slope and sky line for you at the crest, pausing for just a moment before he crosses the divide. If you are quick in judging the head and

equally quick in making a fast shot at fairly long range, you should down him. Trophy bucks seldom dawdle on the sky line unless a respectable distance separates them from the hunter.

The phrase "respectable distance" provides the key to hunting mule deer. Even in the best of mule-deer areas, the animals are widely scattered and much ground must be covered to find the small herds. Even more searching must be done to find the big, lone bucks—unless it is the rutting season. The Jeep or power wagon is essential in range country, the saddle horse a must in the high mountain areas. Your hunting will involve traveling along reefs (Western talk for ridges), stopping

to check basins from rimtops, all the while glassing the slopes for feeding or moving deer. When you do spot the game it is invariably a fair distance away. If you find a trophy head you want, you plan a stalk to bring yourself within accurate hitting range, and this, often enough, is a "respectable distance," also.

More than other gunning sports, mule-deer hunting is a game for the dim periods between dawn and sunup, and sunset and dark. The deer feed from the first gray light in the morning until the sun bears down. Then they look for daytime beds. With the old bucks the chosen spot may be a ledge of rock or a canyon rim overlooking a wide expanse of terrain below, where 53

Before the rut, adult mule bucks (above) usually travel in
"bachelor" bands, then break up to gather harems. Top, right: Largest
trophy bucks are loners. They are seldom found
with does and fawns (bottom, right) until heat of the rut
dulls their normal, instinctive caution.

approaching danger can be detected well in advance. If all goes well, the deer sticks to his bed until the sun touches the western horizon. He lifts up unhurriedly, takes a few steps, stops to recheck his path, then leisurely picks his way down the slope to the feeding grounds below.

After the sun is well up there is not much chance to find bucks still on their feet. If you insist on hunting throughout the day, you will be forced to look for them in their bedding areas, which means the highest ridges surrounding their feeding grounds. Here travel on a careful saddle horse is hunting of the highest order, since you must find the buck, preferably still in his bed, alert, likely enough, but within killing range. A mounted hunter has a much better chance than a man on foot to make a close approach in range country. Deer are quite accustomed to seeing range horses and riders throughout the year and do not take alarm.

The truth is that a wise buck, if he feels he is well hidden and unnoticed, will allow a hunter to make a fairly close approach, counting on his natural camouflage to protect him. But too close is too close, and if you do manage to get within fifty yards of a bedded deer, he is certain to break for cover or to put on a great burst of speed to get out of your reach. The man with the rifle, of course, has a long arm. He can often grass a jumped buck before the animal reaches 200 yards.

Spotting your quarry in good mule-deer country is not difficult. Approaching for a killing shot after a careful stalk is another thing. A successful mule-deer hunter is rarely an indifferent marksman. Here the contrast between hunting mulie and whitetail becomes increasingly obvious. Where placing a shot at a distance of 100 yards is a rarity in whitetail cover, shooting at mule deer at 200 yards or more is quite usual. In fact, a mule-deer hunter can see and identify his trophy many times at a distance far beyond his ability to place a vital hit. And he must be patient. With modern rifles and scope sights the temptation to take a chance at killing a deer at ranges of 500 yards or more continually arises, and occasionally the shot is taken and strikes home, but it requires a skilled rifleman with top-notch equipment. It usually is possible by careful stalking to shorten the range to shooting distances that are more practical—say, about 300 yards or a bit more.

In the past decade I have killed a good number of mule-deer bucks and can recall no animal—even two-point eatin' bucks—that was less than 200 yards away when I fired the shot. The reason for this in my case is that I almost always hunt for a trophy buck, and if I jump one at close range, there isn't time enough to check the head. Many hunters, however, are looking for little more than legal game, and they will get ample opportunity for fairly easy running shots at ranges less than 100 yards. I always pass these up unless I know beforehand that the buck in question carries the rack I want.

Unlike whitetails, mule deer are seasonally migratory. Deer in the mountain and foothill country, bucks in particular, usually spend the summers high up near the timber line to escape the heat and flies. Here they remain until the urge of the rut stirs them, and the does begin to move to lower levels as winter approaches. With the coming of deep snow all the deer move out of the high country. The big bucks are the last to go. A late, warm autumn with little or no snow in the mountains will find the deer still fairly high, however, even during the rut. Under these conditions it is useless to look for big bucks in the low foothills. The time of year and the weather, therefore, will tend to determine where the mule-deer hunter must go to hunt.

Regardless of the season, it is always good policy to do your hunting from high up, above the area where the deer are likely to be. Most big-game animals do not look for danger from above, and are easier to approach for a stalk. Also, when deer are spooked they usually head up for safety and this can provide some good shooting.

Writers about early Western hunting usually underestimated the mule deer's intelligence and rated him as easy game. And so he was, in the late nineteenth century when hunting pressure was literally nonexistent. Even in more modern times, when rifles were effective only at fairly short ranges, the mule deer tended to be an easy mark. But the high-velocity rifle and scope sight have changed all that. Mule-deer bucks no longer take a few bounds after they are spooked, then stand dumbly to look at the hunter. They will stand, true enough—to look back over their shoulders after you have run them out of their beds or feeding grounds—but rarely until they have put a wide area between you and them. The big, beautiful dumbbell is no longer so dumb. He will stretch your shooting skill to the limit.

The rifle for mule deer is somewhat specialized, but the last decade has seen a number of fine tools appear on the firearms market. The famous .270 Winchester cartridge, effective for more than thirty years at modest ranges, has now been replaced by cartridges even more deadly at much longer ranges. Probably the finest choice in a long-range load is the 7-mm Remington Magnum, loaded with a 175-grain, pointed bullet. If the rifleman does his part, this cartridge will kill any mule deer on the continent at 400 yards. There are many much older cartridges that will also kill at this range, but the flat shooting and sustained velocity of the 7-mm Magnum minimize the hunter's problem of estimating range and wind drift in order to make a clean, one-shot kill. If a hunter zeroes in his 7-mm Magnum at about 275 yards, he can make vital hits at any range from fifty to 400 yards, with his sights still on the animal's body. At the longest range his hold will be at the top of the deer's shoulder. At the shorter ranges he will hold lower, just above the chest line of the animal. At the medium ranges, between 200 and 300 yards, he will hold dead on, and put his bullet within an inch or two of his target spot.

For the trophy-hunting stalker, the minimum caliber that can be depended upon to produce 300-yard kills is the 6-mm Remington or the .243 Winchester (also a 6-mm), both shooting 100-grain bullets. These are cartridges of fairly high velocity—about 3,000 fps—with just enough bullet weight to give ample penetration on deer. There are, of course, many other suitable calibers: .257 Weatherby Magnum, .257 Roberts, 7-mm Mauser, .280 Remington, and others of larger bore.

Most important in the choice of rifle is coupling it with the proper sighting equipment for accurate placement of the bullet. This means scope sights every time and, in the mule-deer rifle, a 4X scope attached with a rigid, low top mount is one of the best additions. Greater magnification than this is not essential, and a lower-power scope will not project the size of image desirable at long range for accurate hits.

Non-trophy hunters who are not choosey about the deer they kill will still take many with the old .30-30 carried in the saddle scabbard. This is good medicine for killing a deer jumped from its bed at short range, but it falls far short of the ideal rifle for gathering a trophy buck farther out.

Tracks of feeding elk make a barnyard of
this alpine slope (left) in Montana's Bitterroot Mountains,
near Idaho border. Prize mule-deer buck (right)
was taken on Dana ranch in foothill
country of Montana, at 365 yards, with .264 Magnum.

ELK

We moved slowly and silently down the north slope of a tall ridge. The game trail through the thick stand of lodgepole pine was dim in the deep-woods gloom of sunrise and barely visible as I followed the guide and my hunting partner. We were stalking a bull elk. The path was soft, the carpeting needles limp and moist from the night's dew. The frost whitening the treetops on these Rocky Mountain crests had not seeped down to ground level. Our footfalls were a faint hush, hush on the trail, imperceptible a dozen yards away.

Perhaps a minute or two passed after we left the upper edge of the timber to slip down into the dark evergreens. In memory it seems less. The bull's long-drawn whistling reply to our bugle had come from far down the slope, and a careful approach lay before us. It was a time for stealth and quiet, for the air was dead still, with no breeze to favor us. A quick movement, the rattle of a stone, the rustle of a branch would signal our approach to the alert herd master. He had challenged our call. He expected trouble. His eyes, ears, and nose would be pointed our way. If we got the first look it would be sheer luck.

Off to the right a twig snapped faintly. A flicker of movement caught the corner of my vision. My head swung to the right and I looked squarely into the face of a big bull elk. From eighty yards away he peered through the slender latticework of lodgepole trunks, checking his adversary. Keeping my eyes on him, I hissed to my buddies, "There he is!" The bull raised his head for a better look. "Take him, Jack," I said.

"Can't see him," he replied. "Better try him before he jumps."

The bull, at first quartering toward us, now shifted his feet to face us head on. The ivory tips of his brow tines picked up light from overhead as he stood buried to his knees in low mountain-willow brush in a small opening in the timber. I guessed we could see him better than he could see us, but his shift of position meant he was ready to crash off in alarm.

Quickly, I picked him up in the scope, noting the blackness of his neck mane against the lighter tan of his brisket. The tip of the scope post swung to his chest, then up into the dark line of his neck as I squeezed off. The .358 belched mightily and the scope reared up to blot out the bull from my line of sight, but with my left eye I saw a spurt of water vapor spray from his neck. He gave a great lurch downhill, then disappeared from view, screened by the lodgepole.

Guarding his harem, the trophy bull elk
in this 19th-century painting stands tense and ready
for sudden encounter as he
listens to the challenging bugle of a
rival from the valley below.

I looked at Wendell, the guide, and he gave me a wide smile. "You got him," he said. "I saw the water fly off him all around."

It was true. We found the elk about fifty feet from the little willow glade, stone dead, his wide rack pushed back against a pine bole. The 250-grain Silvertip from the .358 had allowed him to take a couple of jumps, but that was all. This was an enormous bull, not great as a trophy perhaps, but hog fat. He died on the opening day of the early high-country season, before he had wasted away his prime body fulfilling the procreative urge.

Normally, in bugling—the most exciting of big-game hunting—the bugle is used to locate the herd bull or one of his competitors. Once the bull has given back his keening challenge, the stalk can be planned. This bull, however, played a switch and stalked the hunter, believing he was about to engage a rival. If a bull is hot enough in the rut and has had a few victories within a 57

est harems. Once the cows come in heat the herd bull is a busy individual. He must service the cows while keeping a watchful eye out for less-favored bulls, which are forever trying to cut a cow or two out of his harem for themselves. He will run the intruders off as best he can. If the rival bull is a youngster with less than a full rack, he usually scurries for cover at the first charge from the herd master. But if the new arrival happens to be a bull of equal size and age, a lengthy encounter may take place, with much grunting, thrusting, and tearing up of sod and brush before the victor is established.

Within a few weeks, when the heat of mating has passed, the weary bulls no longer show much interest in the hunter's bugle—no matter how carefully crafted from bamboo, garden hose, or plastic, or how skillfully used. From this point or during the hunting season, the adventurer in search of elk trophies must trust to his eyes and his knowledge of elk to locate his game. This may require a bit of time in the saddle, for elk are wide-ranging animals and think nothing of traveling fifteen miles or more in a day to find food, or to escape the high country when the snow gets too deep for comfort.

Originally, the elk (more properly named wapiti, although this name is seldom used by sportsmen in the United States) was an animal of the Western plains and prairie country. In the days when their only human adversary was the Indian, the elk was also found in the timber country of the Northeast. Heavy hunting pressure in the open country, both for meat and teeth (every Brother Elk needed one for his watch chain), caused a wholesale slaughter of the species. The elk that remained headed for the hills. The early 1900's were the ebb years for elk in the U.S., but rigid protection has brought back the herds in the mountains of the West. Open seasons are now the rule in every state that includes some part of the Rockies within its boundaries. The elk range extends well up into Alberta and British Columbia; its northern limit is probably the Peace River.

The bull elk, largest of the world's round-horned deer, is one of the great trophy animals. During the

short time, he may well turn on the steam and head for the bugler. I have seen it several times in elk hunting; however, the hunter cannot count on bringing in just *any* bull for a shot.

Bugling is but one method of getting your elk. Its success is based on being in the elk country when the rut is on (usually at its peak in September). The elk, both cows and bulls, have spent the summer in high alpine basins, just under the snow line, and do not begin to move to lower ground until after the first frosts. Bulls usually herd by themselves in the summer, high up away from flies and the competition for food from range cattle. The antlers begin to grow in March and by summer's end are hardened, fully developed, and peeled clean of velvet. The bull's attention then turns to mating, and he follows the herds of cows and calves into the lower basins as they drift down from the mountains.

58 The biggest, most virile bulls usually gather the larg-

Guide Howard Copenhaver (above)
glasses a small herd of elk from a high Western ridge.
Still keeping elk under observation,
hunting party (right) moves cautiously down forested
slope at beginning of stalk.

late 1800's, the nobility of Europe made the long trek across the Atlantic and more than halfway across the North American continent to hunt and kill these majestic deer. Certain well-fed, mature bulls will weigh well over 1,000 pounds on the hoof, and average ones will run to 700 pounds or more. Standing five feet tall at the shoulder, with antler tips rising another five feet above, the mature bull is an impressively tall animal. He walks with great dignity and loses none of it when he breaks into a swinging trot or a bounding gallop.

The antler formation is spectacular. Mature bulls of five years will carry beams of at least four feet, if not more, and usually will be six-pointers, Western count, for a total of twelve points. Spreads will run about three feet across, with points off the main beams averaging about a foot in length. A young challenging bull, facing this "basket" of twelve ivory-tipped rapiers, has his work cut out for him.

Bulls of record-book class carry beam lengths of five feet or better, with spreads over four feet, but these big heads are now rare. The five-footers were mostly taken more than two decades ago, before the winter range of the elk was cleaned off by range cattle. Since that time, the Federal government has granted permission to ranchers, for a mere pittance, to graze their cattle in the national forest areas, making it almost impossible for the elk to find food there. An occasional head does get into

the records in this day and age, but cracking the book is probably more difficult with elk than with any other Rocky Mountain game.

The American elk has numerous relatives throughout the world, although none approaches him in either body size or antler development. This includes the Scottish stag, the European hirsch, and the sambar deer of India. The Scottish stag (red deer) of Highland stalking fame is small enough for a pony to pack out "in the round." To pack out a mature bull elk, it must be quartered, with head and neck removed, and even then it will be a good load for three mules or pack horses. One animal packs the forequarters, another the hindquarters, and the third the caped-out head, the hide, and the neck.

Some hunters maintain that shooting an elk is no great sport. These are the sportsmen who wait until the heavy snows drive the animals from their mountain home to winter range in the open valleys. The "firing-line" slaughter of these migrating animals is well known to residents of the Rocky Mountain states, and it is particularly obnoxious when the blizzard-pressed herds are forced to move out of national parks, such as Yellowstone, for lower ground. A line-up of shooters faces them the instant they step across the park boundary, and the elk must run the gantlet to find safety in the valleys. The rifle fire is heavy and sustained, and no

shooter is really certain that the elk he tags is the animal he killed.

This is a sure way to collect meat, but it is hard to view it as sport. In some areas of heavy over-browsing, this kind of shooting does serve to reduce the size of the herds. It becomes a matter of making a decision whether the animals should die of rifle fire or starve slowly to death in the late winter.

Killing an elk is not a difficult task in areas of high elk population, where the local laws permit taking any animal encountered, regardless of age or sex. Usually the "either sex" seasons follow the mating period, and the cows and calves suffer most, since a rutted-out bull is not good eating meat. And when the first elk a man sees is legal game, there is not much to killing one with a modern rifle.

Hunting for trophies is far different. The bull elk is smart, fully as sophisticated as a prime whitetail buck, and he is gifted with a keen nose, highly sensitive ears, and eyes as good as an antelope's. To stalk within killing range of a bull is never easy, and the problem is made more complex by the presence of the cows, who act as watchdogs for the herd.

Bugling the bulls is, in my opinion, not only the finest method of taking elk, but rates at the top for any hunting sport in North America. The hunter, or guide, who uses the bugle at once puts the animal on the alert, so that an air of tension is immediately created as the bull sends back his answer. A man wise in the ways of elk usually can locate the bull from his first reply and can determine with some accuracy whether the animal is a youngster or a mature herd bull from the tone and the length of the notes of the whistle.

The bugling of a bull is one of nature's most beautiful wild sounds. It begins with a fairly low, flutelike note, then jumps to a high, reedy pitch that often is held for a half minute. It is astonishing to hear such a birdlike sound from a massive, virile animal. But it is a penetrating sound, and on a quiet day it can be heard a mile away.

Since elk, like deer, are most active during early morning and late afternoon, this is the best time for bugling.

A bull on his feet and feeding is much more likely to reply to a challenge than a bull already bedded for the day. This means that you must be away from camp at first light and up in the elk basins before sunrise. The guide picks the spot to send out the first call, generally from a point overlooking a valley or basin where the sound will carry a good distance and the bull's answer can readily be heard.

Although bulls in the rut make a variety of weird sounds, in addition to the high whistle of the bugle call, they are quick to detect any false note on your artificial bugle. A musician's skill and ear for pitch are needed to provide the proper effect. Once the first call is given, guide and hunter sit tight, concealed from sight, and await the reply. If none comes, a wait of five minutes or more is advisable before making a second attempt. Repeated bugling at short intervals is taboo. Any bull listening will know this is not the real thing.

If a reply comes, it is smart to remain in cover and give the bull a chance to move in your direction. If a bull is hot, he may come right back with a challenge to the call. Or, after making just one reply, he may circle your position and try to come up to look you over, either to allay his suspicion of danger or to survey his competition. It is a fascinating, exciting game that keeps the hunting at high pitch until the bull either spooks or shows himself within range for a shot.

If the bull decides to stay within protective reach of his harem, a shrewd guess as to his probable location must be made and then a careful stalk can begin. It is best to try to circle his location from downwind, giving a final toot on the bugle if necessary to fix the spot in the timber where he may be hiding. It is a cat-and-mouse game in any case, and it is most unlikely that you will get a look at the first bull answering the bugle.

The kill described in the opening of this section was an unusual one. We had climbed into the saddle an hour before dawn, ridden through dark timber up to the rim of a big basin in Montana's Bob Marshall Wilderness, about four miles from camp. It was barely light enough to see the divide as we tied the horses at timber line. Then we climbed up and over the top of the divide,

60

Prime bull elk from Montana's
Bob Marshall Wilderness Area was taken on upper waters
of the south fork of the Flathead River.
The area also is excellent for
goat, deer, black bear, and occasionally grizzly.

where we waited in a patch of timber for shooting light. When I could pick out a white rock on the far hillside through my scope, the guide blew his first bugle call of the new shooting season.

The echo of this first call had barely died away when a clear, ringing challenge came back from the floor of the basin, several hundred yards below us in the timber. Wendell looked at me and said, "There's a hot one, all right. But I think he's in a wallow down in the bottom and won't move up the hill to us." Five minutes we waited. Wendell again gave out with a pair of long-drawn notes on the garden-hose bugle.

Again, the bull came right back, this time with an angry, belligerent tone, followed by a hoarse grunt. Wendell rose, stretched, and said, "Well, let's go down after him, while he's still in the wallow."

But this bull was mad enough to come to us, although suspicious enough to swing off to one side as he sneaked up the slope through heavy timber. It is likely this was a bull that had been whipped out of a herd by a bigger bull and was cooling off in the wallow with defeat and deprivation still rankling him. If he had been with his harem, it is most likely that we would have had to stalk to within shooting distance, although the odds on our

61

getting very close would not have been good in that heavy lodgepole timber.

On another hunt in the same area, we had successfully bugled up one bull on several successive days. But he was with cows and would not leave them. We were forced to make a stalk each time, and each time we were frustrated by a sharp-eyed cow that barked an alarm before we could spot the bull. We did catch one glimpse of the old herd master as he broke away in fright across a small opening in the timber, but the range was long and the time too short to chance a shot. After this herd was spooked about four times, it decided to leave the area. We did not find the band again for the remainder of the hunt.

A big bull elk can make a swift exit even in heavy timber. These animals jump about as well as any deer and can travel just as fast. I remember a time when we jumped a gathering of five bulls on the Dana ranch, spooking them out of a deep coulee with a shot that killed a fine mule buck. The elk, in single file and with the biggest bull, a six-pointer, in the lead, galloped up the far wall of the coulee. Just beyond the crest of the rim stretched a steerproof wire fence probably five feet high. The elk took this in stride like a string of steeplechase horses, flowing over it without conscious effort, even though their tongues were hanging out after the steep uphill climb.

When the elk are on the heavily timbered slopes and ridges in the early part of the season and in the open-park country in the higher mountains, the hunter will get a good deal of short-range shooting, generally at running targets. In the open country of the valleys, however, the shooting will invariably be at much longer ranges, providing time to look over the trophy, get settled in a comfortable prone position, or to find a solid rest before making the shot.

The rifles used in these two extremes of elk hunting, therefore, must perform two totally different functions. In timber hunting the rifle should be light and quick to handle, preferably a lever or slide action or an autoloader, with a barrel length of 22 inches or less. It is unlikely that you will require anything but iron sights for the timber country, which means you can use a saddle scabbard for easy carrying and quick availability. The elk is a fairly large animal and at timber ranges—often less than 100 yards—is a reasonably easy mark for regular iron-sight equipment.

In the open you will need a rifle that possesses a killing potential up to 400 yards and carries scope-sight equipment to make hits at such ranges possible. This is the place for a high-velocity caliber. It should pack a bullet of substantial weight, which will shoot flat enough to make vital hits at 200 to 400 yards with a minimum of range judgment and holdover on the hunter's part. One of the best of the modern calibers is the .338 Winchester in the Model 70 bolt action. This is a fine, one-shot killer on elk at 300 to 400 yards, and a good choice in cases where the recoil effect is not a serious factor.

In timber, the .35 Remington in lever- or slide-action types is a minimum choice. I prefer the .358 Winchester in a lever action, either the Model 88 Winchester, or the Model 99 Savage, both with a 22-inch barrel. Another made-to-order caliber for elk in timber is the .444 Marlin, packing a 240-grain bullet at 2,700 fps from the Model 336 lever-action rifle.

Many elk have been killed with the .270 Winchester and rifles of this class. However, a big bull elk is a tough animal, with large bones and heavy muscle, and experienced guides prefer to see something heavier in their hunter's hands. The time-tried .30-06 is still a top favorite in elk country and will probably hold the spot for some years to come, although newer Magnum calibers, from 7-mm up to the .375, do have greater long-range potential than the '06.

MOOSE

In the province of Quebec, the Canadian hunter refers to his largest game animal as *l'original*. If by this he means that the moose is unique in appearance, a droll character, an original without duplication on the American continent, he is quite right. For the moose looks like a huge mule with a pair

Preceding pages: Elk now are almost entirely big-timber animals. They bed down in shade during the day, come out before sundown to feed. This bull quietly chews his cud after the night's feeding. Guide (opposite) calls bull moose for sportsman.

of outlandish, hand-shaped antlers set low on both sides of his head.

Jack O'Connor, shooting editor of *Outdoor Life* magazine, tells a story about the first moose he ever killed. He was living in Tucson, Arizona, at the time, and the mounted head of the trophy bull was delivered to his home by a Mexican expressman. The Mexican asked Jack why he had someone put horns on the mule's head.

"That's not a mule," Jack told him. "That's a moose."

Said the expressman, "You can't kid me. There's no such thing as a moose. That's a mule." So Jack passed up the argument.

Certainly there is a resemblance between the two animals. The moose is about as large as a big mule and has the same rubbery, overhanging nose. And if we are thinking of a black mule, the resemblance seems to be even stronger.

But the moose is also unique in many ways. He can be seen in more areas of North America than any other game animal—from Newfoundland across central Canada, up through the Rockies and the Yukon, and out along the Alaskan Peninsula to its southwest corner. That's a few thousand miles. And he is also the continent's largest game animal. The American bison is larger, but we cannot really consider it a game animal.

Some big Alaskan bulls weigh as much as 1,800 pounds and stand seven feet tall at the shoulder.

The moose also is unique in that he is one of the few native animals to retain his Indian name. Actually, the moose is a close relative of the Scandinavian elk and practically indistinguishable from that species, but the English colonists saw our American wapiti first and decided to call these "elk." As a result, we have called the moose by the name given him by the Algonquins.

Another characteristic of the moose is that he shuns civilization, which means that in order to kill a trophy bull you must get back into wilderness country. This alone makes a hunt worth while. There are few moose left in the United States, and these only in the remote northern areas of Maine, Minnesota, and the Rocky Mountain states of Montana, Idaho, and Wyoming. The last three and Alaska are the only states where moose may be hunted and licenses are issued only on a special permit-by-drawing basis.

Moose were numerous in all the northern states in colonial days, but the spread of civilization pushed them north, over the Canadian border, into the last wilderness country on this continent. Hunting is permitted throughout most of Canada, with the exception of New Brunswick (limited permits for residents only) and Nova Scotia. The island province of Newfoundland has a tre-

mendous moose herd, created from a nucleus of a few animals brought there in 1907. Hunters are now being urged to visit Newfoundland to control the surplus.

In planning to hunt moose, the first item of gear on the list should be a pair of rubber boots, short or long, according to preference. For more than any hoofed animal on the American continent the moose loves water. Even the so-called mountain moose of the Rockies would rather squish around in the alpine muskegs than tread the dry, timbered ridges. In my travels in search of North American game I cannot recall ever seeing a moose sign farther than half a mile from water, unless the moose was being chased by wolves or a hunter. Some authorities advance the theory that the "bell," the long tassel of skin and hair hanging from the bull's neck behind the underjaw, is a natural device to help drain the water when the moose raises his head above the surface after grubbing for a mouthful of lily-pad roots. It may well be, for if ever an animal needed a drain spout, it is the moose.

The first moose I ever saw in the wild was called out from heavy timber right to the shore of the lake where we were making camp. While one of the French-Canadian guides was rustling a supply of firewood, the other decided to give a toot or two on his birchbark horn to see if there were any bulls in the neighborhood.

After one or two deep belly grunts into the horn—presumably the amorous wailing of a lovesick cow—the guide cocked his head toward the thick mass of black-spruce timber up the lake shore and said, *"She's* come."

I heard nothing and continued to unpack my sleeping bag, figuring he was hoping to boost my morale after a wet forty miles of paddling and a few lengthy portages. But he was right. *She* was coming. In a moment or two I could hear a great crackling of underbrush a couple of hundred yards away. Actually, it sounded more like the work of a small logging crew than the approach of an ardent bull moose. I did not actually believe it was a moose until the animal crashed out of the underbrush, shaking his great head. He stopped on a high bank overlooking the lake, about eighty yards away.

At this critical moment, both the guide and I were crouched behind a driftwood log, the guide mumbling, "Shoot!" while I was yanking a rifle from the case and pushing cartridges into the rotary magazine. It was a puny .250 Savage Model 99 that I had brought along for deer. The '06 was still under a pile of duffle in the canoe.

But the bull stood firmly on the bank, looking first up the lake shore, then in our direction, wondering where that cow was hiding. He was big, black, and majestic, long-legged, with a massive shoulder hump, and with wide antler palms sweeping back over his shoulders, as he lifted his head high to test the wind. Resting over the log, I placed the red front bead on the little Savage just at the point of his foreleg and squeezed. The report of the rifle and the thunk! of the bullet blended into one sound.

At the shot the bull drew up his front feet, humping his withers still higher. I threw the lever and dropped another 100-grain bullet into about the same spot. The bull grunted, dropped to his knees, then slid headfirst down the bank into the lake. He was half submerged and very dead, and because of his great bulk, very unavailable. We couldn't drag the carcass out of the water. We had to cut it up to get it ashore. I learned my lesson. That is the *last* moose I have ever shot near deep water.

It must be said that normally, for his size, a moose is one of the quietest animals on the continent, and does not go rampaging about in the brush and timber unless he is love crazed and has a willing partner nearby. No other animal of equal size can slip through heavy stands 67

Two bull moose, still in late summer velvet, feed on water plants of Yukon bog. Wherever moose are found in North America, they are rarely far from water. A canoe is standard equipment in Canadian moose hunting.

of timber and second growth as noiselessly as a moose. And bulls are frequently given to standing motionless for long periods of time behind a screening edge of timber. A bull will stare out over a marsh or open meadow without flicking an ear, tossing an antler, or shifting a hoof to betray his position, and his motionless stance may seem to last an hour or more, if you are waiting for him to show himself. Many a bull has been passed up by a hunter glassing the meadows simply because the animal was not given enough time to move into the open.

In the enormous wilderness of thick evergreen timber, muskeg, and lakes and streams that make up eastern and central Canada's moose country, the canoe is a vital bit of equipment. Not only does it get you into the moose country (unless you fly into a camp via float plane), but it is essential for hunting along shore lines at dawn and dusk to spot feeding and watering animals. Many moose are shot directly from the canoe. Many more are killed by spotting from the canoe, paddling silently to a near point on the shore, and carrying out the stalk on foot. The canoe is also indispensable for

Palmated antlers worn by bull moose transforms this ungainly creature into one of the most majestic game animals on North American continent. Right: A bull frightened by hunters gallops for shore of shallow Canadian lake. (He made it.)

getting the carcass back to camp after butchering. No one brings out a Canadian moose in one piece, and I doubt if it can be done in more than one or two places on the continent. Moose usually aren't killed that near to a highway or a railway.

The mountain moose of the American and Canadian Rockies is invariably hunted on horseback after the camping area has been reached by pack train. Here the horse and the pack animals serve the same function as the canoe in lowland hunting. In mountain country, the hunter travels from one meadow to another, each of which is approached through screening timber. The horses must be tied out of sight and the glasses used to scan the meadows and the willow, aspen, or alder edge growth for feeding animals. If you are quiet in approach, and careful and patient in glassing the meadows, you will inevitably find moose in this type of cover, if any at all exist in the hunting area.

A close approach to a bull when he is in heavy timber rarely can be made. His long legs carry him readily over brush and blowdowns that a man cannot navigate quietly. The practical method, therefore, is to hunt only during the feeding periods and in the most likely places —meadows, muskeg, and timber edges where low brush grows, for this is the staff of life for moose.

Feeding signs of moose are easily spotted. The big animals chew willows, aspen, red maple, and other small brush right down to branches half an inch in diameter. Bigger saplings, aspen particularly, the moose will ride down and push over, straddling the trunk with their forelegs to bring the tender upper branches within reach. Such bent and stripped trees are obvious give-

aways in good moose country to the observant hunter.

Before the lakes freeze, and right through the early weeks of hunting, the moose will continue to feed on water plants. Any lily-pad lake is a good spot to look for moose and, of course, one of the finest of all feeding areas is a "burn," where forest fires have destroyed the big timber and second growth is rampant. Nothing beats burned-off forest land for attracting moose.

It has been said, with reason, that moose are one of North America's dangerous game animals. And this can be true during the heat of the rut, when the bulls throw caution to the wind and may even charge a hunter, or any strange object moving across their path of vision. I once spent four hours waiting for a guide on a Canadian deer hunt while a belligerent bull moose had him up a tree. He was unarmed, as required by New Brunswick law, and had no choice but to wait until the bull gave up the effort to shake him out of the spruce tree and moved off into the timber. Still it is most unlikely that a bull moose will charge a hunter as the result of a wounding shot. Their belligerence in attack is not motivated by defense or revenge. When inspired by love, they simply will brook no interference from any living thing, including other bulls.

The mature bull moose carries the world's largest and heaviest antlers. A big set will weigh sixty pounds and spread five feet or more. And of the lot, the moose of Alaska is by far the largest and carries the widest spread, with the *Shiras,* or Wyoming moose, down at the bottom of the list. In any case, a mounted moose head is a major trophy and a magnificent one to display. I had a moose head in my garage for eight years because I had no place for it in my home. I finally gave it away to a tavern keeper, who sawed off the palms so that it would fit under his ceiling. So it is with moose trophies.

Although moose are huge animals, they are not hard to kill. One well-placed shot in the lung area, using any big-game caliber, will put down a moose practically on impact. However, with the exception of that first animal, I have used fairly large bores on moose—either the .35 Remington, the .358 Winchester, or the .300 and .375 Holland & Holland Magnums. I carried the two .35's in heavy-timber country in eastern and central Canada, where shooting distances are not too great— say, up to 200 yards. The two Magnums were used only in the Rockies and Alaska, where the shooting frequently is at any range you believe you can make a kill. The .375 H & H, carrying a 300-grain bullet, made a one-shot kill for me in Alaska at a distance of over 250 yards. The sixty-inch bull it struck expired where he stood. The bullet was placed at the juncture of neck and shoulder as he quartered toward me.

One of the finest moose heads I have seen was taken in Canada by my hunting partner, Bill Browning, with a single shot into the animal's shoulder at about 200 yards. Bill was using a .270 Winchester. Another partner of mine has killed two moose with a shot apiece from a .264 Winchester Magnum using a 140-grain bullet. Both animals were some 300 yards away when hit.

Any rifle and sighting combination that is suitable for taking elk will kill moose just as well if conditions and ranges are similar. The big bulls are quickly susceptible to shots through the lungs. This is the best spot to place a bullet.

Moose of Alaska-Yukon
area (above, left) carry largest
and heaviest trophy of all
the world's antlered
animals. Long legs enable them
to travel in deep snow
(above, right) without foundering.
Young bull (far left)
feeds on marsh grass in a
Canadian muskeg, where heavy moose
populations are found.
Bull (left), responding to guide's
call, comes out to
point of land along shore line
in open view of hunters.

CARIBOU

If you have ever watched the screwball antics of a big bull caribou on the Alaskan tundra, or on a high, barren plateau of the northern Rockies, just before the rutting season gets into full swing, you can be forgiven if you feel that the animal is completely crazy or, at best, confused. One moment he will be standing in watchful attendance near the cows. The next he has broken into a long, swinging trot, clicking as he goes, in an aimless run. Or he may suddenly leap into the air, as if he had been jabbed with a pitchfork, turn completely around, and then dash off. A dozen yards away he may stop stone dead in his tracks and apparently go to sleep on his feet. In a few minutes he'll toss his hind legs high and take off for the horizon, snatching a bite of moss every few rods or so as he runs.

In half an hour he may come trotting back to his harem or, just as likely, never be seen again.

Male members of many species of animals go somewhat loco during the mating season, but caribou most of all it seems to me. Yet it may be that a hunter (who is usually in the field during the rut) has more opportunity to watch caribou than other animal, since they inhabit the open country and are seldom found in timber. Certainly if the caribou is confused in some ways, he has *me* confused in another. I'm never quite sure which of the many varieties I'm watching through the glasses, even though certain ones are common only to certain areas. Even guides seldom agree on which family a particular caribou belongs to.

Biologists say that there are three major types of

Buzz Fiorini, Seattle outfitter, shows
off mountain caribou taken in northern British Columbia.
This remote area offers top-grade hunting
for Stone sheep, moose, and black bear, and is among
best remaining preserves of grizzly.

caribou: the Barren Ground, mountain, and woodland, and all three are spread across the northern part of North America from Newfoundland to Alaska and up into the Arctic. But these are very general classifications. The books list at least a dozen varieties of caribou, all carrying the prefix *Rangifer,* followed by various identifying geographical locations or proper names. It seems that every early explorer of the north country had a caribou named for him: Cabot, Dawson, Grant, Osborn, Richardson, Peary, and so on.

The fact is that all caribou look much alike except for size. In general, the mountain caribou is considered the largest, the Barren Ground variety the smallest. The big Osborn bull, of the mountain race, will usually run as large as an average bull elk—700 pounds or so. The several Barren Ground varieties will be only half this size, even among the mature bulls. In every case, however, the cows are much smaller than the bulls—perhaps smaller than is the case with any other hoofed game. And, as is true of many other wild animals, the female is a drab, dull creature compared with the striking appearance of the male. Most noticeable is the bull's magnificent white neck mane, which will attract your eye at a distance of three or four miles, glowing like a beacon in the clear, sunlit high-mountain air. The massive headgear of the male is also striking, completely out of proportion to the size of the animal. A big bull's antlers will tower four feet or more above his head, often equaling and sometimes surpassing, his body height at the shoulder. The antlers will be heavily palmated in the front and on the top, studded with many points decorating the "rocking chair" sweep of the main beams, which roll back from the apex of the head then rise in a gentle, smooth curve. It is a distinctive formation, unlike that of any other deer, with the most prized heads carrying "double shovels" thrust well forward over the bull's muzzle.

Compared with the bull, the cow's headgear is wispy and unimpressive—obviously no trophy—but it does give her some status. And unlike the females of other antlered game, the antlers of a caribou cow are a normal characteristic.

So much for the trophy. It is relatively rare among American hunters, dramatic on the den wall, and a prize that every sportsman with the yen, the time, and the means for a hunt in the Far North should have.

Hunting caribou, however, is hardly great sport, and it is something that I can either take or leave alone. I much prefer to watch them than to shoot them.

I'm never sure whether caribou are dim-witted, unsophisticated, afflicted with myopia, or suffer from all three, but I have seen them trail along with the pack string for the full length of a mountain meadow, the way a herd of range cattle might do—filled with curiosity, their broad square muzzles held high as they sniffed to identify their strange new brethren. I have walked, completely in the open, toward a bull bedded on a grassy hillside and apparently was unnoticed as I photographed him from a distance of sixty yards. I have dropped a big bull, then watched his herd companions stand around in wonder as the old boy kicked his last, allowing me almost to put my hand on his fat carcass before they galloped off a few rods, and even there stopped to stare. It must be said, however, that all these activities were carried out downwind. For if a caribou has nothing else, he does have a sharp sense of smell.

Two simple rules should be followed by the sportsman in search of a caribou trophy: he must travel to caribou country and he must keep his chosen target upwind at all times. Nothing much else seems to matter if you have armed yourself with a fairly powerful rifle rigged with scope sight, a good pair of binoculars, and a spotting scope. The caribou co-operate beautifully by remaining well out in the open—in both high mountain and tundra country. They are easy to spot from far off and ridiculously easy to stalk. In fact, during the rut and/or migration you can pick most any spot that overlooks a fair amount of terrain and wait for the bands to come to you. Caribou are inveterate travelers, moving endlessly and restlessly during much of the hunting season. It is not uncommon to see a band of a hundred or more within easy stalking distance when you stick your head out of your sleeping bag at crack of day.

The hunter's most pressing problem is to hold his 73

lake in good game country. The sport then flies in on a charter float plane, which drops him at the camp door. As I say, there is no good reason for every sportsman not to hang a caribou trophy on the wall if he wants. It requires little more than time and money, and both of these essentials seem not to be difficult to come by today.

If he plans to fill out on all of the antlered trophy animals, the sportsman must constantly tour the continent. If he wants the little Coues whitetail, he must

fire when he spots a fine male caribou within range, particularly if it is his first experience with the big white-necked bulls. The antlers are so huge in contrast to the body of the animal that even a mediocre rack looks like a great trophy. On a good day it is no problem to find fifty bulls carrying respectable racks. Your task is to choose the biggest, the one with the best shape, longest beam, widest spread, best shovels, or whatever.

It is most unlikely that a hunter will make a Northern trek purely for caribou. In my book these are bonus animals that he takes when he is on a hunt for grizzly, moose, Dall or stone sheep, or brown bear, or even polar bear. For caribou are found in or near the areas inhabited by all of these animals, and all of these animals offer more challenge during the hunt.

Hunting any or all of them has been made easier in recent years. It is no longer necessary to slog weary miles on foot through mushy tundra, ankle-deep at every step. Instead, float planes will drop a group of sportsmen on a remote lake in the game country, and the members of the group will set up a spike camp within sight of caribou. The big outfitters are also using bush tractor-trailer rigs for getting into rough back country, carrying a rugged blade ahead to doze trails through brush and saplings.

Today, the usual routine finds the outfitter ready with a dozer road into camp before the sports arrive. If the outfitter uses horses—which is the best way to travel for caribou hunting—he trucks them into the roadhead, then "jingles" the string into the camp location on a

74

For its size, the caribou is equipped with outstanding headgear. Antlers often top body height at shoulders. Not much skill is required to down a caribou, but a trophy head like one at right is a prize.

head for the Southwest, into southern Arizona or northern Mexico. In that area he also has a fine chance for a recordbook mule deer on the recently opened Jicarilla Apache Reservation in northern New Mexico. There the records have been cracked repeatedly in the past few years. Heading north he will hit elk country. It spans from New Mexico right up the Rockies into Alberta. When he leaves the elk in central Alberta, he will begin gunning for caribou and moose. Or, starting from the East, he can take his woodland caribou in Newfoundland (moose, too), a big whitetail in New Brunswick or north-

ern Maine, perhaps another moose in Quebec or Ontario. He must, however, go west of the Mississippi to find the mule deer, far north for the mountain caribou.

No matter what his chosen route, the search for antlered game will carry him into the finest of our wilderness areas, a good share of them still virgin and most of them free of the ravages of man's civilization. Hopefully, much of this productive natural range for the game will be preserved. In any case, the true sportsman, or trophy hunter, will never share in its decimation. May his tribe increase.

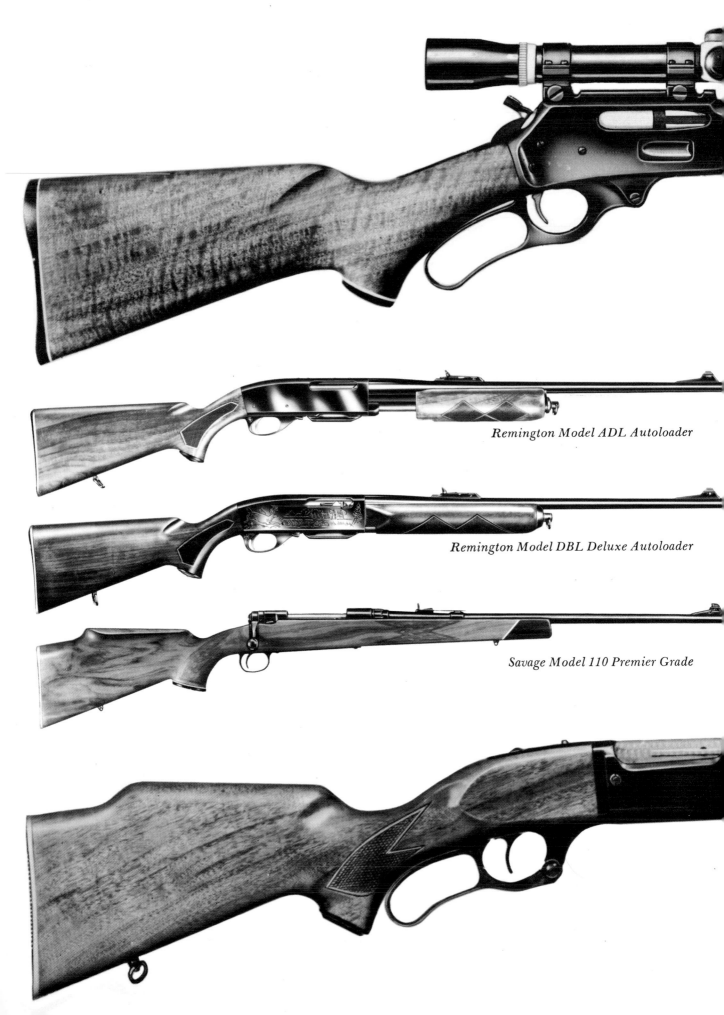

Remington Model ADL Autoloader

Remington Model DBL Deluxe Autoloader

Savage Model 110 Premier Grade

Marlin Model 336, with 4X scope

Winchester Model 94

Ruger .44 Magnum Carbine

Winchester Model 100

Winchester Model 88

Savage Model 99E

HORNED
GAME
3

BIGHORN SHEEP

The ram lay on a steep, sun-bathed slope of black shale at the head of a huge grassy basin. His piercing, golden-yellow eyes wandered slowly over the snow-topped horizons encircling his mountain pasture, shifting now and then down to its far end, where a cleft in the mountains made passage for a stream. Above and behind him a time-furrowed wall of gray rock rose vertically for 200 yards, its silhouette sharp against the cobalt-blue sky of the Canadian Rockies.

Here, thirty miles from the nearest logging road, a dozen miles from the nearest horse trail, he was in a safe haven. And here he had spent the summer with seven mature rams about his own age; all of them would be bachelors until the heat of the late fall rut sent them down toward the timber line in search of the ewes.

After feeding at dawn in the lush bottom of the basin, the big ram, followed in single file by his fellows, had moved up the slopes to the north end of the valley, where the sun had already cleared the first September snowfall from the steep slide of dark shale. Once on the slide, the dark gray-brown coats of the rams blended with the jumbled background of rock. An observer on the far wall of the basin would have found it impossible to see the sheep if it were not for their large white rump patches. As it was, the band moving across the face of the slope became a string of white dots bobbing and angling toward the base of the cliff.

Near the cliff the lead ram stopped and swung his massively crowned head to sweep the basin. His eyes scanned it all, save for the narrow ravine marking the passage of the little stream through the center of the basin. After a few minutes of searching the walls of the valley, the wide snow fields below the towering peaks, and the serrated sky line of his domain, the ram poked tentatively with a broad front hoof at the loose shale of the slope. Then, with his cohort imitating his action, he dug quickly with both hoofs, scattering the shale until he had smoothed an area about a foot wide and a yard long. Satisfied, he took a long, last look down

the valley and plumped himself to the hard ground.

With the rams securely bedded for the morning, life in the high mountain valley settled into pastoral serenity. The sun climbed above the cliffs, its radiance still retaining enough of summer's vigor to erode the snow patches on the slopes. The melt, seeping down, swelled the little stream just enough so that light sparkled from it as it coursed through the valley.

By midmorning the wind from the west rose enough to send long plumes of snow trailing from the pinnacles guarding the basin. A golden eagle swept in on the western wind, soared in small circles over the center of the valley, and with a single scream of disappointment at the lack of a target glided down through the cleft at the foot of the basin toward better hunting grounds below. The rams, dutifully chewing their cud, followed the flight path of the eagle until it specked out, and all but the leader dropped their heads to the shale for midday siesta.

The silence of high noon in a lofty mountain basin is deep enough to be felt, as well as heard. Only at intervals does a pebble, loosened by melting snow, bounce and tumble over tinkling shale. Sometimes its descent precipitates a small avalanche. But such are the sounds rams have lived with forever. None is alarming—not even the small rattle of rock from the stream bed caused by the carelessly placed boot of the hunter.

The guide, crouching up ahead, turned in alarm, and with finger to lips motioned the hunter along. So far they had been well hidden in their stalk by the rocky walls of the stream bank, but now these were petering out. If they were lucky, the last of the cover would keep them out of sight of the rams until they came within killing range. Nervously, the hunter guessed that any shots he got would be at a target a full quarter of a mile away. If the rams stayed bedded he had a chance, with a flat-shooting rifle and a scope sight. If they spooked, only a lucky hit would pay off this heartbreaking search and stalk, which had begun at sunrise.

At this point, neither hunter nor guide knew just

80

Preceding pages: Rocky Mountain
goat is not a spectacular trophy, but bagging him is
difficult, requires arduous climbing in
high mountain ranges. Opposite: Bighorn rams cross
an alpine slope in Alberta, Canada.

where the rams were. It had seemed best in making the long stalk not to risk taking a peek over the walls of the stream bank as they toiled up the valley. The bighorn ram's eyesight is as sharp as any in the animal kingdom and in this bare valley it would be too much to hope that an exposed head would escape notice for long. It was the guide's hope that the stalk would bring them within killing range before the ravine ran out.

But the rams lay quietly as the sun passed its zenith, so quietly that they seemed to drowse. The warm sunlight raised wisps of vapor from the moist stones of the slope. The air at the base of the cliff, protected from the wind high above, settled in a hypnotic mass. The chunky bodies of the sheep on the slide might have been carved from the same stone as the boulders along the cliff wall.

Yet bighorn rams evidently never sleep. A single flash of light winked from the valley bottom as the guide raised his glasses and peered from his hiding place in the rocky ravine, checking the quality of the heads for his hunter. The lead ram, he decided, the one lying on the left, was the best. He had massive curls three and a half feet long, broomed off squarely at the tips. The guide ducked behind his sheltering boulder and whispered to the hunter lying beside him catching his breath.

The wink of strange light was enough to alert the big ram. He focused his attention on the ragged line of rocks below, watchful for any new, strange movement. It came as the hunter's rifle barrel appeared between the rocks, 81

*Full-curl bighorn rams (above) are top-rated trophy animals
in North America. They have heaviest horn development of any game animal their
size, but trophy specimens can be found only
in remote areas of Rockies. Agile ram (top) finds a vantage point from
which to scan valley below. Hunter can capitalize on
sheep's tendency to expect danger only from below. While both sexes carry
horns (middle and bottom), ewes' are shorter and stubbier.*

and his broad-brimmed hat rose above it.

The ram bounced to his feet. His sturdy, heavily-boned legs were planted firmly under him, ready to launch him up the slide. The entire band scrambled to its feet after him, their eyes fixed on the danger spot. The lead ram took a step forward, then another. At the instant of his move, a white spurt of rock dust burst from the slide beside him. The crack of the shattered rock stung him into a great forward leap, up and away from the valley floor. The snap of the rifle report, a split second later, triggered the full line of rams into a trot. Angling up the slope, firm-footed over the treacherous shale, the rams headed for the saddle between peaks, in the classic "topping-out" maneuver of their kind.

The second bullet tossed rock dust and snow under the lead ram's hind feet. The third sent a jet of mud under the second ram's nose; the fourth hit with a soggy whump, jarring the heavy body. The ram stumbled. He picked up his forefeet, but his heavy legs bent under him. His gray muzzle dipped into the shale. He pitched forward, the wide bases of his horns curled under his thick neck, somersaulting down the slide, a tumbling body already dead.

The last of the rifle reports was still bouncing from the basin walls as the lead ram charged up the snow-filled saddle. His string of followers, minus one, galloped behind until all but the last passed from sight over the divide. The tail-ender, a younger ram with horn tips scarcely broomed, paused for one last look, with only head and horns black against the deep blue of the sky.

At the foot of the slide a dark mound against the green of alpine pasture marked the end of the hit ram's rolling descent. Small boulders, disturbed by his passage, still bounced toward the clear, tiny stream hurrying toward the cleft in the hills. The figures of guide and hunter, moving painfully up the slope, were the only signs of life in the basin. Before the men had reached their trophy the rams were well beyond the divide and heading for a still higher mountain valley.

The wild sheep of North America rate near or at the top of the list of hunting trophies. The casual mention

Hunters of 1880's were more interested
in bighorn meat than in trophies. This buckskinned pair,
painted by Frederic Remington, is trying
for ram on far side of canyon. Successful shot also
will mean a backbreaking retrieve.

of bighorn or Dall among hunters puts a glint of memory in the eye of the experienced, a look of envy in the eye of those less blessed. For of all the hoofed game on this continent, a trophy ram is the rarest. Sportsmen who have achieved a Grand Slam—a trophy head of the four major varieties of wild sheep—can be counted on one's fingers. Those who have made it twice probably can be counted on one's ears.

The principal reason, of course, is inaccessibility. Even in these days of swift transit, wild sheep are not easy to reach. They are the hermits of the remote, high wilderness country. Planes and cars will whisk you to the outer limits of sheep country, but the last weary miles of search must be covered on horseback or on foot.

The pursuit of rams also is time consuming. Hunters often must wait for years before obtaining a permit in one of the few states which allow the hunting of sheep. The desert bighorn means torrid hunting in the Southwestern states or in Mexico or Baja California. Hunting the Stone means heading for the north country, the White Dall the Far North, usually the Yukon or Alaska. Bighorn territory, too, is to the north, through the Rockies and the area south of the Peace River in British Columbia.

Fortunately—and this is only a matter of degree—the bighorn can be hunted freely in the two great big-game provinces of Canada: Alberta and British Columbia. There is no need to draw for a permit. Once you have selected an outfitter and bought the big-game license, you are ready to hunt bighorn. The trick lies in selecting the right outfitter. The right one knows sheep country and is willing to hunt sheep. Finding both qualities in one man is not easy.

Killing a trophy ram is all work. A few sportsmen have "lucked into" a good ram while hunting other big game, but it is nothing that can be counted on. Trophy rams mean sweat, tortured lungs, spavined knees, frost-nipped ears, fingers, and toes, and, often as not, great bruises and bloody fingers. A successful sheep hunter must possess some of the qualifications of an alpine climber, a high-rigger, a bronco rider, and a glider pilot. It helps, too, if he is a fine rifleman, accustomed to accurate

judgment of range in the clear, high-mountain air and an expert in giving his bullet the correct amount of "Kentucky windage" when the gales build thirty-foot drifts among the peaks.

The full-curl ram head hanging on the den wall, therefore, becomes a symbol whose cost cannot be measured in dollars alone. It must take into account months of planning, days of riding, hours of walking and breathless climbing, more hours of endless glassing of slopes, slides, and mountain meadows—the painstaking preliminaries to the moment when finally you find a ram, decide to kill him, and do it.

The gathering of a trophy ram puts the hunter into some of the most majestic, awe-inspiring terrain in the world. The bighorn ram's notion of an ideal social life is to be with males of his own age group. To achieve it he chooses that towering, overpowering, confusing mass of stonework carelessly sculptured by nature and called, expediently, the Rockies. And along the length of this continental backbone he chooses the highest, most remote regions, usually above the range of all other game except the Rocky Mountain goat. These he ignores, along with the females and young of his own kind. On a goat mountain you will rarely find rams, unless they happen to be passing through.

If trophy heads could be evaluated by sheer poundage, the bighorn ram again would take top honors. The massive horns of a full-curl ram, even when broomed off, will scale at least three feet around the curve, with a base circumference of about fifteen inches. This rugged headgear may weigh up to thirty pounds. This can be ten per cent of the remaining body weight of the animal. I believe no other game animal in the world approaches this ratio.

The brooming of the horn tips is a disconcerting feature of many trophy bighorns. The scoring value of the head is reduced one point for each inch of horn that is lacking. On a heavy old ram this can amount to six inches or more on each horn for a total score reduction of at least twelve points.

The best bighorn I have killed measured thirty-eight and a half inches around each curl, with a base circum- 85

*Stone sheep (above) is generally smaller than
bighorn and found farther north. It also has somewhat darker body color
and lighter-weight, wider-flaring horns. Opposite: Dall
sheep (top) is pure white species of Far North, runs smaller than Stone.
Guide (bottom) checks Dall heads in Yukon basin.*

ference of sixteen and a half inches. The area of the broomed-off points measures two by three inches, so it is safe to say that there would have been at least six more inches on each horn if the full growth had remained. The ram would have had well over a forty-inch curl, and forty inches is the goal of most sheep hunters I know.

Brooming is unique among bighorns. Other horned or antlered game animals often will break one or more points from their headgear in fighting with other males, but the bighorn sheep is the only game animal which deliberately rubs off the antler tips. The purpose of the brooming is obvious. When a bighorn ram develops a close curl the tips of the horns interfere with his vision. The ram finds this intolerable and grinds the tips until his vision is unobstructed. This goes on all his life.

Widespread curls do not block his vision and are rarely broomed off. So it is these heads that we find most often in the record book. In general, however, it is only the odd bighorn ram which will have flaring curls; occasionally you see one among a group with well-rubbed horn tips. This odd fellow is the trophy the bighorn hunter dreams of.

The two northern varieties of sheep—the Stone and the Dall—are thin horns and normally have wider flaring curls than the bighorns. Only in a few districts, such as the Kenai Peninsula of Alaska, do the Dall have close, broomed-off curls. The tip-to-tip spread of a Canadian bighorn rarely approaches two feet, but that of Stone and Dall sheep frequently exceeds it.

Horns of the northern varieties are much less massive than the average full-curl bighorn. The Dall sheep, which is pure white in most of its range, has horns of a light color, sometimes golden yellow, which make a pretty and impressive trophy. Actually, the somewhat thinner horns of these species are compatible with their body size. Canadian bighorns are by far the largest of all the varieties, with mature rams often scaling over 300 pounds. It takes a big Dall sheep to weigh 225 pounds and the Stones run just a bit heavier.

So much for the trophy. The hunting of all mountain sheep is incredibly rugged, and in the Far North the hunter usually must depend on his legs to bring him

to the levels where he will find sheep. Horses are not often available in much of the Dall sheep country, although more have been used in recent years in the Stone sheep areas farther south. The routine in the Far North is to fly in to a mountain lake by float plane, set up a base camp, and begin searching for rams—always upward and miles from the tents.

In all mountain-sheep hunting your guide-outfitter is the vital link between you and the trophy. Much sheep country, however "sheepy" it may look, holds no sheep, for one reason or another. Or you may be in hot sheep country where you see dozens of ewes, lambs, and young

*Although bighorns are high-mountain game
animals, they feed mostly in meadows like these at
middle elevations below the timber line.
Sheep rarely descend to low elevations unless
driven there by severe winters.*

rams everyday, but no shootable heads. Moreover, since the hunting season opens long before the breeding season, the mating urge, a big factor in hunting most other big-game animals, will be of no help here. Your guide, then, must know where the big rams are likely to hang out, and frequently this will be a dozen miles or more from the nearest band of ewes and lambs.

But no guide, however keen, can count on putting you on to a trophy ram in any pre-chosen basin or mountain range. He must look for rams—as you will—hour after hour, sweeping the terrain slowly and carefully with the binoculars. He studies the grassy pasture slopes for feeding sheep, the rockslides and ledges for those bedded down after the morning repast.

Of the three distinct varieties of sheep, the two species of bighorn are the most difficult to find when bedded. Their gray-brown coat blends into rock and shale, as wise rams seem to know only too well. Stone sheep are darker in color, almost black in some phases, and usually stand out from their background a bit better. These sheep also graze more open country than bighorns and are thus somewhat easier to locate. The Dall, because of his pure white coat, stands out like a beacon when feeding in an alpine meadow. Even when he beds down in a snow field, the distinct outline of his horns gives him away.

In any case, sheep are great wanderers and the band of rams you locate in a basin four miles away in mid-afternoon may be six miles away in another basin the following morning. Unless rams have an unusually good hide-out, with plenty of food and water and no disturbances, you will rarely find them in the same area for more than a day or so. Once spooked, their chopping, steady trot carries them easily and quickly over the steepest, roughest terrain imaginable, putting them miles away in less than an hour.

It is maddening to spook a band of rams after a long stalk—which happens all too often when things don't go right—and to watch them top out of a basin in a matter of minutes when you know full well it will take you hours to cover the same distance. It is equally maddening to locate a ram or rams a few miles away, make a long,

tough approach, and discover the trophy has vanished.

But this is sheep hunting. Meeting the animal on his own terms is the real challenge. The hunter works along rocky ledges, toils up cliff faces, and runs across treacherous rockslides which might start a small avalanche at any moment. But in carrying out the task of bagging a trophy he develops the feeling that he is as rugged an individual as the ram, a feeling that comes in few other types of hunting.

The rifle for mountain-sheep hunting should be fairly light in weight. Even as little as an extra half pound becomes a burden with the endless climbing entailed in getting a ram. The rifle need not be extra powerful, but it should be mounted with a lightweight scope and light but rugged mounts. A carrying sling is a must; some hunters demand a shooting sling, although I have never found this necessary. As a rule you will have time at the end of the stalk to find a handy rock to support your hand.

Among modern calibers, the 7-mm Mauser is probably a minimum for sheep. Although I have never killed a ram with either the .243 Winchester or 6-mm Remington, I believe that these cartridges loaded with 100-grain bullets will do the job. I lean toward these two loads because each has a satisfactory flat trajectory and is chambered in a lightweight rifle. The Remington Model 600, in either rifle or carbine, is a good sheep rifle. If you feel the 6-mm is a bit light, you can choose the .308 Winchester and shoot the 150-grain bullets.

A ram is not particularly hard to kill, although he may be hard to hit because of his location and distance from the hunter. A bedded ram, lying on a hillside above you, is always a more difficult target than a ram standing broadside on your own level. But among modern cartridges there is a wide choice, any of which will provide the necessary accuracy and flat trajectory. The .257 and .270 Weatherby Magnum, the 7-mm Remington Magnum, the .280 Remington, and .270 Winchester are all fine sheep cartridges. If you must kill the ram far off, then your best choice is the Magnums. If you will stalk the trophy to within 200 yards you can certainly anchor him with the 6-mm Remington.

89

ROCKY MOUNTAIN GOAT

Rocky Mountain goat nanny (with kid)
often carries horns as long as billy's, but
invariably more slender. White goat
shows up well against mountain greenery (right),
but is almost invisible in snow.

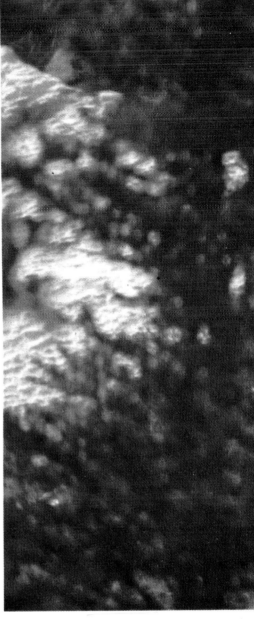

Looking over my horse's ears and through the narrow opening the trail had cut through the tall spruces, I could see the rounded tip of Danaher Mountain framed in the evergreens. We had been riding since sunrise—about an hour—and had camped overnight on the divide between the North Fork of the Blackfoot River and the South Fork of the Flathead, in the middle of Montana's Rockies. Behind me was a pack string of thirty head: mules, pack and saddle horses, guides, wranglers, and my hunting partners. A few yards ahead trotted Cheese, the lead dog of the Copenhaver lion pack, a battle-scarred veteran of a decade of chasing cougars. We were headed into the Bob Marshall Wilderness Area on an elk and deer hunt— and I had a goat permit in my saddlebag.

Within a few minutes, the down-sloping trail, seven or eight miles long and a mile wide, broke from the timber into the valley of Danaher Flats. Down the middle of the valley the South Fork flowed gently, snaking through mountain willow. Off to the west the sheer, gray cliffs of Limestone Mountain rose above green slopes. And on those green slopes, a couple of miles away, lay a couple of white boulders—something like a pair of dice on a pool table, I thought casually as my horse moved along the muddy trail.

I had been looking for elk and deer, had seen no elk, but had jumped a pair of mulies after leaving the camp site. A bull elk had sent out a long two-toned whistle as we were breaking camp, a challenging bugle that carried easily in the still air from his spot in the timber half a

mile above us. But the opening of the season was still one day off and, besides, this bull was out of the Bob Marshall limits, in territory that had a later opening date for the season.

Since I was well ahead of the pack string, I decided to cut over to the creek to look for trout. They were there, well enough, half a dozen or more cutthroat, lying along a submerged log in a clear pool, resting over a white gravel bottom. I unforked my horse for a better look and the trout scattered instantly, heading for the protective cover of the upstream riffle. With the fish gone, I began to glass the mountain sides for game.

At once I saw that the two boulders on the green slope had moved. I sat down and steadied the glasses on my knees for a better look. The boulders now became two white animals cropping the pasture, animals with an odd hump over the withers and the short legs of the plains buffalo. In a word, goat. I dug into my saddlebag and pulled out the 20X spotting scope for a closer look. Each goat had horns—short, black, and sharp—but the distance was too great to tell which was the better head. One was much larger than the other, with a yellowish cast to his coat. I decided to see if my guide thought either might be a trophy.

"Yes," Howard said, checking with his binoculars. "The big goat has eight- or nine-inch horns. They're both billies, but one is a youngster. Maybe he has five-inchers, but I doubt it."

"Anyway," he said, as he climbed back into the saddle, "the season doesn't open until tomorrow and if we 91

nerve to climb sheer precipices on the sort of footing a goat accepts as a matter of course. I have seen goats standing on the face of a cliff with nothing between them and the ground but a one-foot rock ledge and 1,000 feet of air. On the other hand, the goat may not have brains enough to know that he is doomed if he slips. In any case, dizzying heights mean nothing to a goat, although they usually induce severe vertigo in the stalking hunter.

Sheep hunting is tough enough, but only rarely do you get into the kind of tight corner that is so commonplace when stalking goat. While sheep love the high meadows, they rarely go to the top of a cliff unless they are badly frightened. Goats, however, love these precarious haunts, and in a range where both animals are found usually live well above the level of the sheep.

In general, goats are exceptionally easy to spot if they are not bedded down on a snow patch or a slide of light-colored rock. The best time to locate them is early in the morning when they are sure to be up and feeding over the type of cover that reveals their white coats. If you are not glassing them at feeding time, however, they can be hard to find. For despite the fact that they are usually in the open when feeding or bedding, they often will stay in screening evergreens at the edge of the timber line during the day.

Unlike sheep, goats are usually hunted in combination with other game—elk, moose, grizzly, caribou, and, of course, sheep—since they do not spook as quickly at the report of a rifle as do the sheep. This and the fact that they have a fairly wide range on this continent, all the way from Montana to the Alaskan Peninsula—a range that is spreading as more game departments carry on transplanting projects—makes them more and more attractive to the hunter. Probably the best goat country is British Columbia, despite the fact that there is plenty in Alberta, Alaska, and the Yukon, as well as in Montana, Idaho, and Washington. In some states certain goat areas are restricted to permits by drawing and this, of course, limits the hunter's chance for a goat.

As a trophy the goat leaves something to be desired. The head itself has a horsey shape, the horns are insignificant. Indeed, few specimens show horns even a foot

don't nail one up above we'll look for those two on the way back." I was left to ponder how he knew they were billies and how he could check the horns with 8X glasses when I couldn't see much difference between them with a 20X scope. But there are guides and guides!

The next day, riding out from our base camp up Calf Creek toward Foolhen Mountain, we spotted another pair of goats and, after a five-hour stalk, I took a nice billy with about eight-inch horns. More than a week later, on our way back to the ranch, we stopped near Limestone Mountain again to look for the first pair. We spotted them at once, at the very upper edge of the green slope, where the gray wall of the cliffs rose vertically. In a week they had moved perhaps 200 yards. We didn't bother this time to try to take one, but this experience indeed sums up goat hunting. You can find the goat on a "goat mountain," and once you have chosen the animal you want, you can shoot him today or next Friday, as the spirit moves you. He will not go far.

At the risk of arousing the ire of dedicated goat hunters I will say that the goat is dull-witted. I will also say that he has enormous courage. No other animal has the

92

long, and these may well be carried by either sex. For my part, the best trophy a goat supplies is his handsome coat of thick white wool. If you kill your goat well enough along in the season for the winter coat to have developed, he will provide you with an excellent rug.

Since the goat is an extremely tough, phlegmatic animal, he often takes quite a bit of killing. Although he is about the same weight as a bighorn ram, he will not succumb so readily to the same punishment from bullets. Rifles of the type used for grizzly, elk, and moose are most effective on goat—all the Magnums, from 7-mm up, and the heavier .30-caliber rifles. These rifles may be a bit on the heavy side, but once you have found the goat you want it is unlikely that you will have to make more than one stalk to get him.

PRONGHORN ANTELOPE

Perhaps not properly, but at least by common usage, this section on horned game should be entitled "Antelope," since this is the name by which the animal is known in the areas of the West where he is found. The trouble is that he is not really an antelope, but the popular title remains. He is, on the other hand, a strictly American brand of game, with no near relatives in other parts of the world. His hoofs are similar to a deer's but he has no dewclaws. His horns have a sort of bony core, as all properly horned animals do, but unlike all others, he sheds the horns from their core out every year. As a game animal he is a paradox, but withal, a highly popular hunting target throughout the West.

I know several top-notch big-game hunters who rate antelope as their favorite game. In a way, I can agree with this. For antelope stay well out in the open, shunning any sort of cover since it might conceal enemies. And as a result the animal can be hunted successfully at any time of day. You need not be on hand at first daylight to see them before they take to ravines, blowdowns, timber, or brush for their bedding hours. I have killed most of my antelope between the hours of nine a.m. and four p.m., which is most convenient.

Most antelope country is easy to hunt. The wide expanse of plain and prairie is easy to cover in a Jeep or pickup truck. You rarely need to walk a step until you are ready to make a stalk on the particular trophy you have selected. As in hunting sheep or other mountain game, you will do a good deal of glassing to find the herds, but the animals co-operate even in this. Their coats are a mixture of white and light tan—no one has yet figured out whether they are tan-on-white or white-on-tan—and they can be readily seen against most of their native backgrounds. An enormous, pure-white rump patch which blossoms like a sunflower when the animal rises from his bed in alarm is also helpful. When the erectile hairs of this rump patch are fully flared, antelope can be spotted with the unaided eye from as far as two miles away.

For his part, the pronghorn is as keen sighted as any creature in the animal kingdom. I have read many times that his vision is comparable to that of a man using eight-power binoculars. How this was calculated I have no idea. But I do know that when I stick my head over a clump of sagebrush atop a knoll to observe a bunch of antelope half a mile away, they all will be watching me. Obviously, the unobstructed view afforded by open country works as much in favor of the sharp-eyed antelope as it does the hunter, and it is difficult to take them unawares. They know their home terrain well and any strange object, however small—even a hunter's capped head—rivets their attention.

One point in the hunter's favor is that the pronghorn cannot count. If three men spot a band of animals a mile or so away, and are spotted in turn by the band, they can move along until a favorable spot for making a stalk is located. One of the group can then drop out, while the pair strolls on in full view, making sure only that the animals do not become alarmed. The third party, meanwhile, makes his stalk while the band's attention is diverted and, if he shoots well, he should gather his trophy.

The same stunt can be effectively carried out using a vehicle. Commonly, the Jeep hunter rides to the crest of a knoll, quite carefully, so that no more of the top

93

*Spooked pronghorns (below) flare white rump
patches as they take off for sanctuary in hills. At top speed these
animals can do sixty miles per hour, but light coloring
makes them an easy target against blue-gray of Western sage (left).
Old-time hunter (far left) tries for a prize.*

side is exposed than is needed to glass the broad expanse of prairie beyond. If a trophy head is located and the animal is far enough away to minimize the danger of spooking him, the country is studied for making a stalk. When a route is chosen, the Jeep is driven to the take-off point, the hunter is dropped, and the vehicle driven to a high point of ground where the herd can watch it while the hunter makes his approach.

If this sounds like oversimplification, it is. Since a great deal of antelope country is the wide-open spaces, there will be many situations where the animals cannot be approached because of a total lack of screening cover. If the animals are bedded you must wait for them to get up to feed, then try to anticipate the direction they will move. You make a wide circle, under cover or at a discreet distance, then approach on foot to a concealed vantage point, where you wait for them to feed into killing range. Should you prefer not to spend an afternoon in waiting them out for feeding, you will do best to go on and look for another bunch, for antelope cannot be hurried.

In antelope country, a precise knowledge of water holes is of great assistance. Normally, the animals will head for water at daybreak and at dusk, and rarely are they far from a source of water. In the big ranch country we glass the prairies for windmills. With the pumpers working all the time, there is a good supply of water in the cattle tank and, usually, in the overflow catch basin. You can count on finding antelope within a radius of three or four miles of these windmills, unless the area has been heavily pounded by hunters.

The speed of antelope in flight is legendary. No other American game animal can move so fast or so smoothly over rough ground. Biologists say that a hard-pressed antelope can move at sixty miles per hour. I believe this, since I was once riding along a paved road near White Sulphur, Montana, when I nearly ran into a bunch of ten antelope bucks in a little dip over a rise of ground. They immediately went into high gear, running parallel to the road and just ahead of the car—a game that antelope love to play. I checked the speedometer at fifty, with the herd running smoothly ahead, when, for some strange reason, they decided to cross the road. Putting on an extra burst of speed, they flew across the highway, seemingly gaining speed as they crossed. They must have been hitting close to sixty at that point. I would be curious to learn what would have happened if we had begun to shoot at them as they crossed the road. Probably they would have picked up their speed another ten miles per hour!

Although the antelope is faster than a scared jack rabbit, he is not an impossible target at high speed. Unlike other hoofed animals on the run, he does not bob up and down as he goes. Instead, he seems to flow smoothly over the ground with his body moving about two feet above ground level. If you can figure how far to lead him, you need only lay the horizontal wire of your scope cross hair on his body. Then put the vertical wire ahead of him just that amount and squeeze off the shot. There is much luck in scoring on a scared antelope buck, but it can be done. I've done it several times at ranges up to 350 yards.

The real thrill of antelope hunting, however, is in the careful stalk, the approach to a trophy buck as he stands guarding his harem of does. You will have spent some time in glassing him for his head, perhaps breaking out the 20X spotting scope to make sure he is what you want. Then you will have glassed the area to find some cover for your approach: a grassy knoll, a ravine, a shallow coulee, or a clump of sagebrush higher than the rest. You will move up, first in a crouch, then on hands and knees, finally on your stomach, picking up a few cactus spines as you travel. If the wind does not change and you keep your head low as you come in on him, you will have a good chance of getting a shot at 300 yards or a bit less.

The final thrill is in making the precise, one-shot kill after you have carefully calculated range, drop of bullet, and the amount of wind drift, and you squeeze off the trigger with the cross hairs held in the calculated spot. If your judgment was good and the let-off just right, the plunk of the bullet will come back to you the barest instant after your buck hits the gumbo with a dust-raising thump.

SELECTED GUNS FOR HORNED GAME

Browning Safari Grade, with 6X scope

Winchester Deluxe Model 70

Weatherby Mark V

F. I. Mauser Supreme Grade

Remington Model 600 Carbine

BEARS

4

GRIZZLY BEAR

The mountain grizzly, one of the rarest of North American trophies and certainly the rarest in the United States, is killed by baiting more often than not. This method does not rate very high as sport, but it is the most successful way to take a grizzly. For the most part, he is a nocturnal animal, and even in good grizzly country an observant and careful hunter will not necessarily encounter one in the course of a two-week hunt.

Unfortunately, there is no good grizzly hunting left in the United States. The two states with the largest grizzly populations are Montana and Wyoming, which claim about a thousand. But half of these are within Yellowstone National Park and, of course, protected. A hunter's best chance for the silvertip bear is in the provinces of Alberta and British Columbia, where he always has been esteemed and protected as a game animal. He has not had much chance in the States, since ranchers have slaughtered him ruthlessly for more than half a century as a killer of stock. A few bears do turn to stock killing, but this is a poor excuse for the wholesale elimination of the species.

There also is excellent grizzly hunting in the Yukon and Alaska, but, in general, the man who sets out to kill a grizzly is as rare among hunters as the bear is among trophies—except, of course, the spring bear hunter who is after bear exclusively.

Since the grizzly is always found in areas inhabited by other big game, it is usually the sheep, goat, elk, caribou, or moose hunter who gets a chance at him. In glassing the alpine basins and high slopes, both hunter and guide hope to spot a grizzly, but without really expecting to find one. Since bears are great travelers during the fall, just before hibernation, meeting up with one during a brief hunt is a matter of the sheerest chance.

Spring hunting is something else. As soon as the bears come out of hibernation, they begin to work over the slides, where avalanches and sun have bared the ground and the first greenery of spring appears. Rather often these same avalanches will hold the carcass of winter-killed game animals that appeal greatly to a grizzly's shrunken stomach after his winter-long fast.

The technique of spring grizzly hunting is simply to get into good bear country, pick a high vantage point overlooking a number of slides, and use the glasses for a couple of hours after daybreak and before dark, which are the best feeding times. Once the trophy is spotted, the rest is up to the hunter and his guide. They must decide how to approach him, and how to stay upwind and out of sight until they are within killing range. With a grizzly bear it is always advisable to shorten the range to assure good bullet placement and maxi-

100

mum effect with the first shot. Trailing a wounded grizzly in brush and timber ranks high among the hazardous sports of the world.

Although the mountain grizzly is considerably larger than a black bear, it is a rare specimen that weighs as much as a mature bull elk. The rifles listed for elk hunting are, therefore, every bit as effective for grizzly under the same conditions. I would say that a grizzly is no tougher to kill than a bull elk, and I have, in fact, seen a number of one-shot kills on grizzly with rifles in the .270 class. As in all big-game hunting, the placement of the bullet is the vital factor. Although hunters shooting at grizzly are inclined to be shaken by his reputation for power and ferocity, he can be put down with a shot in the brain or through the spine. A bullet into the shoulder, particularly if the bear is facing you, also will put him down long enough for you to finish him off with a second shot.

BROWN BEAR

It was a bright day in early September and I was wading along, tossing an Alaskan Mary Ann hair fly over the clear waters of Battle River in southwestern Alaska. The big rainbows and grayling were coming well, and every five minutes or so I was releasing a fish as I moved downstream.

At the foot of a long riffle the stream was split by a tiny island. Its downstream end was a tapering bar of pure white sand melting into a deep, dark hole. I worked along this bar, scarring the smooth surface of the sand with coarse tracks from my hobnail wading brogues, and eventually hooked a huge rainbow that forced me to shore and down to the tail of the pool before I could release him. Then, with my gear-carrying guide in tow, I moved to the next run, hoping to tie into one or two more of these fine fish before retracing my steps back to camp.

Since I had hooked the big rainbow in the deep hole after the first few casts, I decided to give the pool another try on the way back. But thick stands of alder along the banks made it almost impossible to cover the water,

except from the island at the head of the pool. So I waded across to my original casting spot on the sand bar. Only then did I discover that the sand bar had had another visitor since I had left it just a few moments before.

A line of huge bear tracks, dwarfing those of my hobnails, ran parallel to mine, then swung into the river toward the far side. I was not the only fisherman on that river! As I moved out of the water for a closer look, I was amazed at the size of the tracks of this great bear. I pulled out my De-liar and measured. According to the steel tape, the hind foot tracks were sixteen inches long and ten inches wide, and sank about two inches into the hard-packed sand. The bear must have weighed at least 1,200 or 1,300 pounds. Fortunately for me he was gone from the area, but I was glad that my guide was carrying my .375 H & H Magnum and would have been happier still if he had had a .458 Magnum as well, although at that time this dangerous-game stopper did not exist. I don't think I could have driven off the grizzly with my fly rod!

The coastal brown bear—a subspecies of grizzly—is the largest carnivore in the world. His only rival in size is the polar bear, and it is still a moot question as to which species has produced the largest individuals. Since it is impractical to weigh these huge animals in the field, when they are killed, and equally impractical to move them in one piece, the question of comparative weights is still open. The consensus of mammalogists, however, is that a big brownie will weigh 1,600 pounds.

Among the bears of interest to hunters, the average weights of males seem to double from species to species. The male black bear averages about 300 pounds, the grizzly 600, and the brownie about 1,200, which puts him in a class by himself.

This is a tough animal and should never be hunted with an inadequately powered rifle. The right rifle for brown bear is the most powerful caliber you can shoot well. I rate the .300 H & H Magnum as a safe minimum, with the .338 Magnum and .375 Magnum even better. Currently, the Alaskan bear guides carry the .458 Magnum, in case it should be necessary to follow a brownie 101

*Alaskan brown bear (right), world's
largest carnivore, stands nine feet tall, weighs up
to 1500 pounds. (Only polar bear matches
this size.) Audubon grizzly (below) falls somewhat
short of true representation of species.*

into the brush and dig him out of cover at rifle point.

Although the brown bear has a much more restricted habitat than either the black bear or the mountain grizzly, he is numerous along the Alaskan coast, north of Admiralty Island. Kodiak Island has many, which probably explains why he is frequently misnamed the "Kodiak Bear." The brownie found elsewhere in Alaska is the same as the Kodiak residents, although—as with all grizzlies—there are wide variations in color among individuals. The mountain grizzlies are called "silvertip" because certain of them have a basic black coat with long, white-tipped guard hairs. Nonetheless, grizzlies range in color from black to pale tan, or blonde, as does the brown bear, although the average is, in fact, a medium brown.

In Alaska, which is the greatest bear country in the world, the ranges of the mountain grizzly and the brownie overlap and the animals intergrade. In certain areas, it is not easy for a hunter to determine whether he has downed a grizzly or a brownie. Generally, however, a bear taken about seventy-five miles inland from coastal waters is sure to be a grizzly. The bigger browns are coastal animals.

Spring is by far the best time of the year to hunt the brown bear. The easiest hunting is by boat, one large enough to provide accommodations for hunters and guides. The bears begin to come out of hibernation in April, and they can be spotted from the boat as they work along the slopes and slides, digging out roots or buried animals. At this time of year the bears are in poor condition physically, but will have the best coats. Bears taken in the late summer or early fall usually are badly "rubbed," with large bare spots on the hide. These animals are so bothered by insects in summer that they literally rub the hair from their bodies, leaving their coats quite patchy by wintertime. Hunters looking for trophy rugs will be more likely to find them in the spring.

Once a trophy bear has been spotted from the boat, hunter and guide head for shore in the dinghy to make the stalk on foot. This can be as easy as shooting a woodchuck in a pasture lot, or as tough as downing a full-curl bighorn. It depends on where the bear is located. In any case, both grizzly and brown bear have notoriously poor eyes, an excellent pair of ears, and a good nose. A successful stalk means keeping downwind of the animal until the hunter can get close enough to make a kill—with the first shot if it is at all possible. No hunter should attempt long-range kills on this big, dangerous animal. From relatively short range, he should penetrate the brain, break the spine, or break the shoulders. If the bear isn't downed with the first shot or two, there can be real trouble.

BLACK BEAR

Seated on a big spruce log lying across a trail up in the Allagash region of northern Maine, I watched Joe Willette, my guide, as he sneaked up the trail toward me. He had posted me on this spot, high up the side of a beech ridge, while he circled through the swamp hole below, hoping to maneuver a big buck up to the ridge, where I could get a look at him.

We had a pair of nice bucks hanging back at the logging camp and had one more to go to fill out. This was the afternoon of the last day of our hunt, with perhaps an hour of shooting light left. There wasn't much time.

"You see sum-ting, mebbe?" Joe whispered as he came near.

"No, only a red squirrel," I said, and I went on puffing my cigarette.

"Dese deer mebbe up on dat ridge. Lotta bitchnut dis year. Anyway, you go down dis trail to the logging road and turn." He motioned to the right. "Dat road goes only a leetle way to the end. You stay dere, right at end of dis ridge and I come down to you. Mebbe push buck down." I was all for that.

Quietly, I moved down the old trail for about a third of a mile. Through a clearing in the hardwoods I spotted the gravel of the logging road, made my turn to the right dutifully, then moved slowly toward the end of the beech ridge. A tiny stream, about a foot wide, cut across the gravel. I stepped into it to wash the mud from my boots, sloshing my feet around in it, kicking off a stubborn chunk of clay. As I looked up the logging road, perhaps five seconds later, a shiny black bear walked out of the spruces about seventy-five yards up the road. As his front paws hit the gravel he spotted me—perhaps a half second after I had spotted him. Without waiting for a second look, he made a flash turn into the road, away from me. In another second he was a bouncing black ball heading for the end of the road about fifty yards away.

My Remington 600 Carbine was slung, muzzle down on my left shoulder as I stood in the water. Before the bear had made two jumps it was unslung and at my shoulder. The bouncing ball appeared in the center of the scope, just above the black dot of the reticle. I lifted the black dot until it blended into the black rump and snatched off the trigger.

The bullet whacked into the bear. He made a quick right-angle turn and in two jumps left the road, heading into a small open chopping. As he passed from sight he gave out with a lusty bawl, not the bellow of a bull or grunt of a boar hog, but the squalling roar of a wounded bear. Again and again he bawled and I could hear him thrashing in the brush. His last bawl ended abruptly and I had to decide whether this was his last gasp or whether he had found safety in the blowdowns. If so, I would have to dig him out.

I paced off the distance as I moved along the gravel. Ninety-six steps to where his tracks turned off the road into the clearing. I stood, looking for blood, saw none, then listened carefully for movements in the timber. There were none. After a minute or two I stepped off the road into the clearing and looked this over. Also nothing. I sneaked quietly across the clearing, alert for signs. Nothing. So, I turned back toward the road to renew the search for sign. About fifty feet from the road, I spotted the bear, curled up behind and beneath a topping, with only his hind feet pads projecting. He was very dead, I was sure, and as I came up to him I gave him a good jab in the rear end with the rifle muzzle. This was anti-climactic. He was likely quite dead before I had moved up the logging road, perhaps thirty sec-

onds after the bullet took him square in the rear end. The .308, I discovered later, had passed up under his spine, chopped some liver, and bored onward to make rags of one lung.

He was an adult bear, very fat, very black, with the shiny thick coat of a bear properly pelted for the winter. Unlike many black bears that are killed in spring hunting, he was a trophy animal; his pelt was in good enough condition to make a fine rug.

In hunter's parlance, I had "lucked into" a bear. And this is the only way I have ever killed a black bear—stumbling over one or having one stumble over me while I have been hunting other game. In black-bear hunting in the Northeast this is par for the course. Bears in timber country are not now being still-hunted, or "stalked," with any degree of success.

Despite his unwholesome reputation for ferocity, the black bear is one of the most timid creatures on four feet. He has an enormous respect for the danger that the sight and smell of man represents, and he rarely permits his innate curiosity to delay his swift departure once the enemy is detected.

Although his vision is not of the best, his nose and ears more than make up for it. This makes it virtually impossible for even a highly skilled still-hunter, working upwind, to come to within shooting distance of a black bear. Even if the wind is not working for the 105

Prime black bear was shot by author in Allagash area of northern Maine, with a Remington Model 600 carbine in .308 caliber. Wilderness country such as this is noted for big whitetail bucks and grouse as well as blackies.

After salmon run begins in early summer, an Alaskan
brown bear (left) feeds almost wholly on
fish until hunting season opens. Black bears (above and top),
only species east of the Mississippi,
are deep-woods dwellers, usually come out after dark.

107

bear, those supersensitive ears can pick up your footfalls and away he goes. For about forty years I have pussy-footed through game country, almost all of it inhabited by black bears, and in that time, in the legal bear season, I have seen only five. I have spooked many on deer drives, heard them crashing through brush and splashing through swamps, but have actually seen only these five in hunting timber country.

In the mountains of the Far West and in Alaska it is a different story. The more open high-mountain country permits a hunter to pick up an occasional black bear when he is glassing for other game. Rather often a black will move out of a berry patch at fairly close range, offering a good shot. At other times, the animal can be stalked successfully. In Alaska, particularly in the southern Panhandle area, any salmon stream will produce black bears for a hunter who has patience enough to wait until they appear for their late afternoon feeding. I have seen as many as twenty-eight black bears along one salmon stream in an afternoon, when the salmon run was at its height.

Elsewhere in the country, some states, especially in the South, permit bear hunting with dogs. This is pretty exciting and invariably produces a bear if the hunter is satisfied to gather his trophy by shooting it out of a tree or by backing it into a corner on a rock ledge. It's about as much sport as hunting raccoon, which also has its devotees.

In the eastern Canadian provinces and some Western states, spring hunting is one fairly easy way to kill yourself a bear. When the animals leave their winter dens they are hungry and usually head for the nearest logging-camp garbage dump to pick over the wintered-out remains. Guides with bear-minded sports on their lists usually will have the foresight to bait these dumps with the carcass of a worn-out horse. The bears work this over until only bones remain. Many bears have been killed by potshooting from logging-camp windows.

Some states permit baiting bears in both spring and fall hunting seasons. This is as sure a way to get a bear as the law permits. The outfitter puts out a bait, watches it until it ripens and the bears begin to work on it, and then sends for the hunter. If the hunter has the proper patience he will, indeed, kill himself a bear.

The black bear is not a big animal. An average adult will weigh perhaps 300 pounds in the round, regardless of the many tales circulating about 400- and 500-pound bears. A 625-pound black bear is currently on record in New York state and this is a rare one. The largest black bear I ever saw measured nine feet between the tips of its paws as it hung from its hind feet. This fat, fall bear weighed only 365 pounds field dressed. It may have scaled 450 in the round.

The black bear is not particularly difficult to kill, hardly more so than a big whitetail buck. In timber hunting, when a bear walks up to a deer hunter on his stand, his regular deer rifle—whatever it may be—will quickly dispatch the bear if the bullet is placed well. Pat Lynch, a famous Maine guide of yesteryear, killed many with the relatively puny .250 Savage. How many of these were shot while restrained by a trap chain and drag I do not know, but Lynch always felt that his .250 Savage bear gun was big enough.

I have a Canadian friend who, until a few years ago, shot bears for bounty at the garbage dumps in the spring. He killed eight with the .22 Hornet, shooting most of them only once. He did not lose a bear with this tiny rifle, but he must have placed his bullets well.

There is no problem about the black-bear rifle for Western hunting. It is the same rifle you'll be carrying for sheep, goat, elk, moose, or deer. The choice is endless. If I were forced to choose a black-bear rifle for timber hunting—which seems unlikely—it would be a short-barreled carbine in either a lever action or one of the late-model bolt actions chambered for either the .35 Remington or the .308.

In all conscience, it is difficult for me to look upon the black bear as a game animal. Generally, he is an innocuous clown who does no more harm than his small cousin, the raccoon. In most of his range he is impossible to hunt on a man-versus-animal basis. You can bait him, run him with dogs, trap him, or smoke him out of his den—if you want one badly enough—but none of this makes him a real game animal.

SELECTED GUNS FOR BEARS

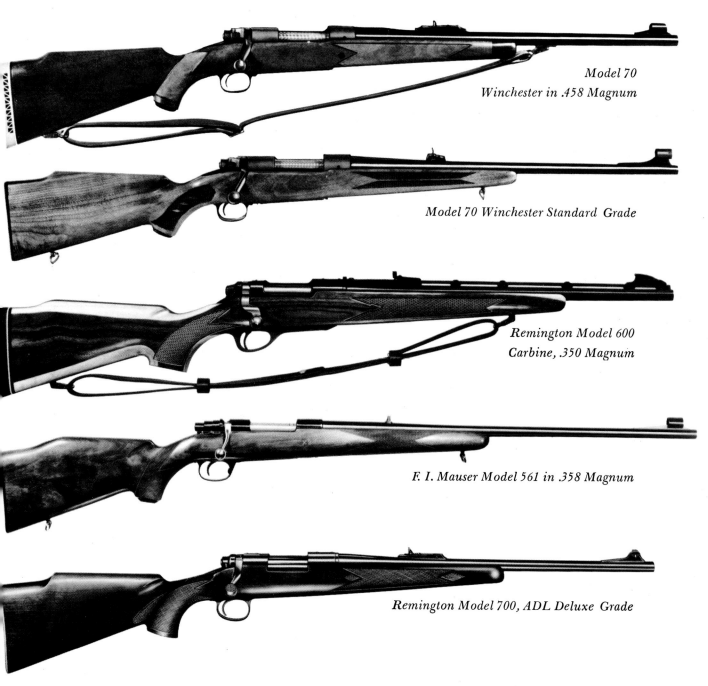

Model 70
Winchester in .458 Magnum

Model 70 Winchester Standard Grade

Remington Model 600
Carbine, .350 Magnum

F. I. Mauser Model 561 in .358 Magnum

Remington Model 700, ADL Deluxe Grade

STALKING &
STILL-
HUNTING

5

When I was a young deer-hunter, the term "still-hunter" had a special meaning for me. It meant being able to move through the woods quietly, without adding to the slight natural noises that make the forest so still. In moving through timber and second growth, the idea was to see your game before it took off in alarm without giving you a shot. This was, and is, still-hunting. It is the purest form of hunting, since it implies that the hunter is searching for his game and planning to make his approach without disturbing it. He matches his eyes, ears, and woods-skill against those of the animal.

Currently, the term still-hunting — as used in most whitetail deer country—has no such connotation of skill. Today's still-hunter foregoes the niceties of careful woodsmanship. Instead, he plants his butt on a stump, log, or rock, and waits there, *still* enough, to be sure, until a deer wanders by. This may take hours, days, even weeks, depending upon how carefully the waiting spot has been chosen. It is a successful way to kill a deer (or other game) if the shooter has patience enough to wait and is warmly enough clothed to keep from freezing. Strictly speaking, however, it is not hunting.

A substitute term for still-hunting is the ancient hunter's word, stalking. The American big-game hunter and varmint shooter does a great deal of stalking, but only in rare instances would he be likely to stalk a whitetail deer in timber country. The man who stalks his game is the one who has spotted it at a distance too far for him to make a killing shot, and who must make a closer approach, using whatever method he can to conceal his presence until he closes the distance for the kill.

In whitetail timber hunting, the deer that is seen is normally within range. Often, however, the situation may not permit a shot. The hunter then simply waits for the deer to move, which will either give him a chance to place his bullet or lose the game entirely. It is unthinkable to attempt to stalk a whitetail (or most other big-game animals) in timber. The deer will pick up the hunter's sounds almost immediately and be off.

So the skilled hunter must be adept at both still-hunting and stalking, and use whichever method the terrain dictates. In either case, he is hunting—not merely waiting in ambush for game to show itself.

No man becomes much of a big-game hunter until he masters the basic rules of still-hunting. It is only by moving carefully and watchfully through game country that a hunter learns how to find the animals, how to read the signs of their movements, and how to see them against natural backgrounds.

Novice deer hunters continually overlook their game, particularly in low growth, because they are watching at their own eye level, expecting to see an animal as tall as a horse. Deer do not stand much higher than three feet at the shoulder. If you expect to see them in laurel, scrub, or low brush you must look down into the cover rather than over it. Except in rare instances, a hunter does not get a full view of an animal. Trees, brush, and other vegetation invariably screen some part of the game. A whitetail hunter more often than not depends upon seeing the mere flick of an ear or a tail to spot his deer's location. In certain covers the entire body may be screened and only the movement of a leg will reveal the animal.

Aside from having a keen eye, a good hunter must know the anatomy of the animal he hunts. Recognizing an animal from a glimpse, or a part of the form, or under confusing light conditions can only be done if its appearance in all possible attitudes is thoroughly well known. The hunter must know the shape of an antler branch, so that he can distinguish it from a jumble of dead tree limbs. He must know that an animal's rump is not the same shape as a tree stump or a boulder. A deer's head, peering from behind a tree trunk, should not look like the stub of a broken branch. A bedded-down animal must not appear to be a log.

The hunter must watch for the signs that betray an animal's presence or his recent activity: fresh tracks, droppings, evidence of feeding, fresh beds, antler scrapings or "rubs" on saplings, pawed-over soil where bucks have been digging in the exuberance of the rut.

Finally, it is essential that as the hunter moves through timber, or any heavy cover, his eyes should continually sweep the terrain ahead of and around him to the limit

*Preceding pages: Mounted hunting party spots
bighorn sheep in Alberta Rockies. (It later stalked
them successfully.) Right: Tracks of
whitetail buck (at right) show toe-drag. Doe's
prints are precisely placed.*

*Winter yard (top) shows heavy browsing of deer on
white cedar. Sportsmen (below) glass a herd of bighorn rams in Alberta
Rockies. Top, right: Distinct trail to
feeding grounds is left by whitetail traveling on runway. Moose
hunter Jim Rikhoff (at right, below) checks bull tracks.*

of his vision. Assuming that his eyes are as good as those of the game he is hunting, he must focus his gaze at the maximum distance at which he can recognize the animal. Otherwise, the game is sure to see him first and go on the alert, awaiting his next move. If he is working through cover that allows him to see objects sixty yards ahead, it does not make sense to look for game forty yards away. The twenty-yard difference will give the game a twenty-yard advantage—a big advantage in timber hunting.

Still-hunting on a dull day puts the greatest demands on a hunter's eyes. The lack of contrast between light and shade, particularly in big timber, makes it almost impossible to pick out a motionless animal unless most of his body is in the open. Sunlight, on the other hand, is enormously helpful. The autumn coat of all hoofed game animals picks up a faint shine in the sun's rays, and quite often the glint of sun on an antler will reveal a buck or a bull otherwise hidden. And, of course, the light-colored rump patches of Western hoofed animals shine like beacons in the sun.

Moving quietly through woodland cover is another mark of the skilled still-hunter. He is ever alert to hazards in his path and tries to avoid stumbling over loose rocks, cracking dead twigs underfoot, and snapping off dead branches projecting from tree trunks. Even so, "moving quietly" is a relative term. No man (or animal, for that matter) can move more than a few yards in timbered game country without making a sound. It may be only the mild crushing of a dead leaf, the whisper of a few blades of dry grass, or the faint thump of a footfall, but sound there will be. The hunter's concern, however, is not the preservation of complete silence, but to make his passage quiet enough so that accruing sounds do not reach the ears of his target animal.

It is generally agreed among experienced hunters that all big-game animals have a better sense of hearing than man. Sounds as such do not, however, put them on the alert. All game country has its sounds: leaves flutter and tree limbs sigh in the wind, bark pops in the frost, crossed branches squeal as they rub against each other, sun-loosened rocks bounce down canyon walls, and dead tree limbs break off to crash on frozen ground. There are

myriad animal noises: the rustling of foraging gray squirrels, the chattering of chickarees, the whistle-scream of the hunting hawk, the thump of the drumming grouse, the cry of the blue jay. All these are part of the natural scene and do nothing to disturb the game.

It is offbeat sounds that put game on the alert. Metallic sounds such as the jingling of coins, the snapping of a rifle safety or the cocking of a hammer, the snick of a cigaret lighter or the clink of a horse's shod hoof—these all are unnatural sounds and game reacts to them instantly. I have had bull elk bugle at the sound of steel shoes on rock as I rode my saddle horse up a dry creek bed. I have also spooked a feeding whitetail buck by carelessly allowing my binoculars to clank against my rifle bolt knob.

A careful still-hunter can usually avoid making metallic sounds. He doesn't carry a pocket full of change. He carries his spare cartridges in a belt-loop holder, so they won't rattle in his pocket. He eases his safety off gently, or cocks his hammer after first holding back the trigger, then allowing it to slip quietly into the full-cock notch.

What is not so easy to avoid are some of the other game-scaring sounds: the cracking of a dead branch underfoot, breaking through an ice-covered puddle, stepping on the unsupported end of a flat stone on a rock slide, the thump of a heavy foot stepping over a blowdown. It is never possible to avoid them all, but they can be minimized by carefully watching the way ahead.

I remember reading, many years ago, in one of the old "Nessmuk" books on hunting in the Adirondacks, a quote which has always come to me each time I step into the woods on a hunt: "A good woodsman never goes over anything he can go around." Keeping this in mind will steer a hunter clear of many noisemakers in the woods. The hunter who charges blindly ahead seldom sees many big-game animals.

A good still-hunter is a slow mover. For, in fact, there is almost never a need for speed. Unless spooked, big-game animals rarely move more than a couple of miles during a twenty-four-hour period. If you find fresh evidence of feeding or bedding during your day's hunt it is certain that you are within a mile or so of the trophy you are seeking. Game is rarely killed by the marathon hunter who rates his day's sport in miles covered rather than in animals seen.

The bonus of still-hunting, if not in game killed, is in better knowledge of game habits and movements. It is a rare day spent in game country when a hunter fails to learn something new about game habits or movements. The signs of animals living in their natural areas are there for the reading if the hunter will trouble to scout the country. The man who sits under a tree all day gains nothing in woodsmanship or hunting lore. The enjoyment of hunting is in learning more about the life of the game, and the timber country still-hunter is the only one who can find an abiding pleasure in hunting without necessarily killing game.

There are basic rules for still-hunting big game, which are part of the accumulated wisdom passed down by numberless hunters through the years. The primary one, which everyone seems to remember, is "Always hunt upwind." It's a good rule since it prevents man-scent from reaching the animal. It is not always possible to put it into effect, however. For one thing, the lay of the terrain, its elevations and slopes, its feeding grounds and resting cover will dictate certain approaches. If the wind happens to be blowing perversely across your planned line of hunt, so be it. You must still move over your area as planned, for there is nothing seriously wrong in hunting across the wind. Your scent will never get far ahead of you. The old rule perhaps might then be rewritten as "Never hunt downwind," which makes more sense. But this is about the only rule in hunting which stands up as written. Others are flexible and must be bent to meet the conditions encountered: location of feed areas, terrain, where the animals hide out in daylight hours, how their movements are affected by changes in weather and the seasons.

A broad rule that applies in most big-game hunting is that the animals feed at the beginning and end of the daylight period and, often, during the night. Night feeding is likely to be the case with the bear family and all species of deer in areas of heavy hunting pressure.

116

Game is usually on its feet, still feeding or moving back to resting areas, in the period from first daylight until sunrise. After bedding down in daylight hours, most game again begins to feed at sundown and continues until dark when it again beds down, often out in the open. These are the times when still-hunting the areas through which the game passes from feeding to bedding grounds is most productive.

Another generality says that game animals go to lower ground to feed, return to higher ground for daylight shading up—sometimes to get away from flies, but most often because they feel safer at a higher elevation than their surroundings. In daylight hours, then, the still-hunter looks for game on its bedding grounds, whether slopes, ridges, canyon rims, or swamps.

The recognition of animal tracks is another essential element of successful hunting. When hunting elk there's no point to following the tracks of a calf moose. When looking for sheep, it's awkward to be misled by the fresh footprints of a bunch of mule deer. And in tracking cottontails on snow, it's time-wasting to pause over the feathery prints of gray squirrels.

No beginning hunter can be certain which animal leaves what track unless he watches it being made. To a novice, a bull moose track looks like a range steer's; the print of a whitetail deer could well be made by a farmer's pasture-lot pigs. In game country, where no domestic stock is found, the tracks of several species will intergrade in both size and shape, except to the experienced eye. The hoofprint of a calf elk can easily be mistaken for that of a big mule-deer buck. A Rocky Mountain goat leaves prints that are quite similar to those of a big horn ram.

Track identification is a complex subject and requires a bit of study, as well as field experience. We will deal with just one facet of the subject here—one, incidentally, that is a source of endless argument: How to distinguish the track of a buck deer from that of a doe. This becomes significant in hunting areas where the doe is on the protected list and only the buck is legal game. It also is important to a trophy hunter who is after a representative buck. Invariably, a knowledgeable whitetail hunter finds the locale of a big buck by its tracks somewhat before he sees the animal itself. Knowing what to look for gives him the clue. He may not—probably will not—find a record-book animal, but he will come up with a mature buck, at the very least.

Observing and studying the print of a single hoof is 117

Antelope hunter tries a long shot over prairie
grass, using steady rest. At shorter range, a hunter in such
open cover would be spotted instantly
by sharp-eyed pronghorn. Some natural screening
is not only advisable, but necessary.

not enough. The hoofs of a large doe and a mature buck are the same. The first clue a hunter must look for is a print noticeably larger than the others in the area, although, of course, this could still be the print of a large doe anywhere that females have been protected. Under these conditions does can get as heavy as bucks.

But a large track is a beginning even if it is not conclusive. Next, it is necessary to find a spot where the deer has left a line of tracks marking his normal walking stride. Soft, smooth soil is about the only place these

will show clearly, except when the ground is covered with light snow—an ideal medium for making track studies. The walking tracks should be examined for the three distinct features of the buck's tracks which rarely, if ever, appear in a doe's.

One: A buck rarely places his hind foot precisely in the print made by a forefoot. The hind foot usually fails by half an inch or more to cover the front footprint. The doe, on the other hand, always covers her prints exactly. A set of walking tracks looks as though

118

Stalk on big mule-deer buck was made through
rolling prairie knolls. Final position for shot is taken
behind yucca clump, from which author
killed buck at 365 paces, using Remington '06,
Model 742, with 4X scope.

The most conclusive clue is the telltale toe-drag a buck leaves in thin snow. Whereas a doe always picks up her hoofs daintily and places them precisely on the ground, the heavier-chested buck tends to drag his. The drag marks will always be found just behind the print of his foot. Often they can be seen after the buck walks over muddy ground, but it's sure-fire in snow.

It is often said that the buck's hoofprint is "blunter," or more rounded off in front, than that of the doe. I have not observed this. I think it is less a matter of sex than of location. Any deer inhabiting rocky country will have hoofs more rounded off by wear than deer living in low, swampy areas. Nor do I think, as is often said, that the two halves of a buck's hoof show more separation than the doe's. Both sexes show splayed hoofprints when they are running over soft ground—but only then. The same is true of the statement that the buck leaves imprints of his dewclaws. It happens with both sexes when on the run and when crossing soft, muddy areas. The one truth about the track which shows dewclaws is that it cannot be that of an antelope. An antelope does not have dewclaws!

Since we have gone on at some length about the importance of track recognition, something should be said, in the spirit of the best romantic hunting literature, about tracking the game to its lair for the final kill. Alas, tracking as such has little to do with successful hunting. Rabbits, yes. Big-game animals, no. It is the rare, and mighty lucky, hunter who can take the track of an elk, moose, or deer, and come up on it within range for making a kill. All game animals are highly aware of the fact that they leave tracks, which can be followed by predators as well as by man, and they continually watch their backtrails for signs of danger. When an animal beds down it invariably chooses a location where it can watch its backtrail, even at the risk of danger from other directions. A hunter following tracks is certain to be discovered by the game before he gets a good look at his target.

The benefits derived from reading tracks are simply that the game you are hunting is in your area, is feeding there, bedding there, mating there, or, in a word, living

it had been made by a two-legged animal. Two: The prints of the front feet of the buck should "toe-out" slightly. Not much, as a rule, but enough so that they are a bit off the center line of the hind footprint. Three: The spacing between the prints of the right front foot and the left front foot of the buck is likely to be wider than those of a doe simply because his chest is wider and his feet come to the ground a bit farther apart. In a really big buck the prints of the forefeet will be noticeably farther apart than those of the hind feet.

there. If you spend time in an area, keeping your ears and eyes open, moving slowly and quietly, you will find game. Without the continual evidence of fresh tracks made by the specific animal you want, it is best to move into new territory. Big-game animals, even in the best hunting areas, are not sprinkled evenly about. They usually are in groups living in "game pockets"—specific areas where the right combination of food, water, and protective cover provides ideal living conditions. The hunter must discover this happy combination, often by seeing the game, but oftener by reading signs.

Here the skilled still-hunter holds the better hand against the stump-sitter. He moves through game country until he finds the most active or populous pocket of game, then concentrates his efforts on it. The stump-sitter usually makes a random choice of his spot. He may have seen a deer there last week, last month, or last year (or someone else did), and he is content to wait right there until another one shows. This is good enough logic, but it avails the watcher nothing if game is not using the area either as a feeding or bedding ground, or a crossing point. Only a careful examination of the area for tracks and other signs can reveal this.

The normal pattern in still-hunting is to work along ridge tops, canyon rims, and over knolls. Big-game animals seem to have a special fear of danger approaching from a lower elevation. They are inclined to watch the areas below them far more than those above and ahead, unless they are on the move to high ground.

Keeping above the game has another advantage. As the sun warms the ground, air currents rise, carrying the body scent of the hunter with them. Rarely will an animal at a lower level be able to pick up the scent unless the hunter is upwind, with a fair breeze blowing.

During the fall hunting season, working the higher ground has still another advantage. Acorns and beechnuts are favored foods of hoofed game and of bear, and in hardwood country most of the mast-bearing trees will be on the higher slopes and the mountain tops. If the crop is good (in many years it is not), oak and beech ridges are the best places to look for game during the feeding periods.

In still-hunting your senses will be on the alert continually. I remember hearing the first whitetail buck I killed cracking brush long before I saw him. To my untrained ears he sounded like another hunter bursting through a thicket. I had been moving briskly along a woodland road headed for a swamp when I first picked up the noise, to my right and a dozen yards ahead. I stopped and waited for the hunter to come out to the trail, for the noise was headed that way. Instead, a nice six-point buck stepped into view between some gray birches and I dropped him with a neck shot.

In another situation, many years later, I would have failed to see a large mule-deer buck, if he had not inadvertently kicked loose a pebble that bounced noisily down a canyon wall. I had already passed this buck, apparently bedded down on the slope below the rim I was working. But after I had moved on, the buck figured he could make his escape by sneaking along the steep slope, in the opposite direction.

When I heard the pebble, however, I stepped to the canyon rim and looked directly back along the slope. The buck was moving through some tiny firs, angling up to the rim. I tucked a .30-caliber bullet right behind his foreleg and watched him bounce all the way down to the bottom of the canyon. He was a buster in more ways than one. It took me and my guide three hours to get him out.

In a sense, the art of still-hunting is little more than the hunter matching his wits and his senses against those of the game he hunts. Since his senses can never equal those of a big-game animal, he must achieve a balance with his brains and the long arm of his rifle. Knowing where to look for the game and how it is likely to behave will usually produce a chance for a killing shot.

A still-hunter's efforts normally are confined to hunting in timberland, or any cover where vision is limited, and a fairly close approach must be made before the game can be seen. This applies to hunting for whitetail in the East, for moose and whitetail in the North, and elk and the three deer species in the lower elevations of the West, which is also timber country.

Photographer Bill Browning (with pack, top, left)
watches as herd of young rams feeds on slope of deep valley in Alberta
sheep country. Horse helps hunter into high country above
timber line (above, right), but will attract attention of keen-eyed
sheep. Below: Author, as he makes a kill on antelope.

But there are several big-game species which are rarely hunted in timber, and many areas of the West and North where elk, deer, and bear are hunted in fairly open country. For example, some of the best elk and mule-deer hunting in America is in the open park country of the Western mountains at, or above, the timber line. This is especially true of the early hunting in the highest areas before deep snow drives the animals to lower ground. Sheep, goat, bear, and sometimes moose, are found in fairly open high country, caribou in open tundra and valleys, antelope in the wide-open prairies. These are the game animals that are spotted at long range, then stalked to within killing distance.

The stalking of any animal implies that you have seen it and that you want to kill it. To see the game in open country sometimes requires a still-hunter's skills, but not often. It depends much on the game being hunted and the type of terrain being covered. In prairie and plains hunting it is likely that some type of vehicle will be used to cover ground. In mountain hunting the hunters inevitably will be on horseback. Neither method of transportation makes a quiet approach, nor does it take advantage of natural screening covers.

But the Jeep and the horse will penetrate game coun-

try and bring the hunter to a point of vantage where he can look for game over a wide area. Antelope can be hunted successfully with a vehicle, since a great deal of territory can be covered and the game located without alarming it unduly. Since antelopes are ranch animals, they do not spook at the sight of a Jeep or mounted hunter, as long as they can stay a safe distance of a mile or more away. At this range a hunter usually can pick a buck out of a herd with his binoculars. If the buck looks worthwhile, the spotting scope comes out and the head is studied more carefully. If it seems acceptable a stalk is planned.

Because of the antelope's extremely keen vision and the fact that it prefers to stay in wide-open, fairly flat country, it is one of the more difficult animals to stalk. Before taking off to kill his chosen buck, the hunter had better make a full study of the terrain with his glasses to be sure of an approach under cover.

The first problem for the hunter is to locate a screen within killing range of the game. This might be a small knoll, a shallow coulee or dry wash, a clump of sagebrush, or a pile of boulders. The problem then is to get in line with this screen, keeping it between man and antelope until a shot can be made. Sometimes this means making a circle of two or three miles, and in sparse cover the chances of getting close are small.

If the antelope are feeding quietly, chances are better than if they are bedded down. A bedded animal has nothing to do but watch the surrounding terrain and chew its cud. It is almost continually on the alert. A feeding animal, however, offers a slight break. When its head is lowered to nip grass or browse, the hunter can move without much danger of detection. If it raises its head to look around, however, he should stay under cover. Remember, too, that antelope, even when feeding, usually have a wise old doe standing watch. An eye must be kept on her, as well as on the buck and the rest of the band.

A good pair of glasses is absolutely essential in hunting game in open country. Only high-quality glasses provide the definition, or resolving power, needed to spot game, particularly when it is in or against cover that closely matches its body color—a moose in the shadows of a cedar swamp, a mule buck lying on a gumbo butte, or a bighorn ram bedded on slide rock. The optical clarity of the glass must be high enough to permit definition of the outlines of the animal against the background. A high degree of magnification is helpful, but not the whole trick. A pair of good 7X glasses will be better for spotting game than a low-grade pair of 10X power.

Stalking big game lacks the element of sudden surprise found in still-hunting. Nevertheless, each stalk will be somewhat different from the one before. The direction of the wind, the height of the sun, the lay of the land, and the amount of cover will always combine to vary the approach. If you keep the wind in your face, your face in the shadows, your body behind cover, your head down—and your movements quiet—your first stalk should be a good one.

123

Guide Howard Copenhaver leads author across
rockslide in Bob Marshall Wilderness Area. They are after
a white goat. Five and a half hours—a long
stalk—passed after goat was spotted and his head checked
before killing shot was made.

BIG-GAME
TROPHIES
6

The chap who goes hunting to put meat in the pot rarely thinks twice about trophies. There is nothing wrong with this. Game animals and birds must be harvested on an annual basis, and with many big-game animals proper cropping keeps the herd in balance with its habitat. With many small-game animals and birds the harvest provides a food supply which normally is wasted through nature's winter attrition.

The trophy seeker, however, fills a somewhat special niche in the hunting scene. Although he is vastly outnumbered by the meat hunter, his contribution to hunting as a whole is on a higher level. First, his target is a male animal at his peak—or just past the peak—of reproductive capacity. Taking these older bucks or bulls makes way for male animals just approaching their prime, with several years of virile breeding ahead of them. Killing the trophy animal rarely imposes a loss on the game population.

A trophy hunter is also a liberal dispenser of funds, usually a nonresident who travels far to find and kill his chosen head, distributing largess along the route—high license fees, often additional trophy fees, travel and outfitter costs, expensive rifles, scopes, and so on. All this, of course, benefits the general coffers of local game departments, providing them with additional funds for game research, habitat improvement, and better management. His individual contributions in both money and influence often reach the highest levels of state and Federal government to promote better game laws, game protection, and controls. Teddy Roosevelt was the father of all such action in the United States.

Trophy hunters fall into two groups: the one looks for the best representative head of a species that he can find; the other is rarely content unless he can crack the record book. Scoring for the record requires both time and money, and even with both abundantly available the project is not often successful. Most of the record-book animals, oddly enough, are killed by the less zealous trophy hunters or, in some cases, by meat hunters, who through their indiscriminate taking of animals will sometimes "luck into" a prize head.

Angus Cameron, a distinguished editor and one of my oldest friends, killed a fine bull caribou soon after we set up camp during his first Alaskan hunt many years ago. He killed for meat, taking the fattest bull he could find. After downing the animal he and Bud Helericks, who was guiding him, decided to make some measurements. Killed in 1949, this trophy made eleventh place in the 1952 record book for Barren Ground caribou.

It is important that the trophy hunter, when he sets out, fix some minimum standards for himself, deciding among other things what he will consider to be a representative head. For unlike the angler, who can take many and release those he does not want, the hunter, once he has taken his animal and filled his license quota, must either wait for another year or head for another state or province if he is not satisfied with his trophy. It is far better to do your estimating with the glasses and spotting scope before pulling the trigger but this demands some knowledge of what to look for in big-game headgear.

As a rule of thumb, when you are looking over a group of herd animals—sheep, antelope, or elk, for instance—the largest-bodied animal among the males usually will carry the best head. If your time for studying the heads is limited, concentrate on the largest animal. With bighorn sheep, the oldest and often the largest rams will be the darkest in color. With bull elk, look first at the animal having the lightest body color; old bulls are a light tan, sometimes a light gray. Among caribou the older bulls will have the largest and most distinct white manes, with the white area running well back over the shoulders. On young bulls the area of the white mane extends only to the point of the shoulder. When glassing a bunch of mountain goat you can usually pick out the oldest billy by his yellowish, off-white coat. The nannies and younger males are dead white.

But this is about as far as you can go with generalities. To pick a trophy head worth mounting, you must be able to make some comparisons of antler or horn size, using some other part of the animal's anatomy as a yardstick. In most cases, of course, you will be hunting with an experienced guide and his judgment of a head usually

Preceding pages: Bull elk carrying
"royal" head, with seven points
on each side, is a top
American trophy. Typical whitetail
(above) ranks well in record
book, along with nontypical whitetail
head (left). Beams of nontypical
heads lack symmetry and have
many irregularly formed points.
Fine as these may be, they
are bettered in the
"Records of North American Game."

Former record holders in mule deer
category: Antlers of typical mulie head (top,
left) branch in paired "Y's";
nontypical specimen (left) sprouts points at
random. Top, center: Record-book
wapiti (American elk) carries at least seven
points on each antler, has wide spread
and better than four-foot beam length. Record
American moose (top, right) shows
long, well-formed palms, long brow tines, many
distinctive points. Alaska-Yukon species
(right) has a wider spread and
wider, longer palms, often with brow palms.

OFFICIAL SCORING SYSTEM FOR NORTH AMERICAN BIG GAME TROPHIES

RECORDS OF NORTH AMERICAN
BIG GAME COMMITTEE

BOONE AND CROCKETT CLUB

Address Correspondence to:
Mrs. Grancel Fitz, Secretary
5 Tudor City Place, NYC 17, NY.

SHEEP

KIND OF SHEEP

MEASURE TO A POINT IN LINE WITH TIP OF HORN

SEE OTHER SIDE FOR INSTRUCTIONS	Supplementary Data	Column 1	Column 2	Column 3
A. Greatest Spread (Is often Tip to Tip Spread)		Right Horn	Left Horn	Difference
B. Tip to Tip Spread (If Greatest Spread, Enter again here)				
C. Length of Horn				
D-1. Circumference of Base				
D-2. Circumference at First Quarter				
D-3. Circumference at Second Quarter				
D-4. Circumference at Third Quarter				
TOTALS				

ADD	Column 1		Exact locality where killed
	Column 2		Date killed By whom killed
	TOTAL		Present owner
SUBTRACT	Column 3		Address
FINAL SCORE			Guide's Name and Address
			Remarks: (Mention any abnormalities)

I certify that I have measured the above trophy on _____ 19___
at (address) _____ City _____ State _____
and that these measurements and data are, to the best of my knowledge and belief, made in
accordance with the instructions given.

Witness: _____   Signature: _____

can be relied on. But there have been times when I might have regretted killing an animal, on the guide's say-so, and set my own standards. I have never killed a record-book animal, but neither have I taken many poor trophies—except for meat!

Judging a head before killing the animal requires a fair look at horns or antlers. Often the background can be frustrating, particularly if headgear melts into either the color or the texture. Snow or light slide-rock is the ideal medium, a gumbo butte probably the worst, with a stand of dead second-growth timber somewhere in between. Somehow, you must see the antler or horn growth, preferably from both a front and side view. If the animal is feeding quietly in fairly open cover, patience and care will give you these views. If the animal is on the move and heading for cover, and if you must take your shot right then, you will need luck to collect a trophy head. It is better to pass up such opportunities, unless you are at the bitter end of the hunt.

Here are some quick rules for evaluating heads of the major big-game animals. Using them before shooting will usually give you a pretty fair trophy that you can mount and display with pride and pleasure. Finally, hunters' luck seems to favor the man who waits and who is content to pass over a few smaller heads before making a kill. A better one usually comes along before the end of the hunt.

WHITETAIL DEER:

Few hunters get the opportunity to examine a whitetail buck's headgear in detail. Often it's only a quick look—and time to shoot. If you can get a fair look, to make comparisons, check the spread against the buck's thickness of body, either from the front or rear. If the antlers spread beyond the body outlines, you are looking at a trophy animal. On a broadside view, it is a trophy buck if the antler height above the head approaches the depth of the body from shoulder to chest line. These will be eight-pointers, or more. These days eight-point whitetails are considered prizes.

MULE DEER:

For a hunter accustomed to the Eastern and Northern whitetail, every mature mule-deer buck looks like a

*Trophies are first scored in the field (above) with steel tape, but
must be officially scored after a minimum drying-out period of sixty days by
a recognized Boone and Crockett Club scorer. Measurements are
entered on official forms (above, right), and totals calculated by official scoring
system. World's-record bighorn (right) scored 207 2/8.*

trophy. The antlers do, of course, average much larger than those of big whitetail and usually extend much higher above the head. The typical head carries five points on each side, although the brow point is often very short, at times only a nub, on even the best heads. If you get a head-on view of the buck, with ears extended, his spread should overhang his ear tips—the more the better—for a trophy head. Many big mule bucks have high rather than widespread antlers. If you find one with a spread matching the width of the ears, and with antlers extending above the head about the same distance as the height from the brisket to the top of the withers, this is also a trophy deer. Many big mule bucks exhibit nontypical heads, with a snarl of points, some extending beyond the spread of the main beams. Such heads are often massive in beam diameter, although generally somewhat shorter than the typical head will be in beam length.

ELK:

Look for a big-bodied animal first. Small bull elk do not carry trophy heads. Next, be certain that he is at least a six-point bull. Then check the size of the last two points, which appear as a fork on the end of the main beam. If these are widely spaced, with the spey (lower or last) point well developed, you should then check the beam length. If the antler tips come well behind the withers as the bull stands broadside with head erect, this is a good trophy head. Another check for a good trophy from this side view is the length of the brow tines. In a fine head these will extend forward almost to the tip of the nose.

MOOSE:

These big brutes are judged by spread of antlers and size of palms. Since the body size varies a good deal, there is no good yardstick to go by. If you get a head-on view of a bull, and his antler spread seems to be about twice the breadth of the chest, with palms at least as long as the distance from the tip of his nose to his ear, you will have a fair head. Choice heads will spread to three times the body width across the chest, and the rare trophies are those having additional brow palms.

CARIBOU:

A side view of a bull caribou should show antler height above the head approaching the total height of the animal's withers above ground. If the top cluster of antlers has many points, with massive-looking main

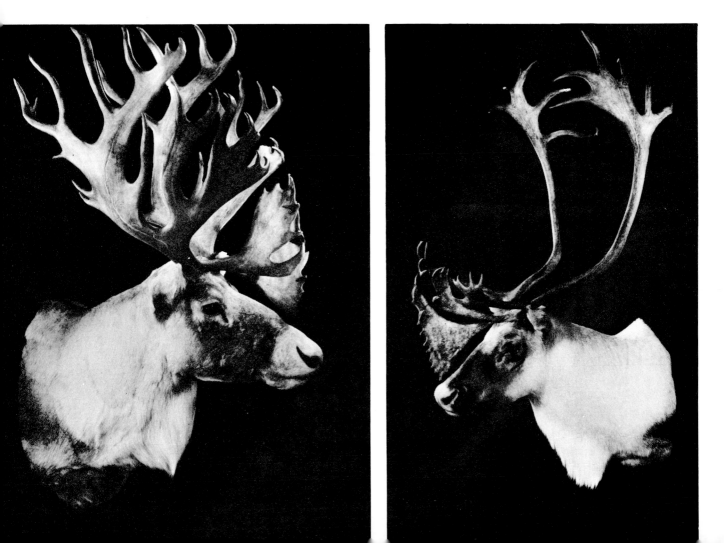

beams, it is a fine head. It is even finer if it has two forward shovels instead of the normal one.

BIGHORN RAMS:

Viewed from the side, a full-curl ram will be just that —with the curl approaching a complete circle. Badly broomed-off horn tips will not quite make it up to the bridge of the nose. If the broomed ends appear to be wide at the tips, and if the diameter of the curl approximates one third of the ram's full height, this will be a head with large bases and a curl close to forty inches.

GOAT:

The Rocky Mountain Goat is extremely hard to judge since the horns are short and very sharp. Their tips are almost impossible to see at any fair distance, so judging the length is largely guesswork. Actually, the difference between a fair goat and a record-book goat is as little as two inches. A horn length of ten inches on a goat is a good trophy and this compares well with the length of the head from the base of the horns to the tip of the nose. If your goat appears to have horns as long as his head, it is time to start shooting.

ANTELOPE:

You should have plenty of time to study your buck, since these are open-country animals and can be spotted far off. You will not be able to judge a head satisfactorily, however, with binoculars alone. Here is the spot for a 20X scope on a tripod—an important tool in hunting any big-game trophy.

A good antelope head has heavy horns which show up almost black. Look for horns with a pronounced hook; these will always measure up longer than straight-tipped horns. If the buck faces either straight toward you or away from you, compare the spread with the width of the ears. If the horns extend to the tips of his ears or beyond, this is a good spread. Next, compare the height of the antler prong, or paddle, with the length of the head from the base of the horn to the nose. If this matches, too, you have a trophy buck.

133

Record-book woodland caribou (far left) and barren-ground
caribou both exhibit the large brow shovels of trophy heads. Goat
(above, left) has short horns, but is still a fine trophy; current record
for goat stands at twelve inches. World's-record pronghorn
(above, right) has nineteen-and-one-half-inch horns.

SMALL
FURRED GAME

7

COTTONTAIL &
SNOWSHOE RABBITS

More men in their youth have cut their hunting teeth on cottontails than on all other small game put together. Hunting the rabbit is fun, truly exciting, and provides an ideal shotgun target. The speed in gun handling needed to connect with a cottontail bouncing through brush and tall grass makes most forms of wing shooting slow by comparison.

The occasional moment of steady, sustained flight offered the shooter by a pheasant or quail is never available to the cottontail hunter. The rabbit is always quick and evasive. First he is in sight for a few feet, then he has darted through an opening into good ground cover, continuing at top speed until he has reached another opening which, like as not, he will skirt to take off in a zigzag flight through a thicket. In typical cottontail country, brush is thick and tangles of briers commonplace. When you connect with a rabbit in this cover, you are doing a good job of gun handling.

Such sport is quite different from tracking the cottontail on fresh snow. Here many of the skills of the big-game hunter are needed. Not only do you have to puzzle out the animal's trail, but you must anticipate where he will head to find the right spot for his daytime form. For these rabbits feed and move mostly at night, and during the day sit tight either in cover that offers good camouflage or below ground in a woodchuck hole. You also need to know on which days they will "set-out" rather than go underground. The warm, moist days of late autumn and the mild snow-melting days of winter after a spell of severe cold will always find a good crop of cottontails above ground. And when they *are* out in their forms, you can count on some fast shotgunning. Their movements tend to be patterned. They will crouch, remaining motionless, until their human adversary is within a few yards, then away they go, cotton-ball tails flashing like a beacon and providing the gunner with a visible target. Most of the time these little rabbits would be almost an impossible target if it weren't for their giveaway tails.

Actually, the cottontail is the most popular game animal in the country and gives the statisticians a good yardstick for recounting licenses sold, ammunition bought, and man-hours expended in the hunting field. A generation ago thirty million cottontails were killed by hunters every year. Today's figure tops forty million.

What is most remarkable about the fecundity of this all-popular American game is that it not only makes gunning possible for millions of hunters, but supplies food for a host of predators, both furred and feathered, as well. Probably twice as many rabbits are killed by foxes, bobcats, house cats, coyotes, hawks, owls, and other varmints, as by hunters each year. To this we can add possibly another ten million killed by cars on the highways—thus making a total cottontail population that is really staggering.

More than any other game, the cottontail is a cosmopolitan animal. You will find him in the grassy sand dunes along a beach, far up in the open parks of the Rockies, on the sagebrush flats of the prairie, and in the deep swamps of the South. Every man with a gun has a chance to hunt and kill cottontails, and if he is the owner of a beagle hound, it's a safe bet that he is a rabbit hunter. Beagles and cottontails go together like ham and eggs. It's good sport to listen to the silvery notes of a pair of hounds tonguing on the hot trail of a canny cottontail buck on a frosty morning. If you're in the right spot when he makes his circle, he'll give you a flash shot as he beats ahead of the dogs from one clump of cover to another.

No game demands less of the hunter in the choice of his gun. Traditionally, the cottontail hunter's firearm is the 12-gauge, double-barrel "meat-gun," but cottontails are being killed with great regularity every season with all gauges and types of shotguns, from the .410-bore single shot to the 12-gauge auto. It doesn't take a big dose of birdshot to kill a rabbit. At cottontail ranges—mostly twenty-five yards or much less—the ½ ounce of the .410 does the trick neatly. Those who use the big double Twelves like to feel that they can clear away the brush with the first charge, then put in the killing blow with the quick follow-up left barrel.

I have killed many cottontails in their forms with a .22 rim-fire pistol, after carefully tracking them down to

*Preceding pages: Bounding
cottontail is country lad's favorite shotgun game,
and supply seems to be endless.
As seen in Arthur Frost painting at right, rabbit
also was favorite with old-time hunters.*

their hide-outs. And I have knocked over hundreds with every gauge of shotgun when I was jumping them out of the brier patches and brush piles. My preference, however, is the small gauges with their more modest charges of shot. I like to eat rabbits, and I don't admire the mutilated carcass that inevitably results when a large-gauge gun is used and the shot must be taken at fairly close range. The little 28 gauge with its ¾-ounce shot load is the cottontail gun supreme. Up to thirty yards it kills neatly without mangling, and it gets on that bobbing white tail just a split second faster than a big 12. And quite often you need just that split second when you're gunning cottontails.

The snowshoe rabbit is almost entirely the hound-dog man's game. Sometimes called the varying hare, and the only member of the rabbit group on the continent that changes into a white coat in winter, the snowshoe has a restricted habitat and is known to relatively few hunters. About twice as big as the cottontail, the snowshoe is also twice as tricky. Unlike his smaller cousin, he will not go underground when pressed by hounds and, therefore, must rely on evasive tactics. And he uses them all, laying a network of bewildering scent patterns as he speeds in and out of the deep, snow-filled swamps of Alaska and northern North America.

The snowshoe rabbit is one of the few animals nature endows with special snow equipment. When his gray-brown summer coat changes to white, the hair of his hind feet grows to great length. When he runs, the hair spreads like a mat, covering an area as large as the palm of a man's hand. Thus the snowshoe acquires his name and his ability to travel easily and rapidly over soft snow that would founder a short-legged hound.

The snowshoe also is no game for the tracking hunter. Although he may squat under a protecting evergreen bush, much the same as a cottontail in his form, the snowshoe will melt away like a ghost when he sees or hears danger approach. The hunter rarely comes upon a snowshoe close enough to shoot.

The trick in hunting him is to put the long-legged foxhounds on his trail, then take a stand and wait for him to make his circle. In the dead of winter, when snowshoe hunting is most practical, this business of waiting for the return of the rabbit can be deadly cold. It's fine sport, no doubt, but I think it's best suited to more rugged individuals than I.

The snowshoe is big enough and tough enough to take some killing. The 12-gauge shotgun with express loads of #5 or #6 shot is just about the best combination for taking him as he slips quickly through the snow-covered evergreens of a northern swamp, pushed firmly along by a pack of loudmouthed hounds.

FOX & GRAY SQUIRRELS

*Snowshoe rabbit (below), really a hare,
is only member of its species to change coat in winter—
appropriately to white. Cottontail (top, right)
crouches in his form during day. Gray
squirrel (below, right) is choice small-rifle game.*

Along with the whitetail deer and the wild turkey, the squirrel was an important animal for the pioneer woodsman and settler—so much so that a rifle was designed especially to bring him down. This, of course, was the famous Kentucky, small in bore, light in weight, but accurate enough to put a ball through a gray-furred head at fifty yards.

Once held in high regard, the gray squirrel has been considerably less popular in the past few generations. It used to be that a man went squirrel hunting and counted on the tasty little nut gatherers to keep him in fresh meat. But today most hunters look down their noses at the man who hunts squirrels—and for no particularly good reason. The truth is that most hunters, even with today's far superior equipment in rifles and sights, fail to achieve the skill demanded to put a bullet through the squirrel's head, or to "bark" him (kill by concussion of shot into the tree near the squirrel's head), a trick requiring even greater ability.

It is my firm belief that a man who fills his bag limit on gray or fox squirrels in any one day—shooting the

rifle—is a good candidate for the title of whitetail still-hunter. The two animals require many of the same qualities of woodsmanship and hunting: moving quietly through the woods, knowing your game and its habitat, watching and listening for it, and making an accurate shot in the off-hand position once the game has been spotted. It is a certainty that no whitetail deer is safe in the woods with the hunter who can knock a squirrel out of a tall oak tree with his rifle. This is the kind of man who can break a deer's neck with a bullet—and we need more of this kind of efficient and knowledgeable hunter.

It must be said that the gray squirrel and his relatives —the fox, tufted-ear, and California squirrels—bear the same relationship to the rifleman-hunter as the cottontail does to the shotgunner. If you hope to become a skilled rifleman, there is no better training than hunting the squirrel, nor is there any other rifle game so easy to come by. You'll find the true gray squirrel in most parts of the northern United States and Canada, the fox squirrel throughout the South, the tufted-ear numerous in the Rockies, and the California variety on the West Coast. The gray squirrel is almost as numerous and available as the cottontail, and just as exciting to hunt.

During the fall hunting season, squirrels congregate in the tall timber, among trees bearing nuts and acorns, and signs of their presence can be seen the instant you step into their territory. Discarded nutshells and hulls litter the stumps and stone walls, and on a golden October day when the sun beats strongly down through branches already becoming bare, you need stand quietly for only a few minutes before the rustling of dead leaves betrays the brisk movement of squirrels searching for winter provender.

If you are not a woods walker by choice, you can get good shooting by simply sitting down at the base of a big oak and waiting for your shots. Once the squirrels have accepted the fact of your presence and recovered from their fright, they become busy again and will appear in the treetops as if by magic. This is one of the qualities peculiar to squirrels. When they are in a tall tree and danger moves in on them suddenly, they freeze tight against limb or trunk until the danger seems to

have passed. Then they begin to move about again and the noisy scratching of their claws on rough tree bark is easily discernible on a quiet afternoon to a good listener.

Personally, I like to hunt squirrels by moving quietly along a woods road through tall timber and listening for leaf rustlings or the squalling bark of one of these gray phantoms as he talks to his neighbors. When the sound locates the squirrel for me, I begin a sneak on him, moving slowly, a step at a time. If he is on the ground, rustling through dead leaves, I step forward when he is noisy and stop when he stops. Usually it isn't too difficult to get within easy rifle range of a preoccupied squirrel. The trick is to wait until he stops whatever he happens to be doing long enough to make him a still target that is possible to hit. If he does take alarm and heads up the nearest tree, he will often stop for a quick look back when he has gained enough altitude to be safe. This may provide an opportunity for a second quick shot. But in any case, he's never going to be an easy target. If you're taking head shots only, you must be prepared to hit a spot the size of a silver dollar—and that's not much of a target at gray-squirrel ranges.

Some men hunt squirrels with a shotgun and there's something to be said for this, too, if a man walks them up and takes them when they're in full flight over the forest floor or streaking up the trunk of a tall tree. A frightened squirrel has an uncanny ability to disappear in a hurry, and taking one in flight is never easy shooting. In addition, the tough hide and tenacity of the gray squirrel make him extremely difficult to kill cleanly

140

Taking squirrels from top of high oak is a job for skilled rifleman. Target is small and game is never still for long. Squirrel hunting produces some of the best big-game shooters in country today.

with a load of shot, no matter what the size. I have lost a number of wounded grays that managed to crawl into their den holes before I could get in a finishing shot.

Nor are these tough little critters easy to kill with a small-bore rifle. I have had them escape even when shot through the chest cavity with a .22 Long Rifle, high-speed ammo, and for this reason it is always a must to use hollow points in the .22 rim-fire for maximum shock power. Years ago I killed a great many with the old .22 WRF in a single-shot rifle, and I still think this is a much better killer than any of the modern high-speed hollow points. The .22 WRF carried a flat-point bullet that would knock a squirrel off a limb just about every shot; it is regrettable that rifles in this caliber are no longer available. However, the .22 WRF cartridge,

which can be used in rifles chambered for the .22 WMR Magnum rim-fire, provides a good substitute. The rifle must, of course, be resighted for the .22 WRF, which shoots somewhat lower at fifty yards than the .22 WMR Magnum.

The .22 WMR cartridge is also deadly on squirrels, particularly the big fox variety, which may weigh two pounds or more. However, the regular hollow, soft-point bullet of this cartridge is devastating in its tissue damage. Use of the full metal-case bullet, instead, makes this one of the best of modern squirrel rifles. In a quality bolt action, such as the Walther or Savage-Anschutz, equipped with a good 4X scope, the .22 WMR Magnum has the accuracy potential to shoot a squirrel through the head every shot at seventy-five yards.

SELECTED GUNS FOR SMALL FURRED GAME

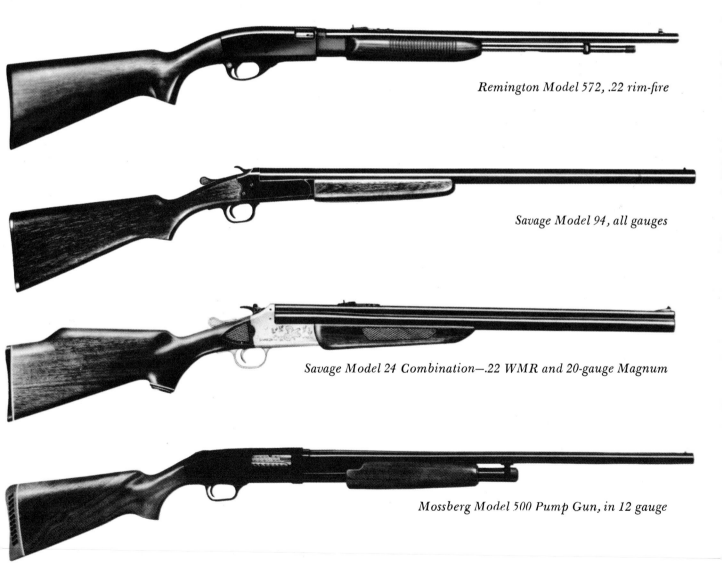

Remington Model 572, .22 rim-fire

Savage Model 94, all gauges

Savage Model 24 Combination—.22 WMR and 20-gauge Magnum

Mossberg Model 500 Pump Gun, in 12 gauge

VARMINTS

8

FOUR-FOOTED
VARMINTS

Not too many years ago the word varmint denoted an animal that no one would eat. It had other unwholesome implications as well. The varmint was predatory, parasitic, and pestiferous. The name derives from the perfectly good English word vermin (by way of the Latin *vermis*, worm), and was altered in backwoods America to *varmint*. To the layman, varmint still means vermin, but to American sportsmen the varmint fills a specialized and highly regarded niche in the hunting field.

Game seasons are short, with the annual or daily take quite sensibly limited to a modest number. A hunter doesn't get to fire much ammunition at game, large or small, during any one year. But the varmint family is large, omnipresent, and with few exceptions, unprotected by law at any time. The list is long and includes woodchucks, coyotes, prairie dogs, gophers, ground squirrels, various members of the cat family, and crows. All are suitable victims for a hunter, whether his armament is rim-fire or center-fire rifle, shotgun, or handgun.

Varmints not only provide a hunter with live targets to develop his stalking and shooting skill, but also offer a shooting laboratory for development of new cartridges and new loads in standard calibers. Some of the most significant recent developments in rifle cartridges have resulted from "wildcat" cartridges designed by long-range varmint shooters. The current crop includes the .224 Weatherby Magnum, .225 Winchester, and the .22-250, all available in factory loads. The latter two resulted specifically from varmint-shooting developments of the past two decades.

The long-range varmint shooter is the most critical of rifle hunters. His target is invariably a small one, and because of the great distances normally involved in this hunting, it seems even smaller. He needs a rifle capable of shooting the smallest of groups—less than one minute of angle, if possible—coupled with the finest of sighting equipment both to magnify the small target and to place the sight accurately on it. And although long-range varminting is a game in itself, the varmint hunter is the sportsman who also rates highest in kills per shot on most of our big-game animals in the North and West. In

other words, the skills gained in varmint shooting are readily transferred to big-game shooting, with highly satisfactory results.

The shotgun plays a minor role in varmint shooting, although crow hunting is now a national pastime. Flight shooting is as exciting as the pass shooting of doves and wild fowl, and without destructive effect on the crow population.

Two members of the cat family provide hair-raising kicks for the hound-dog varmint hunters. Tops, of course, is the mountain lion, largest of the American cats and impossible to hunt without hounds. The bobcat is another great hound-dog varmint, although lately the rifle and handgun hunters have been doing solo acts on these animals and on the red and gray foxes. These hunters call their prey into killing range with the squeal of a frightened rabbit. Since the cottontail is a major food for the bobcat, imitating its cry of terror with a mechanical caller and successfully concealing oneself in a good blind produces results.

The man who coined the phrase "Cowardly Lion" must have had the American cougar, or mountain lion, in mind. Of the thousands of these big cats which have been shot at close range in the past few decades, or captured alive by roping, only a scattered half dozen have made a defensive pass at their human adversaries. The mountain lion is shy, wary of man and almost entirely nocturnal. It is rare for a hunter to see one, even in the best lion country in the Rockies, unless the cat has first been treed by dogs.

The cougar hunts at night and preys mostly on deer, although in ranch country he would rather have a young colt. After making his kill, he usually drags the carcass into some underbrush, eats his fill, then covers the remains with sticks or leaves. He finds a spot somewhere in the area to sleep it off before returning for the next feed. Generally, he stays with a kill until he has consumed it, or until it has become putrid. He then takes off to make another kill, averaging about one deer or other animal each week.

A few years ago in Alberta, Canada, we cut the track

Preceding pages: Mountain lion, America's
largest varmint, is most difficult to take. When treed (top),
he snarls viciously, belying his true, cowardly
nature. Bobcat (right) has been treed by hounds. Lack
of foliage leaves him at hunter's mercy.

the hunter, and a sudden, frantic burst of speed on the part of the lion once he has been discovered and leaves his bed. For the first hundred yards probably nothing on earth can catch a cougar, except a cheetah. But after this quick dash from the hounds, he is likely to pick a tree, or jump to a high ledge, and come to bay before the dogs. For successful lion hunting, then, there are two basic requirements: well-seasoned dogs and good lion country for them to maneuver in. The best hunting ground these days is in the Southwest.

of a cougar as we were returning to camp. The prints, obvious in the six-inch snow, headed into the heavy pine growth above the valley, so our guide took a ride up the slope for a look. He found the fresh remains of a wolverine kill, and after checking the lion's departing tracks, decided that the cat was lying up somewhere nearby. Since there was a good hour of daylight left and we were in no particular hurry to get back to camp, which was only a mile away, the guide left us and rode back to camp for his two dogs. He saddled up a fresh horse and came roaring back with the hounds. The dogs hit the cold track, worked it up the slope to the kill, and then found the trail to the lion's lay-up. Within two minutes, and with a chorus of frenzied squeals and bellows, they jumped the lion. Within another two minutes, they had him up a tree, and perched on a limb about twenty feet above ground. He glared at us malevolently as we rode up.

The guide grabbed the hounds and secured them to a tree at a safe distance. We tied our horses, yanked our rifles from their scabbards, and prepared to back up the guide in case his shot should leave us with a wounded cougar on the ground. But the guide was pretty sure of himself with his .22 rim-fire "Trapper" revolver, and he knocked the lion out with one shot through the earhole. The animal was dead when he thumped to the ground. This is the easy way to get a lion. Most lion hunters are not this lucky.

The dog work on cougar almost always involves hours of patient, cold-trailing on the part of the hounds and

The bobcat, or wildcat, is another hound-dog varmint. Run with dogs in the Northeast and South, the bobcat behaves much like a snowshoe rabbit. It makes the traditional circle, giving the hunters a chance to cut ahead of it and to take a stand where they may get a shot as the cat swings around on its return. In the big-timber country of the Northeast, the cat is somewhat reluctant to "tree," although the Western bobcat seems to tree almost as readily as the lion.

In some parts of the South the bobcat hunter leaves the entire job of finding, trailing, and killing the cat up to his pack of hounds. This provides no shooting for the hunter, but it does offer some of the greatest hound-dog music in the land. For the houndman this is reward enough. However, after a fight to the finish with a big

145

male bobcat—and these animals often weigh as much as twenty-five pounds—the dogs usually need an hour or two for patching up noses and ears. The whole thing is exciting sport for the hunters, and the dogs seem to enjoy it even more, regardless of claw marks suffered.

For shooting cats ahead of the hounds in timber country, I like a fast-handling 12-gauge double, loaded with #2 shot in the right barrel and BB shot in the left. When the dogs are hot on the trail, the cat very likely will scoot past the hunter's stand at high speed, and it isn't often that there will be time for more than two cracks at him. Up to thirty-five yards or so, which is about as far as you will be able to see one in the timber when he is under way, the 2's and BB's will stop him dead in his tracks.

Since the English gentry first adopted fox hunting with hound and horse as a major pastime centuries ago, the fox and the hound have been traditionally coupled. In fact, the term "hunting" in England originally referred only to riding to hounds. All other forms of hunting were called "shooting," with the hunters always looking down their noses at the shooters.

To the British horseman, the fox is a noble animal, created purely for the chase—the hounds hot in pursuit and followed, often at a breakneck speed, by the rider.

Shooting the wary little animal in Britain is unthinkable. He must be run to earth by the pack, seized, chewed, and torn by the dogs, but, hopefully, delivered up with the "brush" still intact to provide a trophy for the day's hunt.

The fox seldom enjoys such status in America, except among the membership of the hundred or more riding clubs that dot the South and East, where pink coats are donned on Sunday mornings for the "breakfast hunt." To all other American hunters the fox, in both red and gray varieties, is just another varmint.

American sportsmen have not always considered the fox "just another varmint," however, nor has the fox always been hunted in the same manner everywhere in the United States. At one time, when mink wasn't the only fur that made an American woman ecstatic, the red fox was an important fur bearer and, as such, was the target of a considerable group of houndmen. But today, when red fox pelts bring a ridiculously low price on the market, and with the nearly universal lifting of bounties, hunting the fox with hounds has become an almost exclusive sport of those dogmen who are stimulated by the baying of the hounds and who achieve their fullest gratification from the spirit of the chase.

In the North, the desired end to this pursuit is the gunning of the fox, but in the South, as in Britain, the hunter seems to prefer allowing his dogs to capture the quarry. Unfortunately, permitting the dogs to take the fox is not always feasible in America. On this side of the Atlantic, there seem to be more places for the fox to den up, safe from the onslaught of the dogs. Like it or not, if the Southern sportsman expects to have a trophy, he will usually have to flush the fox and take the animal while he is on the run.

Occasionally, in the North, fox hunting is done with a mechanical caller, rather than with hunting dogs. After first concealing himself in a blind, the hunter blows into a gadget that imitates a rabbit's squeal. Since the fox and the rabbit are old enemies, the fox appears from hiding to take his prey, but is instead taken by the hunter. The method is simple enough, but the fox is both canny and quick. To lure him into the trap a hunter must possess infinite patience, as well as a full understanding of the fox's habits and a knowledge of his runs. He must also be fast and accurate with his gun.

Sitting and waiting for an animal to appear has never been particularly enjoyable to me. I much prefer the excitement of stalking, and the fox is perfect game. He can always be counted on to provide a good chase and to use a full bag of tricks to throw the dogs off the scent.

Still, many hunters today will not go after fox because they are afraid of losing their best hunting dogs. The reason is an unfortunate one. During the past generation, an ever-increasing number of whitetail deer has moved into fox country, making it nearly impossible for a hound running on a fox to run very far before the hot scent of deer cuts his trail. If the hound is "deerproof," he will stay with the fox track, but hounds with such a gratifying singleness of purpose are hard to come by, and deerproofing a dog involves such stringent measures that the practice has been more or less abandoned in recent times. It seems inevitable that the dog will pick up the deer track, and it is equally certain that once he does, he's a gone dog. He may not turn up for days—if at all. To avoid the disaster of losing the dog forever, it is best to attach a metal identification tag bearing name, address, and telephone number to each dog's collar, and hope that the dog's finder will honor it. All too many do not.

Of course, the same irksome problem often occurs when the dogs are running a true course on the fox. But then it becomes part of the exciting game of the hunt and is accepted as such. A smart old fox will often lead the dogs out of the hunting area, throw them off the scent by taking to the nearby streams and rocky regions, and leave the dogs to their own devices. By the time night falls, the pack will probably be miles from the hunters. But if a hunter knows his fox country well enough to pinpoint his quarry's runs, he can anticipate the path of the fox in his circle in much the same way as the wildcat or rabbit hunter does, and cut the cunning little varmint off on a ridgetop or at a barway with a well-directed load of #4's in a 12-gauge shotgun. The Twelve is a standard gun for this type of game.

With the coyote we enter the sphere of the long-range precision rifleman, the kind of shooting that modern varmint hunting is all about. Although coyotes have been run with dogs, driven by horsemen, shot from airplanes, and chased in Jeeps and snow planes—all shotgun shooting—this wary animal is also very likely the favorite target of dedicated varminters. In the wild, open areas he frequents, there is no limit to the powder capacity of the cartridge you choose for killing him. It is unlikely that you will disturb neighbors or nick a farmer's dairy cow with your shooting.

Coyotes can be found—if they haven't been indiscriminately poisoned off the range—in every area where there is a heavy concentration of jack rabbits or prairie dogs, the favorite coyote food. (If no coyote appears, you can get some good shooting at the other two varmints.) They can be found near ranch haystacks looking for field mice, or, since they also are fond of carrion, wherever a big-game animal has been killed and field dressed. After a day has passed and the man scent has faded, coyotes will begin to feed on the gut pile, if the magpies and golden eagles haven't found it first. As a matter of fact, it's a good idea to watch for magpies and eagles. They often will lead you to carrion, and to a coyote or two skulking nearby.

Red fox (left) provides an exciting chase
for hunters when matched with the long-legged hound.
Coyote (above), favorite varmint target
of long-range Western shooter, is now being found
in Eastern regions, as well.

*North American varmints include: Young red fox (top, left) running
before hounds; prairie dog (top, center) in classic pose atop burrow; Eastern
woodchuck (top, right), feeding warily with an eye out for hunters;
and stealthy bobcat (bottom, left). Preferred varmint targets of riflemen
are coyote (bottom, center) and jack rabbit (bottom, right).*

Dawn is a good time to find coyotes on the prowl for food.

Coyotes respect the hunter and will sit in the sage-brush, keeping him under observation at fairly safe distances of 300 to 400 yards. It takes a lot of looking to spot a sitting coyote in prairie country. His gray-brown coat blends into the grass, sage, and gumbo buttes so well that a fine pair of binoculars becomes as important in coyote hunting as in big-game shooting.

The bigger varmint rifles, rigged with scope sights of 6X to 10X, are the right medicine for coytes. A minimum caliber is the .224 Weatherby Magnum or the Winchester .225, each loaded with 55-grain bullets. The .243 Winchester and 6-mm Remington with the lighter bullet weights also are potent killers. But the .257 Weatherby Magnum and .264 Winchester Magnum, loaded with the 100-grain bullet, probably top the list for long-range coyote shooting.

The coyote is not large. When you get beneath his shaggy coat, his body offers a kill area of about six by eighteen inches. So, if you expect to make 400-yard kills, you will need a rifle capable of minute-of-angle accuracy. In proper bolt actions, any of the above cartridges will deliver this performance, with the latter two Magnums providing the flattest possible trajectory over the 400-yard range. These, zeroed-in at 300 yards, are positive coyote killers at 400 yards, if your allowance for wind drift is based on good judgment.

West of the Mississippi River, the several species of jack rabbit give the off-season shooter more rifle practice than all other varmints combined. Although these large hares have been persecuted, poisoned, and pursued by dog, horse, and man for generations, their incredible reproductive capacity provides a never-ending supply.

You can hunt jacks just as you would coyotes or prairie dogs and in the same country: by spotting them at fairly long range and picking them off with a hot center-fire varmint rifle. And this is the way a great many are killed. But the varmint hunter who gets the most fun out of jacks, and the best running big-game practice, is the shooter who walks them up and takes them on the run, as they break out of their forms. Actually, the system is much the same as hunting cottontails with the shotgun, except that as a rule a jack won't allow you to come within shotgun-killing range before he breaks away.

Since the advent of rifles shooting the .22 Magnum rim-fire (WMR) in 1960, the jack-rabbit hunter has the perfect cartridge for this kind of varmint shooting. A jack hunter usually burns up quite a bit of ammo in a day, so economy is a consideration in choosing a cartridge. Most jack hunters used to use the .22 Long Rifle rim-fire, but today this little cartridge is considered barely marginal for making clean kills, particularly at ranges over seventy-five yards. The .22 Magnum, on the other hand, has the extra wallop to drop a big jack kicking with one shot, and in modern pump- or lever-action rifles, such as the Winchester Models 275 and 255, and the Marlin Model 57-M, it can be fired fast enough to give the varmint hunter half a dozen cracks at the running target before it gets out of killing range. The .22 WMR cartridge, with its 40-grain hollow-point bullet driven out of the muzzle at 2,000 fps, has power enough to anchor a ten-pound jack at 150 yards. If the rifle is rigged with a good 4X scope with a fairly wide field, the jack-rabbit shooter can take his animals running, or wait for them to stop within 150 yards, as they often do, which will give him a fairly long-range shot from a steady sitting position. This, incidentally, is the most practical shooting position for taking the occasional long shot at a jack. While the prone position is a bit steadier, the jack hunter usually cannot see his target above the grass and sagebrush when he is stretched out on the ground.

The prairie dog is a miniature version of the Eastern woodchuck and, like the chuck, lives underground. He is different, however, in that he is far more gregarious. When you find prairie dogs you usually find a lot of them. Their "villages" vary in size from a patch a dozen yards square up to a hundred acres or more, depending on how long they have been established and to what degree they have been menaced by poisoners, shooters, and coyotes. The big villages are becoming rarer. The prairie dog is extremely destructive of alfalfa and other cover crops and farmers frequently must use poison gas to combat him. Also working against the prairie dog are losses of livestock and big-game animals that can break legs stepping into burrows.

Still, the so-called sod-poodle offers a lot of sport for varmint hunters. Once a village is located, a hunter can pick a spot within the hitting distance of a .222 Remington, or other small-bore varmint rifle equipped with a good scope and fine cross hairs, and pot the little pests as they pop up from their holes.

Shooting prairie dogs is something like a game of jack-in-the-box. As you settle down at your shooting stand, about 200 yards from the center of the village, you will probably see three or more dogs above ground, ready to drop into their burrows when you let off your first shot. As the rifle cracks, they sound their alarm whistle and disappear. But others in the village, made curious by the rifle report, usually will stick up their heads. And every time you fire, the dogs above ground will disappear, but will be quickly replaced by a new crop, giving you fresh targets.

The woodchuck is unquestionably the most important varmint animal in the country from the shooter's viewpoint. In the Northeast he's called a "chuck," in the South ground hog, and in the West rockchuck. But no matter what he's called or where he makes his home, he arouses more shooter interest then any other varmint animal. As a result, much of the research and development in high-velocity, deadly accurate, small-bore rifles and cartridges has been aimed at him.

Intensive hunting in farm lands has made the woodchuck furtive and wary. He seems to feed with one eye on the clover and one looking out for the hunter. In most chuck hunting areas now it is difficult to get shots closer than 200 yards, unless the hunter is willing to do some careful stalking behind fence rows and other available cover. Usually, however, the chuck shooter prefers to accept the challenge of making the long-range killing hit on the small target, rather than attempting to sneak into positive killing range.

Besides the normal shooting problems, the quest for chuck today is complicated by the gradual reduction of open hunting lands. In some cases, the chuck hunter himself has created the problem by shooting from the road or from roadside fences without first getting permission from the landowner, and by shooting rifles that make an annoyingly loud report, which farmers, among others, often take to mean death-dealing damage to their livestock.

Proper choice of a chuck cartridge for use in settled farm lands can help the situation. The .222 Remington is made to order for such varmint shooting. It's superbly accurate, with power enough to kill the animals at 300 yards, and has a frangible bullet that is light in weight and has virtually no ricochet potential. Better cartridges for longer range kills are available. Any of those listed under the section discussing coyote fill the bill nicely. But the shooter must be aware that the more powerful varmint loads can be a nuisance, and weigh this factor when selecting the rifle for a particular hunting area. 151

Long-eared, long-legged Western jack (left)
is sporty, running target for hunter with fast-action repeater
in .22 WMR Magnum caliber. Eastern
chuck hunter (above) steadies his aim on long-range
shot with aid of stone wall.

WINGED VARMINTS

About a mile from my home the gentle slope of a hardwood ridge rises from a deadly curve in the road to the village, and eventually makes its way to the knob of Schunnemunk Mountain. For some reason I have not fathomed, the low ridge, densely covered with maple, beech, oak, and other deciduous trees, is the winter gathering place of thousands of crows.

Usually, when the pale winter sun drops behind the ridge at end of day, I can see long strings of the black rascals winging silently over the meadow to the west of my office window, heading for the ridge. Occasionally, I can open my office door and hear, faintly, the raucous babbling of the congregation as it settles in for the night. But as a rule it gathers silently, for crows can be furtive and wary when they choose to be.

These evening flights always stir some memories for me. I remember many windy afternoons in late October when I was a young hunter and crouched behind a stone wall on the north side of another hardwood ridge, watching great flights of crows on their way South. On the windy days they would fly low, swooping down at times almost to ground level, then flaring sharply up as they approached the tall oaks at my back. In those days my pet crow gun was an old 10-gauge lever-action Winchester Model 1901, marginal in strength perhaps for heavy loads, but I always had the tubular magazine and chamber filled with Super-X's, carrying $1\frac{5}{8}$ ounces of shot. The gun had a fearsome kick and because of its low, sharp comb, kept my right cheek overly fat during the entire period of the crows' migration—usually a couple of weeks or more. I could have shot some crows with my little 20-gauge upland double gun, but I wanted everything going for me on those days when the black varmints flew high and steady over the tall timber. I willingly endured the punishment from the big 10-gauge in order to be able to pull birds out of the sky when they were sixty yards or so above ground.

Raucous crow is a favorite varmint target of both riflemen and shotgunners. Right: To achieve best results a combination of a good blind, an owl decoy, and either a reed-type or electronic caller is needed. Famous crow-hunter Bert Popowski (opposite, top) surveys field of slaughter after an hour's shooting in which more than fifty birds were gathered from one blind. Despite heavy shooting, crow population remains steady.

As the most-sought winged varmint in the country, the crow is taken in many ways with rifle and shotgun, but I've always preferred this form of pass shooting. It is not only sporty shooting, but wonderful gunning practice for wild fowl and dove. In many respects it can be even tougher than game shooting, for crows are erratic and unpredictable in flight. This, coupled with their innate suspicion of any object representing man with gun, produces some wild deviations in their flight path when they see, or suspect, danger ahead.

The most consistently successful flight shooting comes from waiting in concealment along their flyways when they are moving from feeding grounds to night roosts. If you are lucky enough to have such a roost in your area, incidentally, don't do your shooting near it. This will drive the crows away and they will never return to your neighborhood for roosting. Instead, pick the most heavily used flight paths, which you can observe by watching the flocks as they come in for a few nights.

153

They will vary, of course, with the feeding areas; crows commonly come to roost from all points of the compass. But after a while you will discover the most frequently used flyways. Now pick a spot at least half a mile away from the roost for your shooting stand. If the birds come in over a ridge or knoll, the elevation will give you better shooting, at a more deadly range, than a blind setup or a stand on low ground.

Probably more crows are killed through the use of decoy owls and mechanical crow calls than by all other methods combined. Watching and waiting while a "green" flock comes in and begins to dive and swoop over the owl decoy can be highly exciting. If you have a good blind nearby and stay well hidden, you can shoot crow after crow before the flock finally takes alarm. Crows have a particular hatred for owls, probably because the owls move into their roosts at night and take the crows when they are at a disadvantage. It is a rare crow that can resist the urge to attack any owl he sees.

Corn shocks make a good crow blind. The owl decoy can be set right on one of the shocks in the cornfield. Once the hunter is well set in the blind, he can begin calling with a mouth call or, if he is lucky enough to have one, with a portable electronic caller. The electronic callers are deadly. I particularly like the recording which includes the alarm-whistle of a hunting hawk. Hawks are also traditional enemies of the crow, and crows will flock to attack a hawk just as readily as an owl. The recording of excited crows bedeviling a hawk, coupled with the predator's shrill whistle, drives the crows who hear it into fits. Generally, within a few minutes in good crow country the shooter will find himself surrounded by wheeling, diving, loudmouthed black birds attacking his decoy.

Crows are good for livening up a regular upland hunting day when grouse, quail, woodcock, or other birds are scarce. I always carry a good call in my shooting vest or gamebag and use it when shooting is dull and the caws of migration-bound crows can be heard. The migrating crow is usually an easy victim. By simply backing into a hedgerow or slipping into concealment along the edge of tall timber the hunter will have a

blind that works well enough to get him a few shots at the crows as they come in to investigate.

Using the calls properly and successfully demands a certain knowledge of crow language. The short, high-pitched shrieking call, repeated many times, is the alarm call. Hunters using it will never bring in a bird. Too high a pitch always frightens the birds. Too low a pitch does not sound natural and no crows will be attracted. The best calls are those appropriate to the time and place—a distress call when predators are about, a nestling's screech for its mother in the spring. For the novice who is not accustomed to these nuances of crow tones the best bet is to buy a crow-calling record, listen to the various calls, and practice them. Usually the tone can be varied by adjusting the reed.

For pass shooting, the regular 12 gauge, loaded with the Short Magnum load carrying $1\frac{1}{2}$ ounces of shot, is pretty deadly. However, no gun is too big for this type of sport, and I occasionally use the 3-inch shell in a Magnum gun, loaded with $1\frac{7}{8}$ ounces of shot. For decoy shooting, a normal trap load of 3 X $1\frac{1}{8}$ ounces is enough. You will get many fast, close-range, wildly erratic shots when the excited birds are milling over the blind and decoy.

No varmint hunter can kill just any hawk he sees in the field with a clear conscience. There simply are too many "good" hawks about. The Audubon Society, as a matter of fact, says there are *no* hawks whose reputations are bad enough to justify shooting them. Sportsmen will dispute this warmly, but I think the Audubon point is nonetheless well taken.

Actually, the problem often is an academic one. Few hunters and outdoorsmen can differentiate among the many varieties of hawk, anyway, so the best rule is to avoid shooting any of them. Otherwise, buy a book on hawks and study it diligently. Then observe the birds in the wild until identifications can be made positively. The following are among the best-known of many varieties found in the United States and Canada:

The Buteo, or mouse-catching hawk, is a broad-winged

154

Golden eagle is a Western bird which
preys heavily on varmints and rodents, occasionally
on livestock. Now protected by Federal law,
it may be taken legally only
with special permits in specific areas.

type with a short, wide tail. These hawks are the soaring variety which can be seen making lazy circles high in the sky on bright, clear days. The species includes the red-tailed and red-shouldered, the rough-legged and broad-winged hawks, which—among many others—are quite often protected by local law.

The Accipiters include the sharpshin, the Cooper's hawk, and the goshawk, each of which is reputed to be either a songbird, chicken, or small-game killer. Accipiters have fairly short, broad wings and long, slender tails. Their flight pattern combines a series of quick wingbeats with a short glide. They travel in a fairly straight line, usually flying from one tree to another, and rarely soar or circle.

Hawks can be decoyed to a mounted owl just as readily as crows, and provide even faster shotgun work. When the hawk decides to attack, he appears silently from nowhere and dives directly on his victim. It takes some shooting to keep him from tangling with the owl and, if the decoy is a mounted specimen rather than a papier-mâché model, to prevent him from destroying it.

Shooting hawks from their dead-tree perches with small-bore high-velocity rifles is risky business in most parts of the country. If the bullet misses, it can stray for a mile or more and do serious damage to persons, livestock, or property. It is recommended sport only in truly wild country, where no one or thing can possibly be hurt and no danger from stray bullets exists.

155

For the past couple of years, the golden eagle has enjoyed Federal protection. However, it is not likely that this will save many eagles from the rifle of the Western or Canadian sportsman when the opportunity to kill one arises. For unlike our national symbol, the bald eagle, which lives almost entirely upon fish, the golden eagle is a meateater. He would just as soon eat carrion as fresh meat, but will not hesitate to kill young fawns, antelope kids, and the lambs of the mountain sheep, which soon after birth are fairly easy prey for this giant predatory bird. It is nothing for these big eagles to knock a young mountain goat or sheep off a cliff, then follow it down, and feed on the remains. There have been many eyewitnesses to this type of eagle depredation, and it will continue, of course, as long as the golden eagle lives in big-game country.

This eagle also kills a host of jack rabbits, prairie dogs, and many species of small rodents, all of which are agricultural pests; thus the present Federal protection. In areas where the golden eagle preys heavily on young game and livestock, however, permits to take these birds can be had. A game-warden friend of mine in eastern Montana has been waging war on eagles for many years. At last count his score on these birds was something over 3,000, and I have no doubt whatever that the excellence of the antelope and mule-deer hunting in his territory reflects his zeal in the pursuit of eagles, as well as his skill with a heavy-barreled .243 Winchester, mounted with a 10X scope.

Although magpies are great carrion eaters, these pests also have the nasty habit of picking the eyes out of the newborn young of antelope, deer, and sheep. With the little animal reduced to helplessness, they literally eat it alive. A flock of magpies can make short work of a young animal, or of any game kill a hunter leaves unattended, unless he first "brushes" it heavily with sage, pine, or other screening branches.

One of the best ways to kill magpies is to sit in a blind over a game kill or a heap of offal and wait for the birds to come in. It rarely takes long. Another way to get some shotgun shooting on these cowardly cacklers is to flush them out of the willows and cottonwoods along the creek banks in prairie country and take them as they leave the trees. They are extremely wise and wary, however, and few varmint hunters will ever fill a bag with magpies.

*Magpies are small, vicious, Western birds
with the sanguinary habit of plucking out eyes of young,
newly dropped fawns and kids. Then, in a flock
attack, they literally eat the helpless animal alive.
They are elusive and hard to kill.*

SELECTED GUNS FOR VARMINTS

Winchester Model 70 Varmint Rifle

Browning Safari-grade Sporter

Savage Model 110

Sako Varminter, heavy barrel

Winchester Model 275 Deluxe, .22 WMR

GAME BIRDS

9

RUFFED GROUSE

In the first full light of an October day, the small dark form snugged against the bole of the spruce tree and perched on a slender limb a few yards above ground became the mottled gray body of a bird. Motionless, in keeping with the still hush of a proper New England dawn, the grouse was almost undetectable. But the forest was beginning to stir. A white-footed mouse rustled a dead oak leaf along a rotted stump, and an acorn, loosened from its hull by frost, dropped to the ground with a soft thump.

Then, from up the valley came the keening cries of a wedge of geese, silhouetted against the mellow light of sunrise as it beat southward on rhythmic and powerful gray wings. As the music of the many wild throats peaked in volume directly over the grouse, he stretched his neck erect, ruffled his feathers, snapped open his fantail, and without further ado burred softly out from beneath his shelter in a blur of wings.

His flight path, purposeful and swift, pointed down to the valley, straight through the tall hardwood timber. He followed it faithfully, with only the faintest hint of tilting wings as he evaded contact with the big tree trunks. Near the edge of the woods he abruptly set wings and dropped to the ground, landing on running feet through crisp dead leaves. Now, with head cocked brightly, he strutted toward an old log, flipping out the feathers of his tail in quick jerks. Gracefully, he jumped up on the end of the log, again fanning out his broad, black-barred tail.

Then he extended his wings before him, almost prayerfully, and beat them in a strong double thrust which stirred the leaves below. Again he beat, and again, with the tempo rising until the first dull blows of sound rose to a wild drumming that echoed from the hillside.

His vigor demonstrated, although not with the passionate persistence of the drum roll that accompanies the mating ritual of spring, he walked slowly to the far end of the log, crouched, then took off across the valley floor, over low alders along the brook, toward the tumbling gray skeleton of an ancient barn. He glided into a grove of gnarled apple trees where he came to rest on a scaly limb. From this vantage he considered the apples scattered on the ground below. They were the grubby fruit of old, forsaken trees, yet still carrying the red-on-yellow striping of the Northern Spy.

The bird dropped softly to the ground, near a bright apple. He pecked at it, turned it over, and chipped away at the meat until he reached the seeds. Even as he picked the tiny pips from the firm fruit, the thump of slamming car doors disturbed him.

Raising his crested head, he waited for more alarm sounds. First came the rumbling of male voices and then the faint tinkling of a bell, neither of which he understood. But they were strange, and his first instinct was to crouch close to the ground, among the apples. He was not in screening cover, however, so he thought better of it. He moved on quick feet to a line of small popples skirting the grove and crouched to await events.

He could hear the swish of leather-faced pants through knee-high grass, the thump of feet, and the steady ringing of the bell as the English setter made his first cast. The sound faded and the sharp blast of a whistle, immediately following, made him crouch tighter still. Again the bell sound increased, then it stopped abruptly. Again came the sound of men's voices.

Quietly now, with head stretched low ahead, he moved through the narrow stand of brush. He reached the very edge, crouched for take-off, then burst up and away in a thunderous flurry of wings. But his flight was low, never clearing the tips of the screening popples. As he broke from cover, a swish of rushing air behind, followed by the sharp crack of gun powder, made him swerve slightly in flight. He climbed in terror, heading for the ridge above, where the red leaves of the oaks and yellows of the beeches stained the long slope in bright color. His intention was clear, too clear. The second cloud of shot cut across his path and enveloped him in its deadly swarm. His head dropped, his wings folded, and his plump body arced to the ground.

The killing of a ruffed grouse in the midst of his tempestuous flight is the most soul-satisfying experience a bird shooter can have. The ruffed grouse is a symbol of dynamic power, of unleashed, disconcerting speed. He flushes from the ground, as the poet says, "With a whir-

160

Preceding pages: Eyed, vermiculated,
and subtly colored plumage of the ruffed grouse matches
autumn's somber tones. The King
of Game Birds, he fans his tail and struts (above)
in preparation for rolling drum call.

ring spring like an Indian bow," and any gunner who has hunted him in woodland covers must agree with that line. He has never been dethroned as the King of Game Birds and it is unlikely that he will be.

Yet, paradoxically, the ruffed grouse can be at once the most idiotically stupid of birds and the most brilliant in protective evasions. It all depends on where you find him. In grouse-hunter's country, which includes most of the United States, he is wily, confounding, maddening. His thunderous take-off stuns the novice into immobility and induces a split second of hesitation in the seasoned gunner which usually is sufficient to guarantee an escape. In wild country, in the North, however, where hunters waste neither time nor shells on shooting grouse on the wing, he can be incredibly inept.

I have seen a guide kill four birds as they stood in a Jeep road in northern Ontario, taking one after another with a single-barrel, .410-bore shotgun. As each small shot charge decapitated a bird, his fellows would calmly watch and await their own execution. I also have seen a guide snatch roosting birds off tree limbs, using only a loop of copper wire rigged to a cut branch, which was dropped over each unsuspecting head in turn. But as a rule you'll find grouse only at the two extremes: extremely smart or extremely dumb.

The wild instinct which keeps these birds alert and dynamic in almost all bird-shooting areas must be instilled by generations of experience with hunters. I am reasonably sure that the majority of birds a hunter encounters each season are the young of the year, yet each displays the masterful escape tactics of its grandparents.

For one thing, the ruffed grouse is a tight-cover bird.

Undisturbed, he walks into open areas for feeding, or exposes himself in the middle of a back-country dirt road for dusting. But cover is never more than a few yards away. When the hunter and his dog appear the bird scurries for safety and sits tight until he finds out what is going on. If he thinks he is well concealed, he may stay put almost until you step on him. If he's a "wild one"—which half the grouse population seems to be—he will flush out noisily at the first appearance of the hunter. Or, if he's a sneaky specimen, he may just rise quietly from the spot, as he can readily do when he chooses, and fly off on soft wings, keeping some part of the cover between you and him. Possibly you'll get a flash of him through the brush, but only that and no chance for a shot.

The tight sitters are the birds that give us the shooting. If you have a sharp-nosed, grouse-wise dog along, ruff will let you get well within gun range before roaring off. Most times, he bursts through the cover, not out of it. If you do catch him in a clear spot he will duck behind a tree trunk, just before you pull off the trigger. His timing in this respect is top grade.

You simply must be a better-than-average gun handler, carry a light, short gun with open bores, and be dedicated to the proposition that every bird that flushes within range is a fair target. You will cut a lot of leaves and branches with loads of fine shot, but you will also kill birds.

Experienced grouse hunters develop a "sixth sense" as to where the bird is going the instant he takes off. Once the flight path is determined, a quick snap shot just ahead of the bird often will intercept him. The idea is to stick with the flight line whether he goes through leaves, branches, or whatnot. It's the gunner who doesn't hesitate to shoot through obstructions who kills grouse—often inexplicably.

Even in top grouse country, the population varies from year to year. Game biologists call it the "grouse cycle," and it seems to go on cycling, with peaks about every seven years, regardless of weather, terrain, or hunting pressure. The grouse is virtually impossible to raise in captivity, at least on an economically feasible basis, 161

so stocking "for the gun" just does not happen with grouse. Nature's way with the bird seems to be the only way to bring them to maturity.

You will find ruffed grouse in almost every timbered area, except the Southwest, from northern Georgia to the interior of the Yukon. Essentially a forest bird, the ruffed grouse has adapted himself remarkably to "fringe" areas of farm land and, in fact, loves an abandoned farm, with its old apple trees, berrybushes, and clover patches. An omnivorous feeder, the bird can support himself almost anywhere suitable cover exists. Studies show that grouse eat more than six hundred species of plant, insect, and animal life, although their preference is seeds, berries, mast, and tree buds. In a bad apple year, when late frosts have killed off the spring blossoms, I have found grouse crops stuffed with sweet clover in the areas of abandoned farm land where their normal autumn diet is principally apple seeds and thorn apples.

It does not take much to kill a grouse, if you can center him in your pattern. I much prefer the lightest, 20-gauge double gun I can get, with open bores and shooting the one-ounce load of #8 shot. The fine shot, rather than a larger size, gets through leaves and branches with more left in the pattern to kill the bird.

A wounded bird has an amazing will to escape. He will crawl under a log or stone, burrow under creeping pine or dead leaves with the last breath left in his body. Quite often when you find him hidden he will be stone dead. It is a mistake to assume, when you see the bird fall, that he will be lying near the spot where he hit. It is also a mistake not to spend whatever time it takes to find him, even if it means crawling on your hands and knees and puzzling over the dim trail of shot-cut feathers marking his escape route.

The unforgivable mistake when in the company of grouse hunters is to call him a "ruffled" grouse.

162

Woodcock shooting (above) usually is done
in close cover, with birds towering swiftly into the open. Top right:
Often a woodcock will literally climb to clear
low thickets. Right: Audubon's ruffed grouse are shown feeding
on wild grapes—a favorite food.

Pl. 29

WOODCOCK

When I was a youngster I lived on a large farm in the middle of the best woodcock country in southeastern New York state. The birds nested in the early spring along the alder bottom behind our big red barn, and I spent many hours at dusk listening to the cockbirds on their singing grounds and watching them climb into the sky in the strange and wonderful ritual of the mating flight.

This fascinating act of nature begins when the cockbird selects a small open area in the alders. Here he struts about like a miniature turkey gobbler, "peenting" as he goes—presumably to lure the female within earshot. When he is certain that his paramour is within range, though hidden in the brush, he makes his ascent, gliding upward in a wide spiral, trill-whistling as he goes. At the top of his flight, several hundred feet above ground, the smooth spiral has narrowed and he suddenly flutters earthward like a falling leaf, chirping and twittering as he descends to his take-off point. Here the shy female, now enthralled, comes to meet him. The love-making results in a clutch of three or four eggs which are laid on the open ground in the densest part of the alder thicket.

If memory serves me, a woodcock was the first game bird I killed on the wing. I had ground-sluiced a few grouse with a .22 and potted some black ducks on the pond with a big 12-gauge hammer gun, but in those early scatter-gun days, I was essentially a cottontail hunter. There came the day, however, when I was kicking through a brier patch and a long-billed, mottled, brown bird burst whistling from the middle of the dead brier canes and I tossed up my 20-gauge single just fast enough to nail him with a wild shot.

This bird, my first woodcock, fascinated me, and with the passing years I find that the species fascinates me still more. In some respects the woodcock has a clownish appearance: eyes set on top of his head, so he can see danger approaching from any direction; a long bill which hangs down in front of his plump breast—ridiculous, but an efficient worm-gathering tool. His body is short and dumpy, his tail a travesty on tails, his feet weak and wispy, pale and thin, useful mostly for springing him into the air when he flushes in fright.

I like him mostly because he is elusive and mysterious. In his migration flight during the hunting season, he travels almost entirely at night and in daylight hours he buries himself in the most damnably thick alder, birch, poplar, and brier covers he can find. I like him almost as well because he is a tough, erratic target, always unpredictable in flight, sometimes buzzing almost straight up to tower over tall second-growth, just as often heading out into the clear to flutter as erratically as a bat. And, finally, I like him as a delicious morsel of food, as tender as a young squab, with rich, dark flesh as tasty as the best wild mushrooms you'll ever find.

Hunting woodcock is a special game for both man and dog. The man must know the right kinds of cover: for "native" birds it's low muckland covered with tag alders of just the right height—not high enough to make take-off difficult, not too low to offer good protection. The "flight" birds are somewhat less selective. They will use the alder bottoms, too, but are just as likely to be found on gently sloping hillsides densely covered with small birch, poplar, and other low growth.

The bird insists on rich soil, since he feeds principally on earthworms. It is useless to look for woodcock on mossy ground. Moss indicates soil acidity and few worms. A happy combination is a low piece of farm land actively used as cow pasture, with scattered clumps of alders and small birch. Cows, bottomland pasture, and woodcock seem to go together.

A woodcock dog must be a slow, cautious traveler.

Woodcock's protective, dead-leaf coloring makes him difficult to spot on ground, and eye placement near top of head makes him impossible to take by surprise. Ringneck pheasant (right) is heavy bird, but strong in flight.

The birds do not move around much in daylight so their scent is not spread widely for the dog to pick up. A fast dog will usually "bump" a woodcock before he knows the bird is around. I prefer an English setter with the wisdom of several years won in the alder patches. His long coat protects him from the tough going he inevitably finds in woodcock cover, and the large areas of white in his coat makes him easier to see in dense thicket. The breed has the stamina, the caution, and the bird sense to make a perfect woodcock dog.

Since woodcock shooting can be as fast as gunning ruffed grouse, the grouse-formula gun works well here. In fact, I like even a smaller gauge, the 28, when I can get it in a very light double gun, either side by side or over/under. Woodcock are easy birds to kill. One or two #9 shot will down them and you can toss quite a few #9's in the ¾-ounce shot load of a 28 gauge. If you insist upon the 1-ounce load for early shooting, when foliage may be heavy, you can get it in the Magnum load for this gauge.

PHEASANT

The flamboyant foreigner we call the ringneck has been in the United States so long that we think of him as a native bird. Actually, of course, he comes from China, but he has adapted to his new home so well that he has been largely responsible for spurring—and maintaining—the present high interest in upland bird shooting. For millions of gunners he has largely replaced the quail, prairie chicken, and other game-bird species not so well equipped to withstand heavy hunting pressure and the spread of civilization.

The ringneck does well on farm lands and in the suburbs, wherever cover is heavy enough to hide him and where he can find weed seeds, berries, wild rose hips, and the farmer's corn to feed on. In the same areas he thrives on grasshoppers all summer long. He's a swamp lover in Eastern farm lands, but he is at his best in the big grain country of the Midwest where he has feed and cover in the same fields. Anyway you look at a pheasant, he is a farm bird. You will not find him in the wilderness or in forest country. The tall-timber is definitely not to his liking.

Pheasants are our gaudiest game birds, the cockbirds exhibiting gorgeous combinations of bronze, metallic blues and greens, a bit of purple, plenty of golden yellow, and a dash of brilliant red. The first ringnecks were brought over in the early 1880's and released in the Willamette Valley of Oregon, and they have been here ever since. Intensive stocking throughout the United States has given the birds almost native status, except in the Deep South, where they are almost unknown.

Any ringneck rooster will give a hunter a good go for his money. The wise bird would rather run through heavy ground cover than take wing. He seems to sense that taking to the air makes him vulnerable to a load of shot, and he would rather stay out of sight on the ground. Thus, for one or two hunters a good, wide-ranging and fast-moving bird dog is almost as important to good shooting as their guns. Inevitably the bird will keep moving ahead of the hunters so long as there is concealing ground cover, but a dog smart in pheasant ways will circle ahead of the bird, cut off his escape, and hold him tight on point until the gunners come up.

In the great cornfield country of the Midwest, where the birds are as thick as starlings on a newly seeded lawn, the hunters gang up in big parties for pheasant drives. Half of the party takes stands at the end of a corn strip and the other half moves toward them through the corn. The birds run ahead of the drivers, usually following the rows, until they emerge under the guns at the far end. When the barrage begins and the ringnecks realize they are trapped between two lines of hunters, they take off in great confusion.

These pheasant drives are wild shooting and a world of sport. The dogs used are generally Labradors or other

retrievers, and they usually stay put with the standers until the birds begin to fall. In this hunting, pointing dogs are almost useless except to run down singles—and where birds are this plentiful no one bothers with a single. The retrievers prove their worth when it comes to recovering cripples, of which there usually are a number in every shoot because the ringneck is such a tough bird to down.

Mature cockbirds weigh about three and a half pounds on the average and measure about three feet in length when extended in flight. Much of this, it should never be forgotten, is tail. In many shooters' eyes the image of a three-foot bird is disturbing. Time and again they underlead ringnecks because of the long tail. Result: tail feathers only, or a bird badly wounded by shot through the abdomen.

In shooting pheasants the target should be the head. Judge your leads only from the head. This will place your pattern either on the head or neck, or, if your lead is a bit short, in the vital chest cavity. Shots at birds going directly away are always uncertain for clean kills, unless the range is short and you are shooting a gun packing a good load of shot. The birds can take a number of pellet hits in the rear abdomen without showing it. They will scale off some distance away and hide until they die, but you will fail to recover all of them even with the best dog work. On rear-end shots your pellets will not penetrate to the vitals unless you are within about thirty yards. I regularly pass up going-away shots when I'm shooting 20- and 28-gauge guns, unless the birds make a close-range rise.

Many ringneck hunters are using overly large shot sizes. Last fall I met a pheasant hunter who was using #4's, losing birds in the swamp, and crying because he didn't have #2's. Big shot is never the answer to killing birds of this size. A strong cockbird can take three or four #4 shot in the body without a flinch and without the gunner ever knowing he touched him. The load that puts down the birds is fine shot, in a pattern covering the head and neck. This is deadly. After having killed several thousand of these birds in the past forty years, I would never consider using any shot size larger than

#6. In a 12-gauge gun, shooting at tower-released birds, I have had top-notch results with the three-dram, 1⅛-ounce trap load of #7½. At a recent release shoot, I downed thirty-four consecutive birds, killing each with a single shot, except for one which required another load to drop him. Here also I was using the standard trap load.

As is true of most game, the pheasant's current rate of survival is based on his ability to find proper food and cover throughout the year. Given good living conditions, the bird thrives under even the heaviest hunting pressure. It is absolutely impossible to wipe out a pheasant population by legal shooting. The birds are much too smart. After the first day or two of gunning, pheasants find new hiding places and neither dog nor man can dig them all out. There will always be survivors, provided the ecology of the habitat is good enough to assure seed for the next year's broods.

Probably the most significant characteristic of the ringneck is his adaptability to private preserve shooting. The bird is largely responsible for the thousands of these shooting areas now in existence. The private preserve, conducted for public shooting, is a great source of sport for millions of hunters who would get little bird shooting otherwise. And the pheasant is the one species, among several which are raised for preserve shooting, which can be counted on to give the closest possible match to wild-bird shooting.

Even though ringnecks may be farm raised, hand-fed, and penned up from the day they are hatched, they revert to the wild state almost instantly upon release. They skulk, run, and hide like their wildborn brethren, and when they are finally forced to flush they take wing with the same strong, driving upthrust that springs them into the air to give the gunner a fair, clean shot.

Unlike native ruffed grouse and woodcock, the pheasant is a clear open flyer when he takes to the air. He is without question the first bird the novice upland gunner should take on for his indoctrination in wing shooting. The ringneck is a big target. He towers up nicely for the shot and he is never so fast in flight that you can't get the gun on him before he moves out of killing range.

*Preceding pages: Released game-farm
ringnecks give same exciting sport as wild birds, lie
better to dogs, and flush from low ground
cover with a strident cackle and blur of wings.
Ringnecks (below and right) are
most brilliantly plumaged American game birds, powerful
on the wing, sneaky on the ground.
Bottom: Well-built blind in Midwest cornfield.*

QUAIL

Some years ago I read a statement by Bernard M. Baruch, the eminent elder statesman and financier, that there are two things a man cannot stand being kidded about—his prowess with the ladies and his skill in shooting quail. As to the matter of the ladies, I prefer to remain silent, but Mr. Baruch's judgment falls close to the mark when he speaks of the quail shooter, and is equally fitting for almost any other sportsman, although it probably applies more appropriately to the Southern gentleman than to his Northern counterpart.

The bobwhite quail is the basic upland game bird of the South. When a Southerner speaks of "bird shooting" he means only one thing—quail—not grouse or pheasant, woodcock or wild fowl. I once had a friend in Maryland who owned a pair of big rawboned pointers that were avid quail hunters. The spoken words "bird," or "birds," were taboo in that household. The instant the familiar and exciting sound reached canine ears, the dogs headed for the nearest window—whether it was open or not. My friend had frequent recourse to the local glazier.

Once south of the Mason-Dixon line the American hunter is in quail country. This is not to say that quail aren't found in the Northern states, but it does mean that they have never reached in number or importance the game-bird status they have in the South.

With the fairly recent introduction of this bird to private shooting preserves, the bobwhite is becoming better known to all American gunners, even in the Northland, where he vies with the big ringneck for popularity. And his stature as a game bird is certain to increase as new methods come along for propagating birds suitable for release on shooting preserves. Only a decade ago the quail was thought hopeless as a game-farm bird, but now game biologists have produced plump, strong-flying bobwhite for release shooting—a sport that provides all the thrills inherent in gunning the wild birds.

My own experience in quail hunting, I am sorry to say, has been somewhat belated. All my early years as a hunter were spent in New York state, where the birds were rigidly protected. In hunting other game, I'd occasionally bump into a small covey of bobwhite and could do nothing more than stand and watch them flare up and scatter as they headed for the nearest thicket. In the spring, I often heard the cheery whistle of the cockbirds during the nesting season, and before I reached maturity I had already classed quail as songbirds in my mind. I still have reservations about gunning them.

Not so the Southern hunter. Youngsters are brought up on quail, as I was on woodcock and grouse, and, it must be said, some of the finest wing shots in the country have grown up solely on quail. A covey-burst from the ground occurring close at hand is a disconcerting experience for a hunter new on quail. Often, as the birds leave in a tight formation, he is tempted to "shoot into the brown." This gathers no birds, except by sheer accident. The skilled quail gunner learns to separate the individual birds as targets quickly and shoots for each bird. It is true enough that rather often a shot held for one bird will catch another in the pattern, but this is a bonus bird and must be chalked up to accident rather than skill.

Bobwhite quail is a bird of farm country, a lover of small grains and weed seeds. He hides in the grass and grainfields and needs the protective cover of hedgerows, rail fences, and strips of brier patch along stone walls to escape from predators. The "clean" farming of New England and the Middle Atlantic states, where rail fences were replaced with virginal barbed wire and the brushy margins of stone walls were cut away, spelled doom to the bobwhite. The farmers' reduced interest in growing his own small grain for poultry also has made the habitat difficult for quail survival. And the increase of semiwild house cats, foxes, hawks, and other vermin predators has sealed his fate in many Northern areas. Apparently the Southern farmer is less dedicated to neat housekeeping than his Northern counterpart and more likely to grow small-grain crops which quail love.

By every test the bobwhite is the ideal bird shooter's game. He is in complete rapport with a pointing dog, lying close to his "find," crouching firmly until flushed, then breaking away with great speed and at all possible angles—and usually in the open. But these birds are small, about a third of a pound, and are not as easy to spot in the air as the much larger, gaudy ringnecks.

Quail hunting is regarded as a gentleman's sport and, as such, is given traditional treatment. In good Southern quail country the gunner does not rise at dawn, nor does he need to. He can lie in bed until well after sunup, take a leisurely breakfast, then climb into a buggy or Jeep which already has been loaded with the wire crates holding a few brace of lean, rangy pointers. Once on the feeding grounds, a pair of dogs is turned loose by the handlers and the first "cast" of the day begins, with the dogs moving at full speed in a wide half-circle, downwind of likely cover, to pick up the scent of a covey. When the first dog hits he checks, then moves in slowly on mincing feet until he knows the birds are only a few yards away. Here he stops rigidly on point. His brace mate honors his point by moving in behind, checking, and holding rigidly in his "backup" point until the guns arrive for the flush.

If this all sounds rather easy, it is. The essentials in good quail hunting are good quail cover and good dogs. The first flush of a covey is almost certain to be in open shooting. When the shots to the flush break up the birds they will scatter, some of them heading for thickets or timber. These latter are left for next year's "seed," and the handler puts the dogs onto the singles dropping into open covers. Quail shooting in timber or heavy thicket is not easy anyway. The birds usually flush out of good killing range, despite fine dogs.

The quail gunner's biggest problem is to make a good showing on the covey flush. This requires quick judgment in picking out the first bird and fast footwork —which becomes instinctive in time—to get into just the right swinging position. It also demands rapid but accurate work with the second barrel to fill out the "double," a factor which tradition insists upon for any quail gunners worthy of the title.

For quail, the lightweight 20-gauge double gun has been the accepted standard arm for more than a generation. Top-notch gunners favor the 28 gauge and many, including former President Dwight Eisenhower, take their birds with the .410 bore. Since the birds are small and are always taken at fairly short range, these small bores with their standard loads of #8 shot are big enough. A bobwhite is a tender bird, a choice table morsel, and there is no point in mangling his carcass with a big dose of bird shot.

Left: Valley quail, also called California
quail, are great runners and do not hold well for a dog.
Bobwhite quail (right) is greatest
of game birds for pointing dogs and an easy
target for a good shotgunner.

*Top: Great thrill in quail shooting is
in burst of covey from ground, as though all birds had
been released with the pull of a
string. Problem lies in picking right single bird as
target, then switching to a second for
classic "double." Shooting "into the brown," as
birds leave in a bunch, seldom
puts quail in the bag. Gunner on left in photo opposite
is ignoring quail-shooting etiquette which
holds that paired shooters only
take birds on their side of the rise. Unlike birds
shown in print (above), quail lie tight
to ground before covey flushes.*

172

DOVE

Each year, about mid-March, when I step out the back door before breakfast for a peek at the thermometer, I begin to hear the eerie, plaintive cooing of the first dove arrivals from the South. Every morning from then on I can see them as they begin nest building in the big spruce trees in my frontyard—one pair sitting on the power line between the house and my shooting range, another couple picking gravel in the driveway. For years I have watched and listened to these lovely blue-gray birds, noted their steady increase in numbers and marveled at their quick take-off and swift flight.

We do not have an open season on these birds in my home state, which pleases members of the Audubon Society no end, exasperates the resident hunters, and contributes little to sport and good game management. For protecting the birds in their northern range is only a stopgap. When they flock up in the early fall and head South they run the full gantlet of guns all the way to their wintering grounds. Except for a few states in the Northeast, doves may be hunted legally almost everywhere they are found, for they breed in every state.

In spite of its classification in the Northeast as a songbird, the mourning dove is actually a canny, sophisticated bird, well adapted to the changing works of man and with all the attributes of a fine game bird. In some quarters, farmers accuse him of destroying

grain crops, but there is more fiction than fact to this. The bird is almost entirely a ground feeder. When he does feed on grain, which is whenever it is available, it is the grain that has fallen from the plant and is lost to the harvest anyway. On occasion he also feeds on the harvested shocks before they are threshed.

So the autumn grainfields are the most likely spots to hunt doves. They flock into these areas thick with growing wheat, barley, buckwheat, and other grains, often by the thousands, just at dawn and just before sundown. Mourning doves also require daily watering, so in dry country a water hole in late afternoon is also a great gathering place for them.

Dove hunters usually work the big grainfields in scattered groups. Taking a stand, with each shooter spaced seventy-five or eighty yards apart along the perimeter of the area, gives everyone his chance at the birds once the shooting starts. Pass shooting between the roost area and feeding or watering grounds is also productive—if the gunner knows dove shooting.

Doves are one of the trickiest targets in all wing shooting. They are fast flyers, seeming to move at about the same speed as a mallard. But because of their small size, they are easily missed when the gunner does not give the bird enough forward lead. When you begin on doves and fail to connect, which is inevitable at first, the rule is to double your lead, and then double that, until you begin hitting. Duck shooting is a good preliminary course to dove hunting. The flight pattern of both birds is much the same, except that a dove is given to erratic dips and dives, under full speed, either when shot at or when traveling on a windy day.

Despite the fact that the mourning dove is a small bird, he is usually hunted with a big gun. Dove hunters feel that doves are as difficult to hit and kill as a duck, so most gunners use the 12-gauge full-choke gun for all pass shooting, with express loads of #6 or #7½ shot. I have had good results with the 20 gauge modified, shooting 1 ounce of shot, but I must admit that there were many days when I wished I were shooting a 12-gauge duck gun.

As in duck shooting—and dove hunting is closer to

*Mourning dove (above), although classed
as songbird throughout Northern states, is prime target
of upland gunners in South. Opposite: Wild
turkey, once near extinction, is making a surprising
comeback in much of his former habitat.*

that than any other upland-game shooting—you will burn up plenty of shells for each bird downed until you learn the pattern of flight and the correct amount of lead. A gunner who kills two birds for every five shells, taking all in-range shots as they come, can count himself among the top echelon of dove shooters.

WILD TURKEY

Wild turkey, the noblest game bird of all, provides a prime example of how the forces of man and nature can combine to restore certain game to areas where it has been absent. For almost a century the wild turkey flourished only south of an imaginary line extending through the central part of Pennsylvania, a line which separates the oak-pine forests of the South and the beech, birch, and maple timberland of the North.

Every schoolboy knows that wild turkey was a mainstay of the colonial New Englander's diet. The great birds were numerous then as far north as Maine, and remained so until relentless harvesting by market hunters and the felling of great sections of big timber for lumber, tanbark, and wood alcohol doomed him to the same fate as the plains buffalo.

Since the turkey is a shy bird—shyer than any other American game bird—and demands the type of feed provided by mature hardwood forests, only the restoration of these woodlands could bring him back. Brush and second-growth timber, ideal for grouse and deer, is shunned by turkeys. There is too little feed for them in the immature woodland, and heavy cover impedes their movements and makes it difficult for them to flush from danger.

During the past fifty years, however, the great second-growth areas of the North, created by extensive cutting of the big hardwoods, have grown up and once again produce the proper food to sustain the turkeys during the critical winter season. The American chestnut, once the top-grade winter feed for turkeys, is still not available, but acorns and other nuts are plentiful enough. Unfortunately, as these forest lands grow, becoming more hospitable to wild turkeys, they become less so for the whitetail deer.

When the birds began to move north of their own accord once more, game management men were quick to restock turkeys in the newly grown timberlands. At first all such efforts failed, for a combination of reasons, but now properly reared wild birds are establishing themselves.

Northern Pennsylvania has a great population. Even with a one-bird "season" limit, Pennsylvania turkey hunters are killing more than 75,000 gobblers each year. New York has a limited open season, destined to be expanded soon. Even a state as far north as Montana has had a limited season for several years now, and Missouri, as the result of a ten-year restoration program, boasts a good crop of birds in forested areas where turkeys had not been seen in decades. The comeback of the wild turkey is extremely encouraging. It seems certain that the great birds will provide exciting hunting for Northern sportsmen in the future, just as they once did in the past.

In many ways the wild turkey is as difficult to hunt and kill as a whitetail buck. He is innately wary and suspicious, possesses extremely good perceptive vision, can run faster than an Olympic sprinter, and flies higher and faster than a ruffed grouse. He must be still-hunted with the same skill as a whitetail deer, or, if this fails, he can be called into killing range, but only by a man 175

*Dove shooting (left) is
pass shooting everywhere. Small size
of birds, coupled with
their speed, makes them extremely
difficult to hit. Most
gunners do not give them enough lead.
Wild turkey (above and right)
is a wary bird with acute
vision. A good blind and camouflaged
clothing are essential.*

177

who knows how to use a caller with the greatest skill. There are a dozen different calls in a turkey's repertoire, and to get within range a hunter must be able to produce most of them.

Because of the turkey's visual acuity, the hunter who sits awaiting birds as they come to their feeding grounds or respond to his call must be partially concealed and motionless until the birds are close enough to make a kill. If he situates himself where he is more or less exposed, at the foot of a tree, or against a boulder, the turkey will easily recognize his form. Unlike the deer, which would seldom detect a man so cached, the turkey rarely confuses his human adversary with natural terrain once he gets a clear look. The most successful turkey hunters wear camouflaged clothes, grow beards or wear face masks, build screening blinds of natural vegetation, and learn to keep still for hours at a time.

Turkeys are also highly perceptive when locating the source of a sound, "yelps" in particular. So all of this deception is extremely important to successfully calling the birds. The turkey will be particularly alert and looking directly at the spot from which the call emanates. A gobbler will often sneak toward the hunter's blind, staying out of sight in cover and also staying out of shotgun range, while he carefully and thoroughly inspects every clump of brush where a man might be concealed. At this stage a false yelp or the slightest unnatural movement will spook the bird into a sprint or a quick, booming flush into the air.

Turkey calling is an art that combines much natural talent with almost as much practice as it takes to play a violin. The yelp of the hen bird varies in tone and pitch, depending upon whether she is calling in her scattered brood or is giving out with a plaintive love call during the mating season. The gobbler's yelp also has sexual overtones. These calls are used, of course, only in those parts of the country which have open seasons during the spring mating period.

The standard, and probably the most effective, method of calling turkeys is to locate a flock, either by finding a roost or still-hunting as the birds feed in the early morning, and then flushing the birds by running toward them or firing your shotgun, or both. Anything that gets them into the air in a wildly confused state is acceptable. Once they have scattered, you pick a spot near that point of flush and hide yourself in a natural blind or build one quickly. Once you are settled and well screened, get out the caller and give a tentative yelp. Try again in a few minutes. Usually the birds will gather once more near your hiding place—that is, if your calling is artistic.

Although the turkey has always been regarded as shotgunner's game, especially in the South, many hunters kill their birds with a small-caliber rifle. A 12-gauge Magnum, using the heaviest loads, will, of course, kill birds up to sixty yards, but the rifleman can count on making his kills at 100 yards or more in open, big timber. Probably the best compromise is the combination gun or "drilling," a three-barrel job with two shot barrels and a rifle beneath. Savage Arms makes an over/under, Model 24, combining a 20-gauge Magnum with a .22 WMR rifle—now a popular turkey gun.

SNIPE

The woodcock and the jacksnipe are so closely akin in general appearance, in their love of damp climates, and in their unpredictable flight patterns that the novice gunner can be forgiven for mistaking one for the other. Both are classified as shore birds, both feed on earthworms principally, and both have been equipped by nature with long bills to carry on their worm probing. In addition, the snipe's movements, like the woodcock's, are mysterious. He migrates when he pleases, feeds mostly at night, and crouches in the short grass of his feeding area until disturbed by the hunter or a predator. But here the similarities between the two birds end.

The snipe is a slender little bird, gray-white in color, and on close comparison quite unlike the woodcock, which tends to be plump and sports a brown plumage that, when held by the hunter, resembles a handful of dead leaves. Probably the snipe's most distinguishing feature, however, is his affinity for water. The woodcock hates to get his feet wet. He keeps to heavy cover and is rarely seen along the lake or seashores, or in the open bogs and marshlands that are the normal habitats of snipe. A shooter who goes after jacksnipe will do his gunning in high boots or waders for maneuvering over these grassy wet flats, and he'll be zeroing-in on a target about half the size of the woodcock.

As a matter of fact, there is no trickier target than jacksnipe, as the shotgunners of fifty or more years ago will testify. Although the bird is much neglected today, the old-timers had high praise for him.

Why snipe gunners have become such a scarce breed in recent years one can only surmise. Certainly the snipe is one of the most cosmopolitan birds, available at varying times in any fresh- or salt-water marshland from Ontario to Texas, and from Vancouver to Nova Scotia—and, for that matter, in almost any other part of the world. Perhaps the lack of interest stems from the fact that good snipe country is also good wild-fowl country. Today's gunners seem to prefer the larger game. It may be, too, that the old gag about "holding the bag" has always been keyed to snipe hunting.

One obvious trouble with snipe shooting is that it's tough work. Whether the hunter is working with or without a retrieving dog, he usually must plunge into marshy regions, sinking ankle-deep in the mire with every step, and at times, when the going is at its worst, sinking up to his knees. At best, a few hours of jumping snipe in their normal feeding grounds will leave him as leg-weary as if he'd been climbing for bighorn sheep.

In 1964, along the St. Lawrence River between New York and Quebec, the snipe were in by the thousands. Although there were ducks on the river, too, it was bluebird weather, early in the season, and the ducks did not fly. Duck gunners wasted days in the blinds waiting for the birds to take to the air. It didn't happen. For days no one had any shooting, and then I talked one of the local guides into gunning some snipe. We had a ball.

Shooting snipe is a combination of the fast quail-covey work and the tricky snap shooting of ruffed grouse. For the snipe is a flock bird. When you find one you will usually flush half a dozen, or a dozen, or per-

haps a hundred. On take-off these birds get into the air quickly, moving in a corkscrew pattern at first, then straightening out once under way, although by that time they are usually out of gunshot. Unlike quail coveys, the snipe tend to stay together after flushing and usually move only to the other end of a marsh before settling down again.

A successful method of hunting snipe without dogs is for the gunners to split up into two parties and work toward each other from the opposite sides of the bog, moving slowly and carefully. Birds flushed by one group will often head toward the other, then wheel about and come back to the first group. It can be wild shooting, with many shells fired per bird bagged.

The gun used on quail and woodcock is also top grade for snipe. A light, quick-handling 20-gauge with open boring will give you more doubles on a flock rise than a heavier 12-gauge with tight chokes, however. The smallest shot size purchasable—#9's—are about right, although if I could still get #10's I would prefer them for these tender little birds.

179

One of the trickiest targets is the
snipe in his normal corkscrew, zigzag flight. Popular
with gunners of a century ago,
snipe get little attention from today's hunters,
perhaps because they are so small.

*Sharptail grouse (below) enjoy a wide range, from
Southern prairies to Alaska. Slightly larger than ruffed grouse, the sharptail
is more of a covey bird than his woods-dwelling
cousin. Pinnated grouse, or prairie chicken (bottom, left),
is now making comeback in prairie states
where he was nearly exterminated in Thirties by drought. Sagehen
(bottom right, and top, opposite page) is largest American
grouse. Prairie chicken shooting is best in grainfields.*

PRAIRIE CHICKEN

What the bobwhite quail is to the Southern hunter, the prairie chicken is to the sportsman of the Middle West, with one major difference. Actually there are two species of prairie chicken: the pinnated grouse, which is most frequently called "prairie chicken" in the field, and the sharptail grouse. The sharptail is slightly larger than the pinnated and enjoys a broader range, but in most other respects—flight pattern, coloring—the two are so similar that at a distance it is difficult to tell them apart. Indeed, differentiating between them is hardly important to the shooter, since they are hunted in the same manner.

Only on close inspection does the pinnated's cutoff tail reveal itself as dissimilar from the pintail of his counterpart. And only then can the contrast between the sharptail's distinctly gray and feathered legs and the pinnated's lightly feathered, yellow legs be seen.

Probably the easiest way to differentiate between them, however, is by range. The pinnated grouse is a bird of the middle United States and seems to prefer to flock in or near farm lands, while the sharptail and its several subspecies is more of a wilderness bird and can be found anywhere from New Mexico to Fairbanks, Alaska. He has, in fact, the broadest range of any Western grouse.

Along the eastern slopes of the Rockies and through the foothills, the sharptail mingles with the blue grouse and the Franklin. Farther north and east, in the Dakotas, Minnesota, and Wisconsin, his range overlaps that of the pinnated grouse. I have even seen and hunted sharptails in the prairie and sagebrush country where the sagegrouse makes his home.

At one time, the Plains Indians, particularly the Sioux, relied on the sharptail as a mainstay of their diet. They knew the bird and his habits well. So well, some students of Indian lore contend, that many of the ceremonial dances practiced by the Indians derive from the peculiar antics of the cockbirds of both prairie chicken species during the mating season.

Each species has an air sac on either side of the neck. The sharptail's are bluish in color; those of the pinnated grouse are yellow. These become distended during the mating display, and in the pinnated grouse, a pair of stiff, pinlike feathers on either side of the neck become erect. Once the sacs balloon out, the birds go into a crazy dance to lure a mate. First, one bird struts, erects and spreads his tail, then twists and whirls about, beating the ground with his feet in a quick tattoo. Before long, more male birds join him, until soon there is a furious circle of action. In the case of the sharptail it is accompanied by a gurgling sound, as air is expelled from the swollen sacs. The pinnated grouse emits a resonant "chick-a-boom" sound that rolls out over the prairie at the dawn of a spring day like the throbbing of an Indian drum. Occasionally, if you are lucky, you may have an opportunity to witness this frantic and unique display. When the situation presents itself, be sure to take advantage of it.

Today sharptail is the great bird-dog game of the West. He flocks in the open grainfields, where wide-ranging pointers can sweep the terrain freely and catch his scent. Once found, he lies well to the dog, usually holding for flush until the guns are within easy range. Late in the season, after the birds have been exposed to their share of heavy gunning, they tend to flush far out of reach of a scattergun, but normally the sharptail gives you a fair break, with a covey rise at about twenty or thirty yards. As the hunting season advances, the sharptails also tend to stay along the edges of bushy thickets and coulees and in the foothill country adjoining farm lands. It is in these areas that the hunter will find some of the finest shotgunning he has ever experienced, with the hardwoods in glorious fall color providing a magnificent background for the birds to burst forth from.

One baleful habit of the sharptail young during the early days of the gunning season is a tendency to straggle forth, single file, when the covey is flushed. The market hunter of half a century ago, armed with a pump shotgun, literally slaughtered these birds on a covey rise, taking a mature bird at first flush, then accounting for a bird with every shell in the gun, as the young rose heavily into the air, one by one.

182

Pinnated grouse gets name from
"horns" on each side of neck, just below head. Horns
are erected and air sacs distended
as a preliminary to
the mating dance of the species.

Today's limits and later season openings have virtually eliminated this type of easy shooting and I, for one, have never had it anyway. Every sharptail covey I have gunned over left the ground in a great rush, all together, almost as though a blanket had been lifted away. They would hold well together, sometimes so well that a shot meant for one would kill a neighbor. When flushed from a hillside, the flock would drive down and out over the valley below, beating and gliding on strong wings, tilting in unison as a vagrant breeze caught their little bodies, until all had passed out of sight. Then the flock would drop to the ground to rest.

In close cover sharptails can be as difficult a target as a New England ruffed grouse, and in the open grainfields they are certainly no easier to hit than bobwhite quail. Most hunters use a 12 gauge, in either full or modified choke, for on an average rise the birds will be thirty-five to forty yards away before you can bring the gun to bear on the speeding target. A quail gun is not big enough for these birds. I have had good results with a light 16-gauge double firing 1⅛ ounces of shot, which is a good minimum combination. It can, however, be duplicated now with the 20-Magnum guns carrying the same shot load in the short Magnum shell.

Pinnated grouse—or simply prairie chicken, as this bird has been known for more than a century—requires high grass for protective cover and nesting. Without it he disappears, as was almost the case in the Thirties, when drought destroyed the grasslands and farming areas of the Middle West and dust storms carried away the precious topsoil.

Because of the near extinction of the pinnated grouse during this period, few upland gunners saw them, much less hunted them, for a number of years. But the restoration of the grass country and good game management have helped to revitalize the species. Although most Mid-western states are still carrying on management programs to restore both the habitat and the birds in areas where they were once so plentiful, Kansas, Nebraska, New Mexico, and Oklahoma now have limited open seasons, and South Dakota, where probably some of the best grouse hunting is done, offers the sportsman a six-

week season with a daily bag limit of three.

The pinnated grouse holds as well to a dog as the sharptail, and offers as much sport when found in open country. As the season advances, these birds grow wary, however, and begin to flush wildly from both man and dog, often taking off sixty yards away. In cold, windy weather they are wilder still and fly much farther before setting down. A good early season load for the chickens is a 12-gauge trap with #7½ shot. Later on you can switch to a duck load of #6's. In any case, the same minimums in gun and load for sharptail apply equally well to this grouse.

SAGE GROUSE

Sage grouse have been in a decline for many years. The best sage-grouse country has been taken over by commercial sheep herds, and these play hob with the birds on their breeding grounds. The grazing sheep trample both the nests and the young birds with their sharp hoofs and crowd the mature birds away from the water holes. When the grouse then look for shelter in the creek bottoms, they are easy prey for the man with the gun.

Most hunters do not rate the sage grouse very highly, however. This biggest of the grouse species is a slow flier and not a very tasty table bird. These two facts seem to be related. At one time, because the sagehen was such poor eating, open seasons were begun in August, when the young birds were little more than half grown and still tender. The young are notoriously poor fliers, however, and once flushed they seldom fly very far before settling down. They must be flushed again and again. It was probably after a few such seasons that the gunners' low opinion of sagehens was formed.

Actually, later in the fall, the more mature birds and the oldsters can be tough targets—not in the sense that they are difficult to hit, but because they take a lot of killing. Ringneck hunters who admire the ability of the pheasant to absorb and carry off a well-directed load of shot will have a new experience when they tackle full-grown sagehen. I have gunned the great, fan-tailed birds in their Western prairie homelands with native hunters who insisted on using 12-gauge Magnums and #2 shot.

Sharptail grouse (opposite) begin mating
dance. Blue grouse (top, left and right) are largest of America's
woodland grouse species and resemble ruffed
grouse in many respects. Franklin
grouse (above) is known as "fool-hen" in West.

This makes a certain amount of sense, since a mature cockbird will run eight pounds and be about the size of a young Canada goose, for which such a load would be standard.

As the name suggests, the bird is never far from sagebrush. A physical oddity is that he has no gizzard and is thus unable to digest seeds and grains as do other members of the grouse family. So the hunter of sage-hens must plough through sagebrush most of the time.

Without pointing dogs it is not easy to get the mature birds into the air. They like to run ahead, from sage clump to sage clump, never letting you get close enough to put them up. If you find them in clipped alfalfa, clover, or crested-wheat fields, they usually will lie tight until you are on top of them. With pointers trained on pheasant, however, it is no problem to get the birds well nailed down for a flush in any cover.

Yet for all their great size and slow take-off, the sage grouse can be deceptive. As they roar up they sometimes give out with a "keck, keck" cackle similar to that of a cock ringneck. And, if you are a pheasant shooter, you will find yourself giving them far too much forward lead. But once you get onto their flight pattern, they are remarkably easy shooting.

BLUE GROUSE

Some years ago, I was riding along a mountain trail in the Bob Marshall Wilderness Area of Montana, heading for Scapegoat Mountain on the Divide. As the trail moved through a heavy stand of pines, my horse suddenly shied to the left and nearly tossed me out of the saddle. I checked him roughly, then saw that he was staring at an enormous burned-out stump on the edge of the trail to the right. Perched on it, apparently unafraid, was a big blue grouse. As I urged the horse ahead, the bird stretched its neck, shuffled its wings and feathers, and fluttered up to a low branch overhanging the trail. I had a little .22 handgun in my saddle pocket and was about to knock that fat blue grouse off the limb when my guide, coming up from behind, cautioned me about shooting. We were in good elk country, he said, and he didn't want to spook any bulls that might be around. So we rode under the tree, and the grouse sat there until we were out of sight, apparently quite undisturbed by the close passage of two mounted hunters.

In some ways, the blue grouse of the Western mountains behaves much like the Eastern ruffed grouse. In true wilderness country, both birds are unafraid of man. Near civilization, on the other hand, where they are frequently hunted, both are more wary and sophisticated. I have gunned blue grouse when they took off from the tall pines, just like ruffed grouse, buzzing out from high overhead and giving you only a flash and a mighty difficult shot. I have also hunted them in the Canadian Rockies, where they will hold in a patch of shin-tangle for a dog, then burst forth with a great flurry, dipping and darting between the big tree trunks in a getaway that would please their Eastern relative. And then there are places where it is sinful to shoot them with a shotgun; you are forced to "ground-sluice" them if you want them. Even running at them won't put them into the air, although they may lift onto a low branch and then sit there staring stupidly at you. No wonder many Westerners still call them "fool hens"!

There are several varieties of blue grouse: dusky grouse, sooty grouse, Sierra, and Richardson's. They differ widely in range. They can be seen from New Mexico far up into Canada and Alaska, and each displays some subtle variation in color. But in general they are all a handsome blue-gray—whence comes their name —and sport a wide, dark tail with a broad, light gray band at the tip. The plumage is appropriate, for the blues make their home in the evergreen forests of the Rockies. In addition, they are the largest woodland grouse in America, and of the entire class of grouse, second only to the sage in size.

Like the prairie chicken, the blue possesses booming sacs on each side of his neck, orange-red in color. These distend during the mating season and with them he sounds his resonant love call. It is ventriloquistic in character, and closely resembles the mating "drum" of the ruffed grouse.

It is unfortunate that the native Western hunter has little regard for the sporting qualities of the blue grouse. And to a large extent this is true simply because he does not hunt the birds with pointing dogs. When good dogs are used there is mighty little difference between hunting blue grouse and ruffed grouse, despite the fact that you will be shooting them 2,000 miles apart. However, it is equally true that the local hunter in the West is usually after big game when he treks into alpine country. Even though he may encounter grouse along the back roads and trails, he will not hunt them as game. If he shoots one, it will be from a tree or on the ground, more often than not, and with a rifle or a handgun. This puts meat in the pot, but it isn't much sport.

In mountain country where much lumbering has been done, the blue grouse, like his Eastern cousin, tends to feed along the edges of the clearings, where the cutting of timber encourages the growth of berries. And if you have a good grouse dog, this is where to hunt these birds. When you find them you will also find some fast gunning. The blue is at least double the size of a ruffed grouse and takes much more killing. Also, on the open prairie and in the big-timber country of the West, you will have to take your grouse with a long shot. A 12-gauge gun, with 1⅛ ounces of #6 shot fired from a modified bore, is as close as you can get to a perfect gun for blue grouse.

187

Mating dance of sage grouse (above, left)
is believed to have been inspiration for dances of many Indian
tribes of Great Plains. Below:
Inflated air sacs emit booming sound as cockbirds
circle hens with tail spikes flaring.

*Chukar partridge (top row)
have become an excellent game-farm and
shooting-preserve bird, and
have "gone native" in many Western
states with fairly high
elevation. Smaller than ruffed grouse,
chukars are similar to bobwhite
quail in their tendency
to lie well to pointing dogs and to
covey up. Chukar was brought
to America from Northern
India, is one of the gaudiest
of partridge family and
a fine table bird.
Below: Gunners work their dog over
choice bit of sharptail cover.*

FRANKLIN GROUSE

As far as I am concerned, the Franklin grouse is the true "fool hen" of the Western mountains. In fact, he is closely related to the spruce grouse, a bird found throughout southern Canada and universally referred to as "fool hen." I have never found one member of either species that deserved to be classed as a sporting bird. On big-game hunts we kill Franklins for the pot, with sticks and stones, and when we have gathered a dozen or so—which means we have run into a few flocks along the trail—we have a "chicken" dinner in camp.

The Franklin was named after Sir John Franklin, the nineteenth-century English explorer of northern Canada, and seems to have been first noted as a species by Lewis and Clark on their expedition in 1804-06.

In appearance the bird is much like his Eastern cousin, the ruffed grouse, though smaller. The coloring of their plumage is particularly close. But in character the Franklin is a bird of the deep wilderness and shows none of the wariness or cleverness of the Eastern grouse species.

Apparently the Franklin does not even profit from his brief encounters with man, for it is virtually impossible to flush a covey even by firing a charge of shot into the ground beside it. When the birds are roosting in low tree branches the situation is even more impossible. You may as well take a stick and rap one on the head as try to have some sport with him.

HUNGARIAN & CHUKAR PARTRIDGE

Hungarian partridge, so called because most of the birds purchased for release here came from Hungary, is one of America's finest game birds and certainly its top-grade import. In his native land, where he is known as the European gray partridge, he is a bird of the open grainfields and so has taken well to the great wheat regions of the western United States and Canada. (Alberta and Saskatchewan have the largest Hungarian partridge populations.) Attempts to stock "Huns" in the East have not generally been successful, but Pennsylvania has a crop in the Cumberland Valley area, and a few counties in northern New York state, bordering on the St. Lawrence River, have limited open seasons on them. For years, too, Prince Edward Island offered fine Hun shooting. Recently, however, the birds there were wiped out by disease.

The Huns make extremely provocative targets. They are small birds, weighing only about twelve ounces, and they are magnificent flyers, taking off in great covey bursts and flying much faster even than bobwhite quail. It is impossible to break up the coveys by shooting.

Franklin grouse are deep wilderness birds, completely unafraid of man since they rarely see him. Although not really a game bird, Franklin is excellent food and can be easily gathered with sticks or stones.

Each flock seems to adhere to the lead of some wise old bird, and unlike quail, does not allow the shooter the chance to follow singles and pick the membership off, one by one, over a dog's point.

Besides being difficult to take in flight, the Hun has long legs for his size and is an unusually good runner—and a deceptive one. When a flushed covey drops into a grainfield and the hunter follows up with the dog, the Hun will always leave a puzzling track, hiding in the stubble and moving ahead of dog and shooter just enough to keep out of sight. Unlike the maneuvers of the ringneck pheasant, which also enjoys a great reputation as a runner, the Hun does not move in a straight line or along a hedgerow, but zigzags his trail, confusing even the best of dogs. A smart dog may circle a ringneck and cut him off, but no one knows which way a Hun will go. While hunter and dog are searching, the partridge will often circle his adversaries in the tall grass or stubble and take off somewhere behind them.

One of the disconcerting aspects of shooting the Hun, aside from his swift, unified flush, is the fact that he will never allow the gunner to get within close killing range. Most covey rises will be as much as twenty-five to thirty-five yards away. No shooter will bump Huns as he might quail or a crouching ringneck. To get on target he will have to be fast with his gun. A man who has had a big yardage handicap shooting at the traps and who also can kill ruffed grouse in the New England thickets may get onto the game of shooting Huns fairly quickly, but a hunter of less ability will have his troubles. In addition, he will have to use dogs. If he does not, the partridge will lead him a merry chase, running just ahead of him, out of gun range, and at a pace that's fast enough to prevent the hunter from getting close enough to put him into the air. To corner a Hun—and cornering one is rare—the hunter must have a dog.

Again, as with most Western birds, a 12- or 16-gauge gun or, at least, a 20 Magnum is required. The consistently long-range rise of the coveys keeps you shooting at the limit of your gun's killing range. Also, since the birds are not large, a modified- or full-choke barrel gives the most effective killing pattern.

Chukar partridge are one of America's most recent—and successful—game-bird imports. The species originates in the Himalayan foothills, but is now thriving in California, Oregon, Wyoming, Nebraska, and Nevada. The bird seems to do best in the Northwest, in semiarid and prairie country, where he makes insects and weed seeds his principle feed. He also does well in fringe farm land where the crop is small grain.

Perhaps the most spectacular success with chukars has been seen on the private shooting preserves. Apparently these birds are as easy to raise as pheasants and, like the ringneck, revert to their wild state immediately upon release.

In size, they resemble the Hun, but not in color. Chukars are brilliantly plumaged birds. The upper portions of their bodies are a startling blue-gray that contrasts sharply with the white of their throats and the off-white with heavy dark bars seen on their undersides. Their bills, legs, and feet are a bright orange-red.

I first gunned chukars many years ago on a private preserve in the East and found them almost the same as bobwhite quail with respect to dog work and hunting. They covey up, hold well to the dog, and flush remarkably like the quail, their singles spreading wide apart once they have been broken up by the shooting. However, they are tougher than quail, and once flushed, the single chukars will fly much further before dropping down. Some will go as much as a quarter of a mile or more before they set in, often taking them beyond the limit of the preserve.

On most small preserves your first flush of chukar will be your best, and many times it will give you your only chance for a shot. After the flush, the chukar, like the ringneck and the Hun, will do a lot of running, and generally flush wild in open cover. It takes a considerable amount of leg work to run down chukars with a dog.

I would not suggest hunting these birds with any gun carrying less than a full ounce of shot. Chukars are more inclined to tower high than other open-cover game birds once they take to the air, so you will be in for some long shooting, even over good-working pointers.

191

Valley or California quail—Audubon version

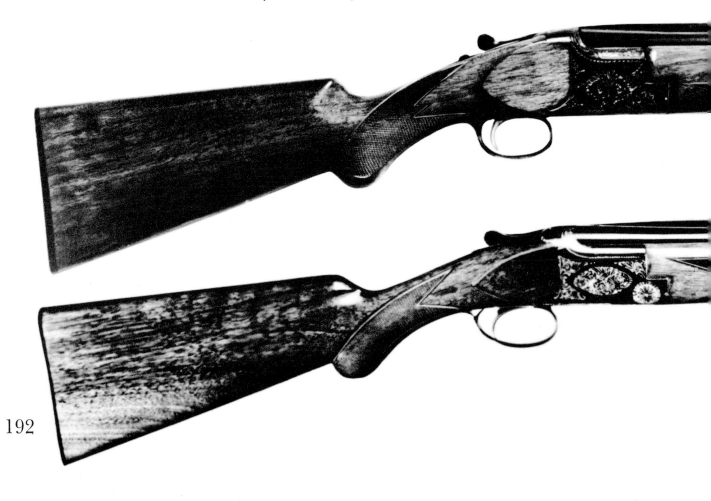

SELECTED GUNS FOR UPLAND GAME BIRDS

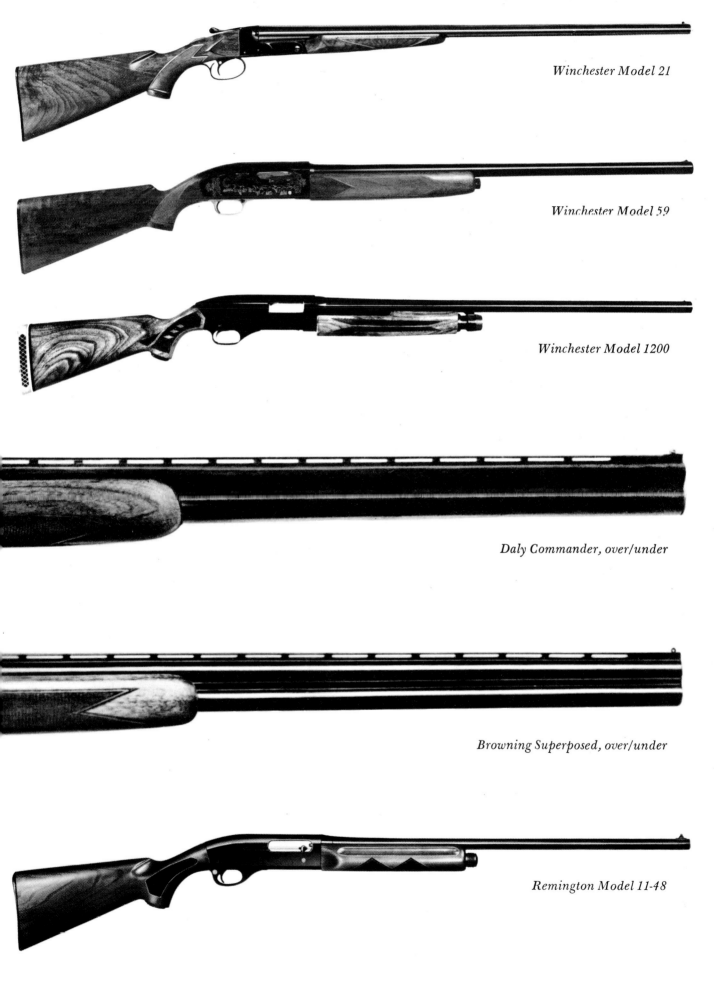

Winchester Model 21

Winchester Model 59

Winchester Model 1200

Daly Commander, over/under

Browning Superposed, over/under

Remington Model 11-48

WILDFOWL

10

CANADA GOOSE

As the first streaks of dawnlight cracked over the low horizon of Maryland's eastern shore, the big gray gander lifted his head from the corn stubble in the final act of feeding. He and his fellows, 300 strong, had spent much of the night in the freshly harvested field, picking up the scattered grain. The moon was late in rising and they had left the calm waters of Chesapeake Bay long after sundown to sweep inland over the flat farm country for their usual moonlight feeding period.

With the growing light the big birds became restless. Heads, coal black with a broad white chin strap, came out from beneath gray wings as the resting birds stretched their necks and waddled between the stubble rows. The big gander suddenly ran a few steps, then launched into the air. He beat slowly over the stubble, climbing gently toward the dark west. The flock followed in scattered strings, forming a wide, wavering line as it gained altitude. The birds' strident, mellow honkings filled the air while they gathered in formation, shifting into a long, undulating wedge with marvelous grace in flight.

In a matter of minutes, the great gray V, stretching out for 200 yards and pointing toward the bay, swept high over the salt marshes. It passed over a sandspit, where a small flock of stiff-looking geese floated quietly in the leeside, away from the fresh breeze now coming from the northeast. The big wedge wheeled over the end of the spit, 100 yards high, then sloped down in a long glide to the choppy surface, well away from shore.

With the coming northeast wind, heavy dark clouds scudded over the eastern shore, cutting off the first rays of the sun. Quickly the breeze stiffened, whipping the waters of the bay into whitecaps, and the two gunners at the end of the spit shook themselves and snuggled down into their goose pit, away from the chilling bite. Every few seconds a head rose above the pit as a hunter checked the flock of geese resting a quarter mile away in the bay. The decoys in the lee of the sandy point of land bobbed gently.

Now the morning grayness deepened as the cloud cover became solid. The wind grew in strength, curving downward the tall plume grass lining the shore line. The geese became restless. The flock now headed into the blow, swimming strongly to keep position. From over the eastern shore a murky wall swept toward the sandspit, and the first hard granules of snow stung the gunners' cheeks.

The lead gander flapped his wings tentatively, striking the waves. His body came clear, his broad black webs slapping the surface in a running take-off. In a matter of seconds the entire flock broke off into the wind, their wings pumping against the driving snow. They wheeled slightly toward the shore line, passing over the decoys, only a dozen yards aloft.

A slight movement in the pit caught the old bird's sharp eye, and he swerved slightly to the right, increasing the beat of his wings. The guns spoke twice, three times, five times, and in quick succession four heavy gray bodies tumbled from the line to splash into the waves like a stick of bombs. Before the last bird of the quartet hit the surface, the dark form of the Chesapeake retriever left the side of the pit and charged toward the birds. Within a minute, the first of the geese had been dragged ashore and deposited proudly at the pit. Within five minutes, the gunners, with the limit of geese over their backs, were heading up the spit in the snow.

Few game birds stir a hunter's imagination as quickly or as thoroughly as a honking wedge of Canada geese. Usually heard before they come into view, the great gray birds, traveling purposefully on rhythmic wingbeats, moving at deceptive speed, always step up the pulse rate of any man who owns a gun. And for all people who have any awareness of nature, the clear, deep calls of geese coming from high above in their migrating flights are both harbingers of spring and messengers of winter's onset—depending upon which way the big V is headed.

The honker is the wild-fowl gunner's big game. Always wary, seldom making a stupid move which will bring him into easy gun range, the great gray Canada is a prize rarely bagged unless wind, weather, and feeding conditions favor the hunter. I have a friend, an ardent and experienced big-game hunter, who always

Preceding pages: Snow and blue geese in
flight toward Western prairie water hole. Opposite: Canadian
honkers leave daytime resting place in prairie
pond to head for grainfields.
These geese are principally land feeders.

says that he would rather kill a goose than a moose. And, at times, it seems that killing the moose is the simpler and less exciting task.

Canada geese, it is good to say, have made remarkable progress within the last generation, particularly in the eastern half of this continent. At times it seems that geese outnumber the many species of ducks, particularly when they are seen in the wintering grounds from Maryland south to the Carolinas. The wild-fowl hunter's money, through agencies such as Ducks Unlimited and other conservation groups, has done a great deal to re-establish breeding grounds in the North and sanctuary areas for the birds during their southern migration. Suitably rigid hunting controls on the Federal level have helped to fix the annual harvest at a proper figure.

Although we traditionally think of the Canada goose as a huge, gray bird—and these the big races certainly are —there is greater racial variation found among this species than in almost any other North American game. The *giant* Canada of the northeastern prairies will often weigh eighteen pounds, while the tiny *cackling* Canada of the West Coast averages only about three pounds. Between these extremes are at least half a dozen subspecies of varying sizes, all looking much the same— with the characteristic black head and neck and the white cheeks and chin strap—except for the differences in size. One or more of the subspecies will be found somewhere on the North American continent, ranging from the north of Alaska down into Mexico, depending upon the season.

Unlike most other waterfowl, the Canada goose is principally a land feeder, rather than a water feeder. They are essentially grazing birds, fond of clover, alfalfa, natural sedge, and other grasses, as well as the farmer's grain crops. They commonly feed far from water, which they use mainly to rest in between feeding periods. Also unlike many other waterfowl, the Canadas travel in their own group. When you find them feeding in a field, you rarely see any other wild fowl with them.

The goose hunter is a specialist among wild-fowlers. He hunts geese to the exclusion of other webfoots and, indeed, must concentrate his efforts on finding the most-used inland feeding grounds, digging pit blinds, collecting a good spread of decoys, and then waiting for good shooting weather. Throughout North America a multitude of gunning setups and methods are used, of course, based on the feeding and resting areas of the birds. The goose hunter picks his shooting spot and type of blind depending upon local conditions, but, in any case, his hunting will be strictly for geese even in areas heavily populated with other waterfowl.

Good goose weather is invariably bad weather. Bright calm days find the flocks well out from shore, whether in fresh-water lakes or along the seacoast, where they sit in comfortable security before leaving for the feeding grounds, usually either before or after legal shooting hours. Storms and high winds, however, often put them up from big open water, and they head for a sheltered bay or a protected inland lake or river. If the gunner picks the right flight line he will get some in-range 197

Canada goose in flight
(above) is most majestic of North
American wild fowl,
with wingspread approaching
five feet. Right: Canadas love to
feed along edges of
marsh grass in Montana
prairieland. All
of several Canada varieties
have white chin strap.

198

Snow geese (above), birds "from beyond the North Wind," frequently make nonstop flights from above Arctic Circle to United States. They winter along Atlantic seacoast, from Maryland south. Left: Snow goose is pure white except for black-tipped wings, a mark seen only in flight.

shooting. In bright, calm weather, even if he selects the right flight line, the birds always seem to come over well out of gunshot.

A few years ago, a group of gun editors was invited to a goose shoot late in December, at Remington Farms, in Maryland. Here geese and ducks gather by the thousands during the fall migration. In fact, many winter over on the small sanctuary pond even after it is frozen solid, since there the birds are fed regularly. But this area of Maryland is great, flat, grain-farm country, and almost all the birds leave the sanctuary everyday to feed in the surrounding farm lands.

Blinds of several types are set up around the sanctuary, none less than a quarter of a mile from the water. Since a great deal of shooting goes on here throughout the open season, the geese are extremely well aware of the gantlet they must run when leaving or coming to the pond. Yet come they do, thousands of them, each morning, after the night's feeding. But they are wise enough to come in high, in long lines sometimes stretching for half a mile, 100 yards or more above the blinds. Once over the water, they sideslip fantastically to lose elevation in a hurry, then drop into the safety of the sanctuary. In bright, calm weather no one gets shooting.

And this was the case for our first day in the blinds. Thousands of geese overhead, filling the air with their ke-RONK cries and great wingbeats, with each bird wary enough to know the safety margin and to keep it. It was a glorious sight and an exciting experience, but no one busted a cap during the entire day.

The second morning was a carbon copy of the first and about a dozen chagrined gunners eventually repaired to the lodge for lunch. Before this pleasant interlude ended, the skies darkened and a cold northeast wind swept over the pond where some 15,000 geese were resting. From the lodge we could hear the sudden cries and loud honkings as the birds became restless. It was time to grab guns and head for the blinds.

By mere chance, wildlife artist Bob Kuhn and I were paired off in a multiflora-rose hedgerow blind, southwest of the pond. Before we had finished the half-mile walk through standing corn strip to the blind, the wind had whipped up to almost gale force and heavy snow had begun to whiten the frozen ground. As we ducked into the blind, the snow became so heavy we could no longer see the sanctuary area, but it was easy to locate from the raucous outcries of the now thoroughly disturbed birds.

Then, out of the swirling whiteness, came the geese. Even before we had hurriedly stuffed shells into the Magnum pump guns, the honkings were coming closer. Like gray ghosts the birds streamed low overhead, long black necks outstretched and wings pumping furiously to gain elevation. As Bob and I stood facing into the driving storm, a group of five loomed out of the gray murk twenty-five yards away. They were almost upon us before they were visible. The leader passed beyond before we could get guns up, but we each took a bird from the left and right, with the two guns booming almost at once and the heavy, whirling bodies crashing down behind us through the standing corn.

Before the handler sent the Labrador off to retrieve, a great flock came over us. The snowy air was filled with their flailing wings. Two more shots, two more big birds down in the cornstalks. Our limit was reached and our day's shooting was over. With the big trophies slung on our backs, we sent the handler off to the next blind to bring another pair of gunners into our favored spot. Within a half hour, the entire party filled its limit, and most of the birds had been taken over that southwest blind—a familiar pattern in goose shooting.

Because of the great size of the Canadas, a wild-fowl hunter is always tempted to shoot at them when they are well out of killing range. At sixty yards a mature gander looks bigger than a mallard drake at thirty yards, and sixty yards is just about the maximum killing range for a shotgun on geese—regardless of what you may read about downing geese with Magnum guns and loads. A goose must be hit hard to put him down at once. Many are seriously wounded and die miserably and unrecovered because hunters shoot into flocks at long range, with little hope of dropping a bird except by a chance pellet or two in the head. This practice is the bane of all wild-fowl shooting, but it is probably more prevalent in goose shooting because of the size and stamina of the birds.

Although #2 shot has been the goose hunter's standard for many years, it is likely that you will make as many clean kills with #4's. Up to sixty yards the #4's give excellent penetration and the extra shot in the load improves the odds of putting two or three into a vital spot. Further, you will not be tempted to fire at out-of-range birds if you are using the smaller size.

It seems unnecessary to say that the smallest practical gauge for gunning the big Canadas is the 12. The 3-inch Magnum 12, carrying the 1⅞-ounce load of shot is even better, and many goose hunters prefer the big double 10-gauge Magnum loaded with 2 ounces of shot in the 3½-inch shell. My current choice in a goose gun is the Browning Superposed 12-gauge 3-inch Magnum, shooting the maximum load of 1⅞ ounces. With this armament you can count on downing a goose every shot at sixty yards—if you lead him just right.

SNOW & BLUE GEESE

The snow geese are beautiful white birds showing black-tipped wings in flight. This is a dress that fits well with their origin, for these are geese of the far northern wilderness. Their scientific name, *hyperborea*, means literally "beyond the North wind." This also fits, since these birds are born beyond the Arctic Circle. Of the two varieties, the Greater is found only on the eastern part of the continent and is rarely seen after it leaves Canada in migration until it reaches wintering grounds along the Atlantic Coast, from New Jersey south to the Carolinas. The greater snow goose is generally protected and, thus, of minor interest to hunters.

Lesser snow geese are not Eastern birds in any great numbers, although they have been appearing more and more in the wintering grounds of the greater snows, along with their counterparts, the blue geese. Ornithologists still are not in accord on snows and blues as a separate species. Apparently, the white bird was the original stock, and, in fact, half a century ago the blue

goose was rarely seen. Some authorities rate the "blue" goose only as a color phase of the lesser snow, and, indeed, the two color phases intermingle and interbreed freely. Many family groups include both color phases, although I still note a predominance of the white geese on the wintering grounds of the East Coast. In Louisiana the blues now far outnumber the snows, the white birds dwindling to a mere five per cent of the total wintering in that region.

Neither the snows nor the blues have the sagacity of the big Canada goose. They are fairly easy to call into range over a blind and decoy readily to almost any object shaped and colored approximately like a goose. Some gunners simply use rolled-up balls of newspaper placed on shore lines or in the fields, near the blind.

The lesser snows and blues are heavy grasseaters, with an equal fondness for small grains in the stubble fields after harvesting. They are principally daytime feeders, usually leaving the water at sunrise to fly inland to the fields and returning to the resting areas about sundown. Both geese are gluttonous feeders and become quite plump before the opening of the gunning season. I have had several literally burst open upon hitting frozen ground after being killed in the air.

Not long ago, the blue geese were noted for making nonstop flights from the James Bay area of Canada to wintering grounds in the remote marshes of Louisiana. 201

Blue geese intergrade with snows
to such an extent that species often are almost impossible
to tell apart. In fact, ornithologists do
not completely agree that blues are a distinct
species. They may be young snows.

*Odds on taking a pair
of Canadas from blind (above) or
lone snow goose (top,
right) heavily favor the gunners.
Dogs shown with white-fronted
geese (bottom row) are
almost essential. Since all geese
are tough, clean kills are
not the rule and
cripples must be retrieved.*

At this time few hunters had an opportunity to become acquainted with the bird. The increase in sanctuaries and feeding grounds between Canada and the Gulf states, however, now finds both blues and snows stopping frequently on their trips to the South. The lush grainfields of the Dakotas likewise are now fine hunting grounds for the blues.

Since these geese are medium-sized birds weighing between four and six pounds, a load of #4 shot in a standard 12-gauge gun is an effective killer. Actually, I have killed a fair number with a 20-gauge gun using the 1-ounce load, but, again, I had to guard against long shooting, and wait until the birds were less than fifty yards away before beginning to fire.

AMERICAN BRANT

This diminutive and succulent little goose was once the favorite target of sportsmen and market hunters along most of the Atlantic Coast. But unlike other geese, the brant is rarely found far from salt water. In addition, it feeds almost exclusively on eelgrass. When the eelgrass succumbed to a fungus blight in the early 1930's the brant very nearly disappeared, too.

But the eelgrass has made a startling comeback within the last decade and with it the brant. From a low estimate of about 20,000 in 1935, the birds have increased to something over a quarter of a million in the peak year of 1961 and are holding their own.

When the eelgrass disappeared along the Atlantic Coast, the relatively few survivors of the race began to migrate over inland waters, developing some new feeding habits in the process. Those still using the ocean coast line acquired a taste for sea lettuce, or sea cabbage, and with it an unsavory reputation as a table bird. Current descendants, as they continue to feed on the renascent eelgrass, are improving in flavor.

Brant are sporty shooting, but, as with other geese, foul weather provides the most action. They travel in large flocks of fifty or more, sweeping low along the coast line, in no particular formation. Their characteristic grouping is a long line, with a number of birds heavily bunched at the head. Their tendency to move in a tight formation renders it not so uncommon to gather the day's limit of birds with one well-directed load of shot into the head of the column.

Brant shooting is salt-water gunning—and probably always will be. In calm weather the birds like to sit far out from shore in great rafts and are not disposed to move until driven off by a storm. A wild northeaster, with huge rollers smashing over sand bars and stinging sleet and salt spray driving into the blind, is supreme weather for gunning brant. Then the birds reluctantly break up their big rafts offshore and seek shelter in the coves and bays, flying low over the crests of the breaking waves. If you have a good spread of decoys set in the lee of a bar, with a comfortable pit dug in the sand within good killing range of the blocks, you will get shooting.

Note: Along the Pacific Coast, the name brant is loosely applied to the white-fronted goose, which actually is closer to the Canada goose in size, feeding habits, and flight pattern. The white front refers to the bird's face, which has a narrow white band across the forepart of the head.

204

Top: Blue goose gunning in Ontario. Until recent years, blues did not stop here during migration flight. Decoys (bottom) could pass for real thing. Successful goose hunter should want and have the best.

BLACK DUCK

North American ducks are divided into two broad categories: the shallow-water, or "dipper," ducks and the deep-water divers. Feeding habits, therefore, determine which type of duck you are likely to find on certain waters. The diving ducks, obviously, won't be found on shallow ponds or streams. The dippers, though, can be found over a wide range of conditions, from the tiniest woodland pothole to the big ocean bays.

The black duck, sometimes called dusky duck and, incorrectly, "black mallard," is one of the largest of the duck species. He is the favorite bird of the inland gunner of the Northeast and, in truth, is not found at all in the West. Wild, wary, and highly suspicious, the black loves inland potholes, often those in heavy timber, which he shares with the wood duck and hooded merganser. Blacks are not gregarious. They stay pretty much by themselves and generally in rather small flocks.

At the opening of the seasons in the Northern states gunners will find many "native" birds which have hatched and grown up in the hunting area, since blacks will nest all the way from Delaware to the far reaches of Canada. Opening-day shooting is usually good on the young-of-the-year blacks, but it takes only a few days of pounding before the birds smarten up and head for open water far from shore lines. Migrating blacks who have run the gunning gantlet from Canada are always difficult to decoy and shy of any type of blind. When they do look over your spread, they will circle two or three times before deciding whether to drop in. Any small movement by the gunner in the blind will send them flaring off. They have a sharp eye for any blind construction that is in the least bit unnatural.

The black has another disconcerting habit of dropping in well away from your decoys, then swimming in cautiously toward them, but staying well out of gun range until he carefully checks both the stool and the shore line for concealed hunters. Most often, he grows suspicious of the whole setup and jumps into the air—still well out of range.

This ability to jump almost vertically from the water when alarmed is a trick used by most shallow-water ducks, but the black does it quicker and better than any other species. When the birds do light to your decoys and you flush them, you must hold your gun well above them if you want to connect. The same thing can be said for jump-shooting blacks from the tall marsh grass when your guide or shooting partner is poling your skiff. They really can take off almost straight up.

The blacks you will kill in inland waters, or fresh from the wild-rice marshes of Canada, are always prime eating. The late-season migrants, usually called "Canadian red-legs," are quite likely to follow the coast, feeding on snails, barnacles, and salt-water plants to the detriment of their flavor. During World War II, when shotgun shells were practically nonexistent for sporting use, I took a morning off from my war-plant chores to gun ducks on New Haven Bay. There were many ducks of different species, but I was careful to pick only the blacks—big, fat birds with bright red legs. With five in the sack I figured that I had a fine company meal in hand. Not so.

After plucking and cleaning the birds and finding snails in the crops I developed a suspicion that these would be poor fare, a suspicion that was quickly confirmed when the birds went into the hot oven. The fishy odor didn't leave the kitchen for a week.

MALLARD

The beautiful green head adorns what is probably the best-known wild duck in the world and, indeed, the most widely distributed, for it is found wherever the feed, cover, and water are suitable. In America mallards are the prime target of duck shooters for several reasons. One is that there are more of them, spread over almost all of the continent, than any other species. Another is that they decoy readily and respond better to a properly used duck call than most others. And if another reason is needed, the mallard is invariably good eating. He's a vegetarian primarily, eats but few insects, and loves the farmer's grainfields, where he gobbles greedily corn, wheat, rye, barley, or whatever small grain is available.

Black duck (far left)
frequents inland potholes and
small creeks. Mallards
(left) are most
widely distributed North
American wild fowl.
Bottom left: Mallard drake and
hen take off from
shallow marsh. In Currier &
Ives print, pre-Civil
War gunners hunt teal
in Maryland, while modern
Carolina gunners
(below) try
some pass shooting.

A bonus with this bird is that he is easy to raise in captivity for game-preserve shooting or restocking. This is not strange, considering that he is the ancestor of most of our domestic breeds. As a shooting-farm bird, he is available to a great number of gunners on a fee-per-bird basis, which is the growing trend in game shooting these days.

On a preserve the birds are raised (or purchased as ducklings) then released on a small sanctuary pond where they are fed daily and which they are not about to leave. On shooting days the birds are trapped, carried to a release point several hundred yards away, and allowed to escape from a chute or tower. Without hesitation they head unerringly back to the pond, crossing over or near the blinds. This provides some excellent pass shooting, almost equivalent to that found in wild-duck gunning. There also is the certainty that cripples will be recovered by the retrieving dogs, always a part of the preserve planning.

There is much to be said in favor of this sort of gunning. It surely eliminates the rigors of wild-duck shooting: the rising before dawn, the slogging through mud to the blinds, the exposure to biting winds and driving rain or sleet, the many leg-cramping hours of blind sitting. And perhaps the most significant aspect is that it does help to reduce gunning pressure on wild birds in many of the popular duck-shooting areas.

The big grain country of the Midwest and Alberta and Saskatchewan is the great mallard-shooting area. Here the birds, like geese, leave their water resting grounds and feed early in the morning and late in the afternoon in the stubble fields after harvest. Grain shocks can be stacked together to make quick, on-the-spot blinds. With a few decoys scattered around the blind, the gunner is ready for business and, in good mallard country, he usually does not have long to wait for the appearance of birds if his timing is right. The birds are almost certain to feed before the end of the day's legal shooting time, regardless of weather. On stormy days the shooting will begin earlier.

WOOD DUCK

When I was a youngster, wood ducks were rigidly protected by both Federal and state law. Time has proved that this was a wise move, but it was a maddening situation when I stalked along the brush-lined creek passing through my father's farm and flushed half a dozen woodies for every black or teal that came off. I must admit that the "odd" wood duck dropped to my gun, but if he was a male he was carefully skinned and the beautiful plumage carefully preserved in a moth-proof box for the winter's flytying sessions. The barred flank feathers of this most beautiful of wild ducks provides the best material for Quill Gordons, Cahills, and many other effective trout fly patterns. In fact, a professional flytier can find a use for almost every feather on the bird.

The wood duck suffered for more than half a century under the guns of market hunters, who sold him to restaurateurs for his tender flesh and to milliners for his plumage. But the drainage of 70,000,000 acres of land which were its major nesting areas, beginning under the Swamp Act of 1849, had a greater effect in decimating the wood duck population than did the market shooting. Now, however, because of rigid protection and the enormous number of nest boxes set up by conservation people during the past two decades, the wood duck population has soared. In limited numbers they are now legal game in most duck-shooting areas.

The Upper Mississippi Valley is an ideal nesting area. The summer population probably outnumbers all other species combined. The Middle Atlantic and New England states also have a high percentage of nesting wood duck and a healthy number of birds for the hunter.

As its name indicates, the wood duck is a lover of timber, principally deciduous timber. He is found throughout this big-timber belt east of the prairie country, wherever there is a pothole, pond, or stream with big trees nearby. Like the hooded merganser, the goldeneye, and a couple of other species, the woodie nests in a hollow tree wherever there is an opening large enough for him to squeeze in. An entrance about three by four inches seems to be ideal.

For the hunter, the woodie is a friendly bird. He decoys readily, without hesitation, and since he is gregarious, he will come in to mallard decoys as readily as any other type. In fact, I know of no gunners who use decoys imitating the wood duck. A black duck imitation does well, as these two species are frequently found in the same area and type of water. Duck shooters who frequent the inland beaver ponds and timber potholes for black ducks are just as likely to fill out on woodies, using the same setup.

*Most beautiful of North American wild
fowl is the male wood duck (above). Although almost
extinct in early part of this century,
woodies have made a great comeback. Left: Pair
of mallards depart a woodland pond.*

Pintails (left) make a suicidal approach
over gunner's blind on Eastern Shore of Maryland. Pintails
are about the same size as wood duck,
second only to them in beauty. Early Audubon prints show
blue-winged teal (below) and widgeon (bottom).

PINTAIL

The pintail, or "sprig," rivals the wood duck in beauty, although the pintail's coloring is more subtle. His long tail—if not his size—gives the drake the title of "water pheasant." He is a smaller bird than the upland ringneck and noticeably smaller even than the mallard. The pintail is basically a bird of the Western and Northern prairies, but a fair number travels well up into Alaska to nest.

East Coast and Gulf Coast gunners get some pintail shooting on birds which nest in the Hudson Bay area and winter anywhere from Massachusetts south to Mexico. But the best shooting is in the Western prairie and the grain country of the Great Plains, where the birds have much the same diet as the mallard and often feed along with him. The basic difference between the pintail and other dipper ducks is that the pintail can and will feed in somewhat deeper water. Because of his longer neck he can forage on the bottom, when he "tips-up," at depths that other shallow-water ducks cannot reach.

Another curious characteristic of the sprig—the name favored throughout the West—is his habit of dropping into remote, isolated water holes in arid country. I have seen hundreds on tiny alkali ponds in Western ranch country where there was no other water for miles. At first I believed that the birds were merely stopping over during a migration flight to the South, but after watching them for several days, it seemed that they came from the west at sundown, then took off for the west at sunrise. I suspect that they had a good grain-stubble field for feeding during the day and used the small pond only at night. Since we were hunting antelope at the time, I had no shotgun along, but I was content to observe the many small flocks of these beautiful waterfowl as they came in to roost before dark. If we had been duck shooting we could have slaughtered them. The entire length and breadth of the pond did not span more than a gunshot, and we could have hidden in the sage and taken them easily as they came in to alight.

Pintails are usually wary and alert, almost as much so as the black duck. They come to decoys with caution, usually circling several times to look things over before dropping in. Among dipper ducks the sprig is also rated tops in speed. Flocks often have been clocked at sixty miles per hour. The long tail and neck of this duck and his general streamlining give the effect of even greater speed. In common with the tyro ringneck-pheasant hunter, the gunner shooting at a sprig often underleads him because of the long tail.

Among Western gunners the sprig is almost as popular as the mallard. Some claim that the sprig eats better, and these gourmets are willing to overlook the smaller size of the bird because of his better flavor. I doubt this, however, since in the same areas the two species will usually feed on the same foods, mostly grain. I have eaten both mallards and sprigs taken on the same day in the same spot and, frankly, can find no difference in flavor.

Duck shooters in the Northern states do not get as much sprig shooting as they would like. These ducks usually start to migrate early in the fall, along with the blue-wing teal, so a good share of the flight has passed before the season opens. But in the wintering grounds on the East Coast, south of New Jersey, and in southern California and Arizona, the pintail gunning is tops until the very end of the legal hunting period.

Male pintail often is called "water pheasant" because of lengthy tail feathers. In the West, where he is much more numerous than in East, he is known as "sprig." Both areas savor him as a delicious table bird.

BLUE-WINGED & GREEN-WINGED TEAL

These two teals, along with the Western cinnamon teal, are the smallest of the ducks sought by wild-fowlers. In spite of their small size, they are highly prized by gourmets, and in the market hunting days the bluewing was a favorite target.

Northern gunners get to see few bluewings during the open season. These are among the earliest, if not the earliest, ducks to leave for the South. They begin to migrate from the Northern states and Canada before September and are usually in the wintering grounds of Mexico and the fringes of the Gulf states within a few weeks. The late-season openings in the North and East defeat the gunner if he is looking for teal.

However, a special early gunning season on a limited basis is now being put into practice in order for game biologists to make studies of the flight patterns and population of these handsome little ducks. Successful permit holders are asked to report details of each kill and forward a wing from each bird to the Fish & Wildlife Service. Since not enough of these birds have been taken in the past twenty years to provide research data, the special season is a must.

Bluewings have always been an easy bird to bag. They seem to be completely unsuspicious and decoy readily. Years ago I had bluewings settle into the decoys while I was out in a skiff, in plain sight, picking up dead birds. At times they also seem to develop a fondness for your stool setup. They will drop in; you can jump them, then take a pair as they leave. As likely as not, they will circle the marsh a time or two, then drop right back in, so you will get another crack at them.

Next to the wood duck, blue-winged teal is the most numerous duck nesting in the territorial limits of the United States, with almost eighty per cent of the young hatched on the prairies of southern Canada. Most of the birds taken by gunners during the season are killed in the Deep South and many of these carry bands affixed in Canada. Most bluewings leave, however, before our gunners get a chance at them.

The green-winged teal is even smaller than the bluewing, is a somewhat later starter, and has a longer migration period. Greenwings are fine shooting, fast and tricky in flight—even faster than the bluewing—and their smaller size makes them seem to be among the fastest of wild-fowl targets.

They are a pretty little duck, often rated second only to the wood duck in brilliance of plumage. They tend to fly in tightly bunched flocks, and it is not unusual to get a pair or three for every shot you fire when they swing in like bees over your decoys. They are as gregarious as wood duck and have no hesitation in decoying to imitations of blacks or mallards.

Both species of teal are easy to kill. A trap load of #7½ shot in a 12-gauge gun does the job quite readily. You will not find the greenwing as easy a target as the bluewing, however. The sprightly little greenwing is given to erratic flight when frightened and can often put on a performance that would shame a ruffed grouse. He probably has more wing power per pound than any other wild fowl.

WIDGEON

The American widgeon, or baldpate, is another dipper duck, like the mallard, which is found almost everywhere on the North American continent during one part of the year or another. Oddly enough, this duck does not rate high with most gunners, either because he is smaller than the mallard or because, under some circumstances, he is poor eating. This is due to the widgeon's habit of feeding on some kinds of vegetation that grow in salt water and impart a strong, musky taste to the widgeon's flesh.

But the widgeon is by no means a salt-water duck. It comes along toward the South with the blacks and, like them, will follow coast lines, but in general he is an inland species, nesting principally in the prairies of the northern Midwest and central Canada. He winters in the coastal regions of the United States, south of New England in the East, south of Puget Sound in the West. He does, however, feed frequently with the sea ducks—the canvasbacks, redheads, and scaup—often stealing the food these divers loosen from the bottom and carry to the surface.

*Left: Setting out decoys for puddle ducks
(shallow-water species) on small, prairie-country pond.
Fewer than a dozen blocks are enough
for these inland waters.
Box blind screen with natural grasses (bottom, left)
provides standard setup for duck
shooting in Midwest. Opposite page: Audubon drawings
show ringneck duck (right) and goldeneye
(far right). In print below, a male canvasback and
two females feed on marsh grass.*

The baldpate is a tricky flyer, an aerial acrobat of sorts. When frightened he jumps almost vertically from the water, like the black duck, then takes off in a fast, weaving, bending flight that makes him extremely difficult to hit. These ducks don't decoy well because they are shy and jittery most of the time. Usually the best service your decoys will perform is to bring the birds toward your blind and, perhaps, within killing range before they pass on. But it is almost certain that they will not "set in."

My first experience with widgeon was on the Carmen's River, on Long Island, in New York, gunning with the late Guy Kibbee and VanCampen Heilner. Our guide had us set up in a big box blind on the edge of the river, just below a sweeping bend and right in a heavy stand of hardwood timber. The river flowed into a sanctuary pond about half a mile below, which harbored a mass of ducks of several species: blacks, pintails, mallards, and wood ducks. After the morning feeding period, many of the ducks would fly upriver to pick up a cropful of fine gravel from the shallow headwaters. They would then trickle down in pairs and small flocks throughout the morning, returning to the pond invariably by following the river.

We had a mixed set of decoys near the far bank of the stream, where they could be seen by the birds as they came down around the bend. Our guide, who was an expert with a duck call, would quack mightily at the first appearance of birds, and the mallards and pintails would swing in close enough to give us some fair shooting at forty yards.

Not so the widgeon. They maintained their course as they swung around the bend, just above the tree line, and although the guide gave out with a most provocative *Whew, whew, whew* whistle at all the widgeon, not one changed his course. But we did connect with a few on their upriver flights, when the guide had a better chance to whistle them in, since we could see them for quite a distance over the trees. Some deigned to swerve a bit in flight to look over the decoys—a little mistake in widgeon judgment that put five plump, nicely colored drakes in our bag for the day.

CANVASBACK

The canvasback is unquestionably the king of the diving ducks. Favored for years by the epicure, the "can" was gunned for market with more zeal than was expended on any other wild fowl, and this duck brought the best prices. Today he is no less esteemed among game gourmets because he has remained choosey about his diet. Wild rice and wild celery are his mainstays and this produces a fat bird with a rich, delectable flavor.

The can is esteemed on other grounds, too. As a sporting target he is probably the speediest of all wild fowl. He has been clocked at seventy-two miles per hour. With a northeaster on his tail he will do ninety without trouble. At times the birds sweep in with alarming speed, flare off over the decoys, and race away before the surprised gunner can get off a shot. This is especially the case in stormy weather when visibility is limited and the flocks come in fairly low.

As is true of all diving ducks, the canvasback is a deep-water feeder, or at the very least a water feeder. All the diving-duck species have their short legs set well back on their bodies, which makes it awkward for them to move about on land. Thus, it is only on rare occasions that you find any of the divers feeding in grainfields or grazing in the inland meadows.

Cans like big water, whether it is fresh or salt. Good gunning can be had on most of the Great Lakes during the flights, and some of the finest late season shooting is offered in New York's Finger Lake area, where many of the birds winter over if the weather does not become too severe. Another top-notch late-shooting area is from lower Chesapeake Bay down to Currituk, on the central East Coast, which is a prime wintering ground for good flocks of canvasbacks.

Since canvasbacks travel in large flocks, it takes a big spread of decoys to bring them in. Yet the canvasbacks are probably more cautious than any of the other diving-duck species, and most gunners will use nothing but the best, most lifelike imitations to fool them. Many old-timers are satisfied only with decoys they make themselves and considerable artistry goes into producing the best examples. As a rule, the hunter with the biggest

flock of the most natural-looking blocks is the man who gets the most shooting on the big lakes and bays.

The profile of the canvasback's head is distinctive. It has a long bill, almost as long as the head, which slopes gently downward in a long, concave curve. This is the profile that the best decoy makers strive to produce, and it is recognizable on the decoys at a fair distance.

Your gunning for cans will most likely be over, or on the edge of, deep water as this is their favorite feeding ground. A fine spot is a pit blind on the end of a long bar, terminating in water ten to fifteen feet deep, over which you place your flock of blocks. Canvasbacks traveling along the shore line but well out of gun range will usually be attracted to such a setup and will swing in toward it, often dropping down for a close look as they speed by. Usually your best chance for a shot is the first time they pass by within killing distance. It isn't often that they make the turn and come back to settle among your deceivers.

REDHEAD

A tyro duck hunter often mistakes the redhead for the canvasback, since both are frequently found in the same areas. They also are confused because their coloration is so much the same, and although the redhead is smaller, this is of little help in distinguishing between the two. Furthermore, distinct differences exist in the much brighter red of the redhead's head—hence his name—and in the shape of his head and bill. The "can" has a maroon-colored head with a black bill and, as mentioned before, a long, sloping profile. The redhead has a high forehead, a shorter bill, and a more typical duck profile.

These diving ducks fly in tight flocks, moving in unison. They are not nearly so fast as the canvasback and considerably less astute when it comes to decoying. Once they decide to set in to your spread—which they do with great and satisfying frequency—only shooting at them will turn them away. I have had them drop into a spread while I was still out in the boat putting out the last few blocks. And they will often drop into the water between the decoys and the shore, close to your blind, something that the wary canvasback seldom permits himself to do.

Redheads usually migrate in large flocks. When they settle down offshore to rest, they stay so close together that they look like small islands, and for this reason are often referred to locally as the "raft duck." When on the feed, the big rafts usually break up into smaller groups, each going its own way to find a good wild-celery bed on the bottom in water ten or more feet deep.

Breeding grounds for the redhead lie mainly in the great "duck factory" area of the northern prairie states and in the southern provinces of Canada. Wintering grounds are in the Deep South and Mexico, with some of the birds heading for the East Coast, between New Jersey and South Carolina. During the migration flights, duck hunters are likely to find redheads on any large body of water. Usually they travel in their own groups, but occasionally they will flock up with the canvasback or the bluebill.

217

Shallow-water "john boat" is indispensable
gear for Southern duck shooter in flatland marshes
and bayous. Equally valuable
is a Labrador retriever for finding downed
birds in tall swamp grass.

The eating quality of redheads is choice. With vegetable matter making up about ninety per cent of his diet, it is unlikely that you'll ever find a redhead with a fishy taste. Duck connoisseurs agree that this species is one of the choice table birds.

And he is fairly easy shooting, since he is slow to take off, not particularly fast in steady flight, and often surprisingly lacking in caution. In the central flyway, redheads top the total bag among all the diving species—when it is legal to take them. However, they are subject to seasonal fluctuation, for one reason or another, and limits are severely restricted at times. There was no open season on redheads during the 1960-61 season, for example, but there has been a one-bird limit in most areas since that date.

At one time, the illegal market-hunting kill of redheads in Mexico may have been a big factor in the off/on scarcity of these birds. But much of this killing has been eliminated on the redhead's wintering grounds, so the birds should have a brighter future.

Two species of diving duck are listed as "scaup," a bizarre name which comes from the raucous, throaty *"scaup, scaup"* sound made by both birds. Informally, the greater of the pair is known as the broadbill, the lesser as the bluebill, although in some localities both are called "blackheads." This probably results from the fact that it is almost impossible to tell the two species apart unless the birds are in hand. Both males have glossy black heads, the greater scaup's with green highlights, the lesser scaup's with purple highlights—a minor difference when the birds are on the wing.

Scaup provide cold-weather gunning. While some birds are heading for their wintering grounds in September, the dipper ducks are still around to test the hunter's skill. And when these have gone south, the bluebill and broadbill take over. The biggest flights of these birds do not come until the onset of winter, and even then a fair number remains to winter in the northern coastal areas. I have seen many on the Hudson

Scaup (above) are deep-water diving ducks,
usually found in coastal areas. Opposite: Ringneck,
another diver, is small, swift, and
erratic in flight. He also is a vegetarian and
thus a fairly good table bird.

River in mid-winter, just below the George Washington Bridge, within the city limits of New York.

Most coastal gunners low-rate the scaup as food. And, in truth, when scaup feed on fish, crustaceans, and other marine life, they are intolerable. Over inland waters, however, the scaup can be as good an eating bird as a mallard or canvasback, as long as he sticks to a similar diet.

No wild-fowler, on the other hand, low-rates the scaup as a target. Some of the best duck-gunning action a hunter can get is on the big flights of bluebills as they are driven down from Canada before a howling storm. With a good spread of decoys on the edge of big water you will get some of the world's trickiest shooting when the birds are moving.

Scaup come in to decoys without hesitation, usually in a direct line and at high speed, without the shilly-shallying of the puddle, or shallow-water, species, or some of the other divers. Often they approach the decoy spread low over the water, like jet-propelled black balls, in tight formation and never wavering in flight. If they decide to drop in, they do so abruptly, all at once and splashing a good deal. If they fail to drop in, then pass over the blocks at high speed, your shots will never make them flare or swerve. They just keep going. And although the canvasback is credited with higher speed, the smaller size of the scaup makes him seem to move faster. If there ever was a duck that demanded a long lead to make a kill, it is the scaup. So when you're missing birds in this type of gunning, just remember to take a good lead—and then double it!

RINGNECK &
AMERICAN GOLDENEYE

The ringneck duck is a small diver, actually an American scaup, with a wide distribution within the United States. He is primarily a vegetarian and, thus, good eating. If it were not for his small size, about one and a half pounds, the ringneck would probably give both the redhead and the canvasback some good competition with gunners who like to eat

their ducks as well as shoot them. He's an unwary bird who takes well to decoys and, except when on his migration course, he is also swift and erratic in flight. So he gives the hunter plenty of action.

American goldeneyes have less going for them than the ringnecks. For one thing, the "whistler," as he is usually called because of his high-pitched wingbeats, is rarely good to eat. Secondly, he is a suspicious bird, difficult to bring in to decoys. Most whistlers are gunned by pass shooting, either as they speed by your decoys or from a point of land as they trade back and forth between feeding and resting areas.

———◆———

The list of American diving waterfowl is a long one, with more than two dozen species. Some, like the mergansers and scoters, are shot mostly for sport, since few men will be tempted to eat them. Others, like the harlequin duck and the old squaw, have a limited range and are, therefore, unknown to most gunners. But the divers provide sport for a great many hunters who like gunning over big water for a succulent bird, and who will brave the elements to get the best shooting. Of all North American bird shooting, the quest for diving ducks is the most demanding. It requires the painstaking preparation of decoys, boats, and blinds, and the most rugged constitution to put them to the best use. But because of its challenges, it can also be one of the most satisfying sports.

219

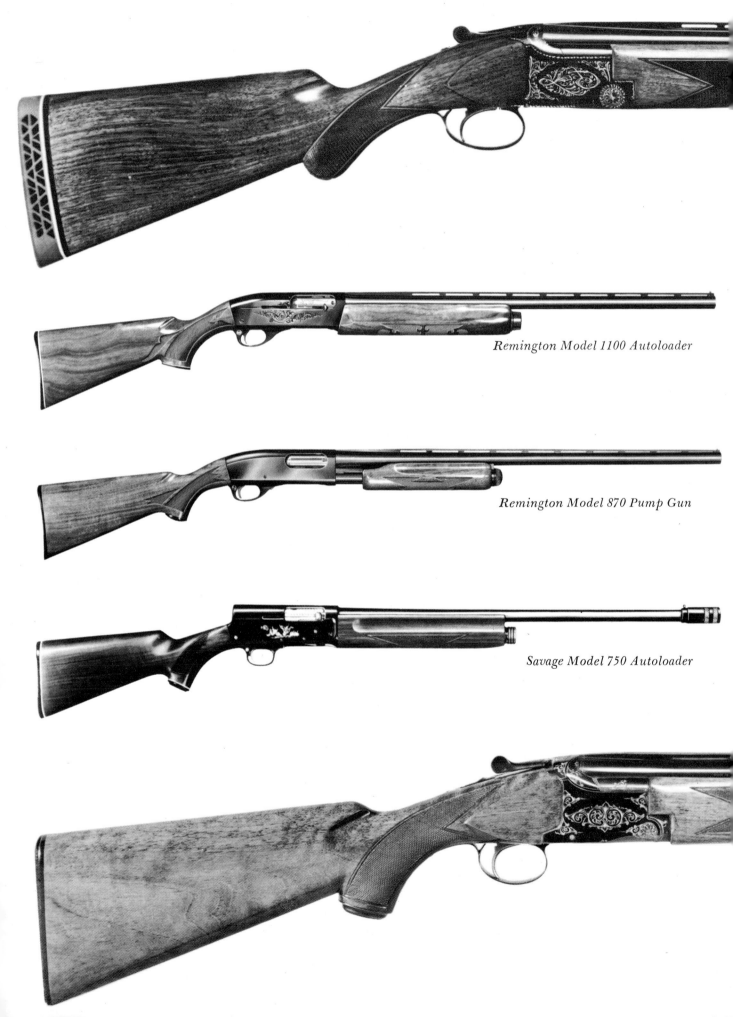

Remington Model 1100 Autoloader

Remington Model 870 Pump Gun

Savage Model 750 Autoloader

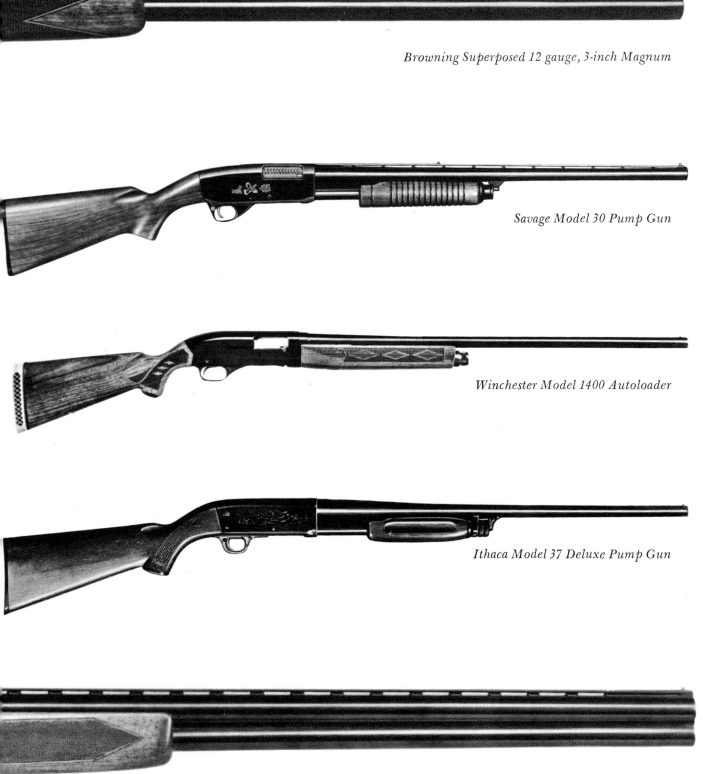

Browning Superposed 12 gauge, 3-inch Magnum

Savage Model 30 Pump Gun

Winchester Model 1400 Autoloader

Ithaca Model 37 Deluxe Pump Gun

Winchester Model 101, over/under

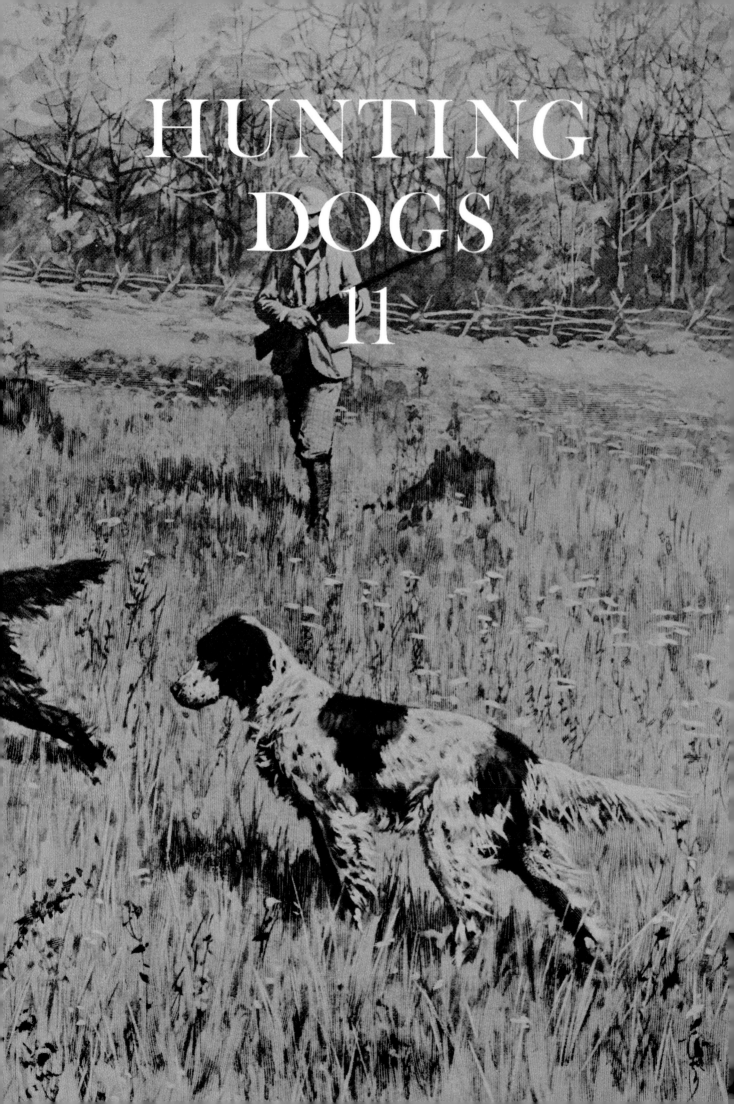

HUNTING
DOGS
11

Probably 5,000,000 dogs, among a total of about 30,000,000, are used in the United States for some form of hunting. A good dog in the field, aside from offering steady, faithful companionship, is a material asset. With a dog along you'll find more game, get easier shooting, recover crippled or wounded birds and animals, and have the enjoyment of watching him work. Several types of hunting are impossible without dogs. Every type is more successful.

Although there are a great many breeds classified as hunters, the hunting dog breaks down into four basic categories: pointing dogs, flushing dogs, retrievers, and trailers. Within these four groups are numerous so-called standard breeds that have been recognized for many years for their hunting abilities, and a fairly large number of breeds which are not generally considered to be hunters but which often are useful in the hunting field.

The first pointing dog used for hunting in America —the English setter—is still the most popular. And with reason. He has many desirable skills. The English setter today is probably more tractable than any other pointing dog. He is generally less high-strung, steadier in his work, and more responsive to the handler's control. He takes the keenest pleasure in ranging far and wide, if that's your desire and if the country permits. But he also works closely and with great thoroughness in tight cover, through brush and briars, swamp and bog. His many, many generations of training have bred in him an innate sense of caution that usually enables him to find the bird before it is flushed wildly.

The English setter has a fairly heavy coat which offers him a considerable degree of protection in rough going. And unless very closely bred to a particular strain, he has a great deal of stamina. I know several English setters, none of them really young, which can take daily hunting throughout the entire gunning season. In some cases, on private shooting preserves, this means at least six months of the year. It is not easy to find another breed in the pointing-dog class that has all of the English setter's qualities.

There are many so-called strains of setters. In their native England there are at least half a dozen. Since the breed came to America a number of different strains has been developed. One of the earliest was the Gildersleeve. Another was the Ethan Allen. These were particularly trained and bred for hunting grouse, woodcock, and snipe. Then there was the Campbell, and the Laverack, from which the strain now known as the Llewellin setter was created. One of the top champions in this particular strain was Gladstone, the ancestor of many of today's Llewellins. There also were offshoots —blue Beltons, orange Beltons, and liver-and-whites.

The pleasing feature of the English setter strains, or varieties, is that their coats have a great deal of white. This makes them easy for the handler or the gunner to see when the dog is standing or working in heavy cover, which is the English setter's strong suit. He is still the top choice among gunners of the North and Northeast, and it is not likely that he will be displaced soon.

In the South, the American pointer tops the field in popularity, for this is quail country and pointers and quail go together as well as ham and eggs.

Wide ranging and filled with energy, the pointer covers the great expanses of open bird country with greater speed and self-assurance than any other breed. This characteristic also makes him the top choice in field trials, for these invariably are run over relatively open courses, so that the dog work can be seen by the spectators as well as the handlers. Unlike setters, pointers usually are operated in pairs, and the skill with which a pair—or brace—of well co-ordinated pointers can handle quail, pheasants, Hungarian partridge, sharptail grouse, and other grainfield birds is a wonder to behold.

The pointer is flashy and stylish in his work. He hunts with head and tail held high, going at full speed until he catches the faintest trace of bird scent. He can check his headlong flight and quickly reverse his field, if the occasion demands, seemingly all in the same movement. No other pointing breed can keep up with him. He's built almost like a greyhound and has a great deal of the greyhound's speed.

If the pointer can be faulted on any count, it is that

*Preceding pages: Setter holding point on quail is honored
by pointer at left and second setter at right. Above are half a dozen
pointing breeds. Brittany spaniel (left) and English
setter are at top, Gordon and Irish setters in center, and a brace
of pointers and a German shorthair at bottom.*

his coat does not give him adequate protection for hunting in dense covers. His ever-wagging tail is continually whipping through briars and thorn bushes, so that at the end of half a day's hunt his tail end is not only bleeding, but his ears and quite often his chest and forelegs, as well. In grass and grain he does well, and these are his proper milieu.

The pointer is a bit more hardheaded than the average English setter and will withstand rigorous training methods without becoming timid. Generally, he's a less affectionate dog than a setter and is not nearly so inclined to be a one-man dog, in the field or at home.

The pointer's generally slim build and thin coat fit him for hunting in hot weather better than any of the long-haired breeds. Since his basic color is white, lightly marked with either black, liver, or orange, he's probably the most readily visible of all the pointing-dog breeds.

Another pointing breed that is steadily gaining in popularity, particularly during the last decade, is the Brittany spaniel. Among spaniels he is unique for several reasons. He has a natural instinct for steadiness on point, whereas the spaniel's normal instinct, training, and breeding is to flush a bird without hesitation. He also resembles a setter much more than a spaniel, and he acts more like one. The Brittany is normally born with a short tail or no tail at all. Those that do have tails usually are docked when they're a few days old.

The Brittany is, of course, a breed that developed in France and many authorities believe that it originated by crossing one of the older red-and-white setter breeds from England with a nondescript dog brought to France by an English sportsman for hunting woodcock.

The Brittany, unlike the pointer, is a sensitive dog and can be ruined by too rigorous training methods. He learns very quickly and has highly developed pointing instincts. Just a few years ago, for example, I hunted over a friend's Brittany on the opening of the ruffed grouse season. The dog was only nine months old and had been trained on barnyard pigeons. It is certain he had never met up with the scent of a grouse. Yet my friend and I each killed the limit of grouse before noon

of that opening day, most of them over this dog's point. His instincts were sure and steady, and even at that tender age he worked his birds with extreme caution.

If you insist upon a pointing dog that carries his tail like a banner when he's working birds, then the Brittany is not for you. But he's a fine little dog, makes an excellent home companion, and is destined to become one of the outstanding breeds among bird-dog lovers and upland gunners in this country.

Another pointing breed also steadily gaining in popularity in America is the German short-haired pointer. This breed comes about as close to an all-around gun dog as a bird shooter could want. Although he is eager enough, he is not a speedy, flashy dog. He does not range widely and, therefore, is relatively easy to control. He's an excellent close-cover dog, and works woodcock and grouse with the same efficiency as quail and ringneck.

The breed is the result of crossing the basic stock of the old Spanish pointer and the bloodhound. Resulting stock was again crossed with the foxhound and finally with the English pointer. The German short-hair exhibits most of the good qualities of these different breeds. The dog is an excellent retriever. In fact, because of his heavy bone structure and muscling, together with his fairly tight coat, he makes a good water retriever even in the coldest weather. More and more, you will find German short-haired pointers in the duckblinds. The breed is not flashy at work nor stylish on point. But it is a steady, reliable dog that will fulfill practically every desire of both the upland game shooter and the wildfowl gunner.

The two remaining pointing breeds, the Irish and the Gordon setters, have now dropped from the high esteem in which they once were held in the United States. Both breeds have been prostituted by the dog fanciers, particularly women, who have downgraded their hunting characteristics in favor of refining their points of beauty—as beauty is rated by kennel clubs.

Half a century ago the Gordon setter had no peer among American pointing breeds as a close-cover dog. He was superb in handling woodcock and grouse. He could be faulted on only one count: the difficulty of

Springer spaniel (top) leaps to retrieve a fallen duck.
Above, left: English cocker returns to hunter with hen pheasant, as
does national-champion black Labrador (right).
Golden Lab (bottom, left) sits proudly by bag of sharptails.
Bottom, right: Hardy Chesapeake retrieves his duck.

seeing his shiny black-and-tan coat in dense cover.

Unfortunately, popular as he is in the show ring, the Gordon seems destined for oblivion in the hunting field. Thirty years ago I owned and hunted with a Gordon that was stolen at the prime age of five years. Since then I have never seen a really good gun dog of this breed in the field.

Pretty much the same applies to the contemporary Irish setter, although it must be added that even years ago he had an unsavory reputation as a hardhead. He always has been difficult to control, and has required rigorous, and sometimes painful, training methods to keep him in hand. This is true of the existing crop of Irish setters, which, like the Gordons, has been largely subjected to the refined breeding which emphasizes show rather than hunting qualities.

The springer and the cocker spaniels are flushing dogs. Neither of these breeds has an inclination to point, although occasionally you'll find a springer who will squat momentarily before charging in to put a bird into the air. The cocker, as you might suspect by the name, was originally bred for gunning woodcock and at this the busy little dog was unusually adept. In the last quarter of a century, however, the cocker has become a house pet, and finding a cocker in the field with a shotgunner now is almost impossible.

The springer, on the other hand, is one of our busiest, hardest-working dogs. He goes through the most impenetrable cover like a vacuum cleaner. If there's a bird or a rabbit there, he will get it on the move. This stocky, medium-sized dog works close to the gun, is relatively easy to control, and when he does flush a bird it is for his hunter.

The increased interest in ringneck pheasant hunting in this country has been largely responsible for the growing popularity of the springer. He does not brook

228

Popular breeds of trailing hound used to run varmints
or big game are: Plott hound (top, left), developed in Smoky Mountain
area for bear hunting; American beagle (top, right);
black-and-tan coonhound (bottom, left), and American foxhound,
which is frequently hunted in packs.

any nonsense from a ringneck. He is not subject to the continual hesitation of false pointing that affects most pointing-dog breeds. Once his moist little black nose fills with pheasant scent, he takes the trail with the greatest zeal, and within seconds the bird will be in the air. If the bird is really running, the hunter must do his own part to keep up with the dog, because it is as sure as death and taxes that when the springer catches up with him the pheasant will be into the air with a loud cackle and a flurry of beating wings.

America has three popular retriever breeds: the Labrador, the golden, and the Chesapeake Bay.

The Labrador is one of the most powerful dogs in the world for his size. He is also one of the toughest. He has a dense coat, and although the hair is relatively flat and smooth, he has no fear of entering icy waters at full speed. Since the Lab is strictly retriever, he has become enormously popular on the private shooting preserves, where birds are released from a tower or from a chute and are killed by the hundreds. The dog's job here, of course, is not to find the game, but to retrieve it after it has been downed. On any one day it is not unusual for one dog to find and retrieve a hundred birds, either pheasants or, perhaps, mallards.

The golden retriever is pretty much a long-haired version of the Labrador. Today the golden cannot even claim the distinction of a light, golden coat, since in recent years golden Labradors, and even white ones, have been bred. However, the golden retriever is an extremely popular dog in the West and Far West, where he is used for retrieving the many varieties of game bird found in the prairie and plains states. The golden fulfills much the same function as the Labrador, except that the breed is rarely used over water. Many people feel that the golden is a more companionable dog than the Labrador and makes a better combination hunting dog and house pet.

The Chesapeake Bay retriever is strictly the wildfowler's dog. He is one of the largest of the hunting breeds; males may weigh up to eighty pounds. He has an extremely dense, oily coat which suits him probably best of all breeds for retrieving ducks and geese from freezing winter water filled with floating ice cakes.

The Chesapeake is certainly no beauty and, in fact, many breeders emphatically resist any attempt to make a show dog of him. He's a utilitarian dog, powerful, strong, steady, and apparently impossible to tire, no matter how much you demand of him in retrieving ducks and geese in the coldest of weather. His first love is water; a Chesapeake would rather play in water than on land.

He has an amazing memory, and sometimes he seems to have the ability to count. If he sees four ducks drop out of a flock to your shots, he will not sit in the blind after retrieving the third bird. Without any urging or reminding, he will again charge out into the water.

Among the trailing hounds, there are many breeds, a large number of them of American origin. The rabbit dogs are the beagle and the basset, the foxhounds, the black-and-tan coonhound, the Walker, the Trigg, and the redbone. The Plott hound is used extensively in the South, particularly in the Great Smoky Mountains for bear and wild boar.

To some degree, the size of the hound matches the game he's pitted against. For example, the small breeds of beagle are cottontail-rabbit dogs. The basset, too, is a good, slow-working cottontail dog. For running the larger snowshoe rabbits, the Walker hound is usually the choice because of his longer legs, which enable him to get through the deep snow that is prevalent when the snowshoe normally is hunted. The American foxhound is, of course, used in hunting foxes, and quite often is run in fairly large packs—particularly when riding to hounds. Other breeds for fox hunting include the Walker, the black-and-tan, the redbone, and the Trigg. The Trigg, which originated in Kentucky, is almost exclusively a fox dog today.

Hound-dog men who run mountain lions and bobcat are not particularly fussy about a specific breed. Their packs are cosmopolitan, usually with some redbones or black-and-tans with a generous admixture of airedale. These cat dogs are not only keen-nosed, but have stout hearts. Courage is needed in large quantities when tangling with mountain lions and bobcats.

HANDLING GAME IN THE FIELD

12

A hunter's first obligation as a sportsman is to kill his game quickly and neatly. His second obligation is to take prompt and thorough care of the carcass. Many tons of fine game meat are wasted each year simply because the hunter is either careless in placing his shots, or careless in handling the game after it has been downed. Besides, a badly wounded animal that must be chased a long way before it can be finished off is never as good eating as an animal that has been killed quickly with one well-placed bullet. So the business of properly caring for game meat begins with the shooting.

When large game is involved, the hunter must be absolutely sure the downed animal is dead before he approaches too closely. If it is still alive, a finishing shot should be taken through the neck, just behind the ears. This will not spoil usable meat, nor will it create problems for the taxidermist should the shooter decide to have the head mounted.

Many hunters make a ritual of either sticking or cutting an animal's throat, because it symbolizes to them the coup de grâce, the final act of killing. But it's really a senseless thing to do. If the animal is not yet dead, it's extremely foolish to try to stick it. Many hunters have been injured by wounded animals while undertaking this symbolic gesture. And if the animal is indeed dead, nothing is gained by cutting its throat. The organs have already ceased functioning, the heart has stopped pumping, and no further bleeding will take place, other than in the draining process during the final field dressing. In addition, if the animal has a head worth mounting, it is the height of foolishness to mutilate the throat with needless cutting. In most cases the scalp is destroyed, and the taxidermist has to throw it away and purchase a new one, or substitute one he happens to have on hand. In either case he will charge you extra. So keep your knife away from a trophy head.

To dress a carcass it should be placed belly up, with the head slightly uphill. This eases the operation of removing the entrails and forces blood and body fluids into the body cavity to drain toward the rear. It is never necessary, or even desirable, to hang a deer or other large animal to field dress it. The whole thing can be done with considerable less bother right on the ground.

The only tool needed for field dressing is a small, sharp knife. A pocketknife will do to make the few cuts needed. Even on animals as large as moose or an elk the surgery can be performed very nicely with a small blade. The larger hunting knives that many outdoorsmen carry in belt sheaths are usually too clumsy and unwieldy, and quite often the blades are not brought to a keen enough edge.

When the big game is being hunted in the back country, away from a camp, two additional items are required, particularly if the weather is warm. One is a sack of common table salt for curing the capes of the trophies (and the hides if you want to save them). The other is a plentiful supply of packing-house tubing, commonly known as cheesecloth. This is easiest to handle on a roll. Automobile supply houses usually stock it (for polishing cars).

Start the field dressing operation by inserting the point of the knife at the sternum, the cartilage connecting the ribs. Once the hide has been pierced, turn the knife blade upward, with the sharp edge on top and make the first cut directly back toward the genitals. Care must be used at all times to avoid cutting through the intestines or the stomach. The best way is to lift the hide with the fingers as the knife blade carries through. When the cut reaches the genitals, remove them. Some states require the hunter to preserve the evidence of sex with the hide. In such areas the scrotum should stay with the hide when the testicles are removed.

If preserving the animal's head is not a consideration, the carcass may be cut from the genitals to the point of the lower jaw. This will permit more rapid cooling when that stage of the operation has been reached.

Next, cut around the rectal tube to free it from the body. This is done with much the same motion used in coring an apple. When the tube is free, it can then be pulled back through the body cavity when the entrails are finally removed.

At this stage, the paunch and intestinal cavity must be pulled free of all the entrails to allow access to the

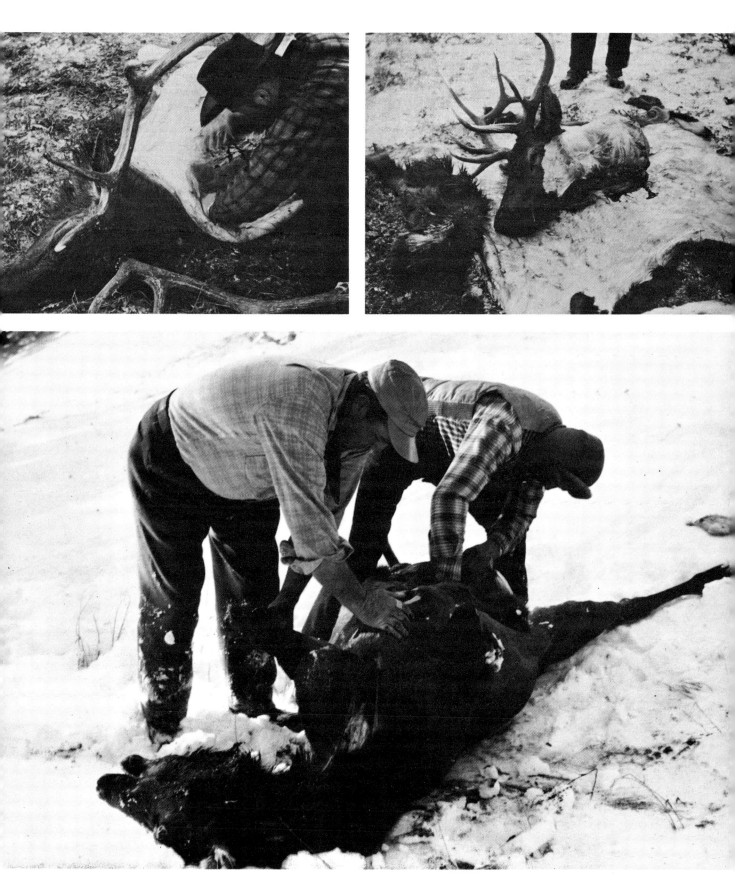

Preceding pages: Three animals bring down one bull elk.
"Caping out" trophy elk before skinning (top, left) assures enough
hide for shoulder mount. Remainder of hide (top, right)
is used as work surface for butchering. When cape is not saved, field
dressing is easier. Carcass may be split to jaw, as with cow elk (bottom)

diaphragm, which is joined to the inside of the cavity at the bottom of the ribs. Cut through the diaphragm all the way around the body cavity until it is completely free. A good part of this will have to be done by feel, especially in the lower reaches of the cavity.

With the diaphragm out of the way, it is now possible to reach well up into the front of the chest cavity and grasp the windpipe and gullet. Simply hold them with one hand and pull them well back while reaching up with the free hand to sever both with a stroke of the knife. Still grasping the gullet and windpipe, pull the entire group of entrails back with one good, quick tug. You may find you will have to do a little additional cutting around the inside of the rectal tube to get it completely free of the body at this time, and you will also have to make certain that no fecal matter remains lodged in the opening between the hindquarters when the tube is pulled back through the cavity. If there is any, it should be pushed out with a stick.

Next, the carcass should be rolled over on its belly so that it can drain. To speed the draining process, spread the hind legs. When the draining is completed, the carcass should then be rolled over on its back again, and the body cavity propped open in one or more places with sticks to allow air to circulate through it, and to permit the meat to begin cooling.

234   This simple method of field dressing a deer has three important advantages over more complete, but also more complicated, methods. The relatively small opening made by cutting only from the point of the sternum to the genitals helps to keep brush, mud, and other debris out of the cavity when the animal is being transported. Secondly, the animal handles better for either carrying or dragging if the pelvic arch is not split at this point. In addition, should you wish to preserve the cape for the trophy, it is important that you not cut the skin any closer to the head than the point of the ribs. Most sportsmen prefer a shoulder mount on an antlered or horned head, and it is easier for the taxidermist to set up the mount if the entire brisket comes to him in one uncut piece.

With the bigger animals, such as elk, moose, or caribou, the field dressing must be a little more thorough. If the cape is to be saved for mounting, immediately after making the abdominal cut and removing the entrails you will have to circle the entire carcass with the knife blade, starting at a point behind the withers, continuing down one side, behind the brisket, across the forelegs, and up the other side until you have reached the first part of the cut. A second cut is then made from a point directly behind the ears, along the topline of the neck, linking it with the encircling cut. Now peel the hide back as far as you can, toward the ears and the back of the jaws, enough to permit you to open the

Left to right: Paunch and lower intestines
are rolled back out of cavity, so diaphragm can be reached with knife.
Pair of hunters pack heart and liver in protective
plastic bag. When field dressing any animal, first incision is made
at sternum. Diaphragm is removed by cutting close to ribs.

animal up through the brisket, and even up to and including the gullet. Most hunters prefer to remove the windpipe completely—Westerners in particular—because they believe it has a tendency to sour the meat. I have never found this to be so, and have therefore never bothered to do it, but I have seen it done many times.

A great many hunters also make a point of removing the metatarsal gland, found on the outside of the hind legs of each deer. Personally, I have never known any meat to be tainted by the failure to remove these glands, but again a great many hunters feel that it might possibly be. If you share this view, by all means remove the metatarsals. It certainly can do no harm and it takes only a few moments.

Since an animal should be allowed to cool out as long as possible, predatory birds are often a problem. This is particularly true on a wilderness pack hunt, where carcasses are usually left out overnight, until pack mules can be brought in to carry them back to camp. To prevent the carcass from destruction and mutilation it's wise to turn the animal over on its belly and entirely cover it with freshly cut evergreen boughs or other handy brush after the initial cooling period. This usually secures it from any scavengers, at least for the brief, overnight period. With larger animals the carcass will invariably be quartered anyway before it is packed for moving, so dirtying the meat in handling need not

be taken into account. Prompt cooling, however, is important in handling any large animal, so do whatever is necessary to field dress the animal as soon as possible.

It must always be remembered, too, that the pelt of a big-game animal provides a thick layer of insulation, particularly when the animal is in its winter coat. It tends to retain the body heat of the animal, often to such a degree that even in the coldest weather a hanging carcass will still be warm inside after several hours. So be sure to allow sufficient cooling time.

To quarter a big animal, a sharp ax is essential. All the best Western outfitters use the double-bitted ax which can be carried in a sheath and stowed with the rest of the equipment. The ax is used to split the brisket of a big, tough elk or moose, and to cut the carcass in half, lengthwise, down the spinal column.

Most experienced big-game guides and outfitters prefer to skin large animals on the spot and use the hide as a surface on which to quarter the animal. This keeps dirt, grass, hair, and so forth off the meat. To keep meat clean during handling and packing, slip each quarter into a large cheesecloth bag, then into a muslin bag with a drawstring top. Both materials are porous, so that air may continue to circulate about the meat.

Some outfitters quarter the carcass without removing the hide. But this method too often permits hair to find its way to the meat. Later, when the carcass is 235

*Getting game back to camp can be a problem: Winch hoist (top, left)
hauls mule out of deep canyon, while large mule-deer buck (top, right) drags readily
over fresh snow. Bottom, left: A poor carry.
Two poles are needed, and game should be rigged higher to prevent swaying.
Horse and stone boat (bottom, right) handle job easily.*

brought into the packing plant, the hairs must be removed, one by one—a painstaking process. Leaving the hide on the carcass does protect the meat, however; the only problem is that the hunter must forego saving the hide, unless he wishes to keep it in pieces.

In hunting in mountain country in the early fall, the shooter often encounters very warm weather in the daytime and cool weather at night, with temperatures dropping well below freezing. The problem then is to keep the meat from getting too warm during the day. This is best accomplished by hanging the individual quarters at night and removing them before the sun comes up. Pile them on a tarpaulin in a shady spot, cover them with several other tarps, and anchor them with rocks to keep scavenging animals from getting at the meat while you are away from camp. Certainly, this is a time-consuming chore, but it must be attended to each morning and evening by anyone staying in a wilderness camp for any length of time if he expects his meat to be in good condition when he gets back to civilization.

There are two schools of thought on how to handle an animal the size of a deer once it has been brought back to camp. The old-timers usually prefer to hang it head down from a tree, or man-made rack. It's the traditional method and is better for photographing because the head is visible. But the modern method of hanging the animal head up is more sensible. It allows the carcass to drain clean, since there will be no pockets in which blood or other body fluids can rest. In the reverse position, any remaining blood or body secretions will drain down into the chest cavity. Furthermore, hanging the animal head up protects the meat in case of rain or snow, because the upper part of the carcass sheds the moisture and the open part of the body is facing the ground.

Two schools of thought also exist on whether or not game meat—or any meat—should be washed. Again, the old-timers insist that no water should reach the meat. If the animal has been killed cleanly with one shot, and handled carefully in transit, there is no reason to wash it. However, if the meat has become soiled in any way

or is excessively bloody, it's entirely in order to wash the inside of the carcass with buckets of water. But then it must be thoroughly dried. As every butcher knows, commercial beef is generally washed down with a hose in the slaughterhouse, so mere contact with water does no harm.

In warm weather, the hunter will also have to deal with the blowfly menace. This is done most satisfactorily by enclosing the carcass in a length of packing-house tubing. The tubing stretches so it will completely cover the animal—head to tail to tip of hind feet. Tie each end with a simple knot. A five-yard length is usually enough to cover a large deer.

If no packing-house tubing is available, there are a couple of alternate methods that can be used to discourage the flies. One is to be absolutely certain that no moisture pockets exist in the meat in the cavity. Blowflies lay their eggs only in moisture. Then sprinkle all the exposed parts of the flesh liberally with black pepper and rub it in by hand. Blowflies are repulsed by black pepper. Smoking will also discourage the flies. A small, hot fire with a good supply of green hardwood sticks, enough to create a considerable smudge or smoke, is needed. Position the carcass over the fire so that the smoke clouds may enter the cavity, and completely cover the carcass with a blanket or makeshift lean-to to speed up the process and allow more smoke to reach the carcass as it leaves the fire.

When big-game animals are killed in areas of good feed, and before the height of the rut, their meat can be as good as the best grades of beef. Yet much of it is wasted each year, usually as a result of carelessness on the part of the hunter or ignorance of the proper methods of handling game. For instance, a good deal of fine venison is ruined by hunters who take a freshly killed, warm animal and tie it to the hood or top of a car. After several hours in the hot sun during the return trip home, the meat spoils.

Too many hunters also fail to follow up wounded animals and finish them off. This is inexcusable. It's the hunter's obligation to deal promptly and properly with the animals he has shot.

237

HUNTING CAMPS

13

unting big game from a wilderness camp set up in a remote area is one of the great experiences a sportsman can have. More and more, the best big-game hunting on the North American continent is being confined to remote areas. It is rare that you will find permanent camps in such places, and it is up to the hunter to establish his own wilderness home if he intends to hunt the biggest of big game. Pretty much the same can be said for the hunter who is looking for a trophy whitetail or mule-deer head. Today the bigger heads are coming from the areas where hunting pressure is relatively light.

One of the great joys of hunting in the wilderness is the absence of other hunters in your domain. The game lives its normal life without false and disturbing elements, such as automobiles and battalions of hunters, which are certain to send it into seclusion or out of a region entirely.

Another bonus in wilderness hunting is the sheer beauty of the land itself. The rolling open lands of the Yukon and the broad, snowy peaks of the Rocky Mountains provide a majestic setting. To live in it even for a short time is reward enough, whether game is killed or not. Under these conditions of quiet solitude, the hunter and the animals are more equally matched in the game of stalking and escape. Here a man has a chance to study the game, to make note of its movements and feeding habits, where it rests or beds down. And here he can take the time to study a number of different herds or animals in order to pick the one he wants as his trophy head.

The simplest approach to making a wilderness hunt is to hire an outfitter who has all the gear. If you will bring the personal items you need—bedding, clothing, and hunting gear—he will provide everything else. Heated tents, a food supply and a cook, pack animals, saddles, and all the paraphernalia of wilderness travel are included in the package.

If you are disposed to set up your own camp without the assistance of a regular outfitter, it is quite likely that you will select one of the national forests for your hunting ground, particularly if you're after elk, moose,

mule deer, goat, and sheep. If you are a nonresident you will be required to have a guide, and he probably will choose the hunting spot unless you insist on a specific area. In any case, your first chore is to determine whether camping is permitted in the area you plan to hunt. The national forests generally permit camping for hunting, but this should be checked. Any of the local state conservation departments or game commissions can provide maps and information.

The rugged individual who likes to go it alone on a camping hunt must assemble a complete camp outfit. For a two-week hunt in big-game country, this can be quite a bit of gear, especially in cold weather. Usually it's possible to rent pack horses and saddle horses to carry both you and your gear into the camping area. In other cases, a local man can be hired to drive you in his Jeep or power wagon to the edge of the remote country where you want to pitch your camp. In no case, however, should you camp in the middle of what you think will be the best game area. Set yourself up in a location offering firewood and good water—and within reasonable walking distance of the country you expect to hunt. Your chances will be better if you stay out of the game area except when hunting.

In most areas during the fall hunting season, the weather will be chilly, at least at night. In any case, you will require a tent that can be heated, and to my mind the best unit for this is the so-called "sheepherder's stove." This little sheet-metal stove, and its stovepipe, folds into a flat package for easy carrying and can be mounted on sticks cut on the spot to bring it up to comfortable cooking level. It will quickly heat a twelve-by sixteen-foot wall tent, which is the standard type and size for a party of four hunters. This rugged tent can be set up with poles cut at the site. It's capable of withstanding a great deal of wind and bad weather, and although among the oldest tent designs, it still is probably the best one for the big-game hunter's camp.

In setting up your tent, it is always smart to select an elevated spot. A high bank along a lake shore or a river is usually a good location. Make certain, too, that there are no large, dead trees that can topple onto your

*Preceding pages: Well-organized camp
in Montana's Bitterroot range. Right: Cook tent equipped
with sheepherder stove, which folds
flat for packing. Supporting legs can be fashioned
from saplings cut at camp site.*

*Top: Author inspects sleeping tent. Among
most big-game hunters, wall tent is choice for permanent setups.
Extra fly over tent (above, left) provides better
protection from sun and rain. An A-pole rig is seen above, right.
Opposite: Old-time hunters gather around campfire.*

shelter. If you're going to be in camp for a week or more in mountain country or northern country, where you can anticipate some rainfall, it is always a good idea to spend a half hour digging a drainage ditch completely around the tent.

When you reach your camp site, your first obligation is to get your animals unpacked. It's not only callous, but plain bad practice to leave animals standing around under a full load, while you pick up firewood or cut your tent poles.

If you're using a wall tent and plan to be set up for at least a week, use the seven-pole A-rig, a skeleton framework inside which your tent can be slung. Lash two end poles together like the letter A for both front and back of the tent, and run a ridgepole over the extended shears. Lash a cross pole to the shear poles on each side at a point about three feet from the tent walls. Then tie the side guy ropes of the tent to them. When this framework is well made, it will hold together for months.

It seems unnecessary to mention that in setting up a camp such as this, it's absolutely essential to have a good bow saw on hand and a couple of good, sharp axes, plus a file and a stone for keeping everything sharp.

Water and wood supply are extremely important. Much of the moose, elk, and bear country is in high mountains and usually has an abundance of good fresh water, far from sources of pollution. On the other hand, low-country streams, particularly on farm land, can be dangerous to drink unless the water is first boiled. In these areas it's always a good idea to have Halazone tablets as well for purifying the water quickly.

During a two- or three-week period a hunting camp will consume a good deal of firewood, and this means something more than dead timber that's been lying on the ground for months, soaking up water. This sort of musty downfall is always referred to by the Indians as "squaw wood," because it's easy to gather. But it is difficult to ignite and when it does burn, it gives off little heat and a great deal of smoke. The well-run camp needs a supply of dead standing timber that can be cut down readily with the bow saw. Many of the national forest areas contain standing timber that has been fire

killed. This is excellent stuff for fire building.

One of the unfortunate features of high-mountain country, however, is that it is forested almost entirely with evergreens or soft woods. These pines and spruces and firs all burn readily enough, perhaps too readily. You will have to cut a considerable wood supply merely to do your cooking and keep your camp warm.

On pack trips, where you'll be using saddle horses as well as mules, it's a good idea to include in your gear a short piece of chain with a hook on one end and a ring on the other. When you fell a fairly good-sized tree, you can take your horse into the timber, hook the chain around your log, fasten your lariat to the chain, and then haul the timber out with your rope wrapped around the saddle horn.

Another extremely useful item in a big camp, or on an extended hunt, is a lightweight chain saw. There are models available that weigh only about twelve pounds. 243

You can easily carry a two- or three-week gasoline supply for its little motor in one can. A chain saw will save many hours of labor in the woods which might better be spent hunting.

Sanitation is an important part of camp engineering. Plan the garbage pit and the latrine so that they are conveniently reached, but will not drain into your water source. Be sure to dig the garbage pit far enough away so that the inevitable flies do not come into your camp. Ditto for the latrine; this can be a simple pit dug in the ground, between two trees. You can nail or wire a timber crosspiece to the trees about two feet above the ground to use as a seat. When you break camp, fill in both latrine and garbage pit with the soil you removed in digging. The army-surplus folding shovel is the best tool to take.

If you decide to camp in sagebrush or gumbo country in the prairies, you will be faced with entirely different problems of water and wood supply. You can never count on water being near your camp or hunting location. And where you do find water, it often isn't fit to drink because of alkalis. The best bet is to pack your water in forty-quart milk cans such as dairy farmers use. These have tight-fitting covers, and two of them can be packed on a single mule using the classic swing hitch employed by most Westerners. The Decker packsaddle is exactly the kind of a rig for this chore, as well as the most certain method for packing meat and camp gear.

Since sagebrush and mesquite are not good firewood, although they are most likely to be encountered on any sort of prairie or desert hunt, it's best to provide other

fuels for your camp. One of the best rigs is the standard gasoline stove, preferably a three-burner which compacts readily for easy transportation. If you are traveling in a big power wagon, it's entirely in order to use a trailer stove fueled either by propane gas or gasoline. A twenty-pound tank of propane gas will give you all the cooking heat you need for a fairly large group of hunters for at least two weeks.

Once you've satisfied yourself that your tent shelter, heating, and cooking facilities are adequate, the most important item for personal comfort is the sleeping bag and an air mattress, or some sort of cot. It never pays to economize on a sleeping bag. In all north country and high mountain areas you'll find that the nights are cold during the hunting season. If you try to get by with

a bag filled with two pounds of down, Dacron, or other insulation, it's inevitable that you'll find yourself waking up at midnight chilled to the bone and unable to get warm again.

Any sleeping bag designed for hunting trips should have a comfort level guaranteed down to zero degrees Fahrenheit. For most people this means a bag containing at least four pounds of down. Needless to say, these high-quality, low-temperature bags are not cheap, but this is the sort of item you buy once in a lifetime. It doesn't wear out, so it's an excellent investment—and the only one that will guarantee your sleeping comfort. The bag should be equipped with a snap-in liner of muslin, and you should carry a spare. It is never easy to have down-filled sleeping bags dry-cleaned, so every 245

Pack string (above), fording a Rocky
Mountain river, heads for elk. Outfitter uses Decker
pack saddle and swing-hitch. Tents that
backpack easily are used in Dall-sheep camp (left),
some 6500 feet up, in Yukon.

effort should be made to keep the bag clean, from its first use. Muslin sheet liners will do this.

Almost as important as the sleeping bag itself is a proper air mattress. Little tree roots and stones underneath your sleeping bag always seem to get bigger and more painful as the night wears on. A good air mattress takes care of the situation. Here again, don't skimp on price. Most men buy them too narrow. It must never be forgotten that the stated dimensions of an air mattress have been measured when it is deflated. As it is pumped up, it loses a few inches both in width and length. For the average man an air mattress should be at least thirty-four inches wide and seventy inches long before inflation. My preference is the waffle type made by Hodgman. This is made of two tough layers of cloth with a layer of rubber bonded between them. These mattresses will give at least ten years of satisfactory use, so they are a good investment.

Another essential is a ground cloth. This can be of light canvas or, better still, of light nylon. A vinyl sheet does just as well, but it will not last as long. The idea, of course, is to keep ground moisture from reaching your sleeping bag through your air mattress. It isn't likely to do this with the Hodgman mat, which is rubberized, but if you should want to turn your mattress for any reason the side that has been lying on the ground will be wet. Hence the advantage of a ground cloth.

The final essential for sleeping comfort is a small pillow. I like a feather pillow, but many hunters use an inflatable one made of the same material as the air mattress. I find these completely uncomfortable. A good feather pillow can be crushed down and tied into an insignificant bundle, yet when you're ready to use it, it can be fluffed out to fairly large size, and it is indeed comfortable to sleep on.

These days the food taken along on a camping trip can be almost anything a hunter wants. There are literally hundreds of fruits, vegetables, and meats in dehydrated form, all of which are tasty and nourishing, yet take up relatively little packing room and are light in weight. Canned goods are fine if you can handle their bulk and weight. There's no need to dwell on the selection of these foods, but a final word should be said on hunting-trip menus: never depend for a meat supply on the game you kill. It often works out, particularly on a trophy hunt, that the animal the hunter wishes to shoot is not found until near the end of the hunt. If he is on a restricted license, he will not be able to shoot meat for the pot, and everyone's diet will be a bit slim.

I was once packed in by a Canadian outfitter up in Alberta on a sheep hunt. I did not discover until after we had arrived at the hunting spot and had made camp that the only meat this joker had brought along was eight sides of bacon. Not that the bacon wasn't delicious, but after five days of eating nothing but bacon I decided I had to kill something to eat before we all began suffering from malnutrition. At dawn on the morning of the sixth day, I set out from camp to shoot myself a deer—any kind of a deer—and did manage to snag a nice, fat four-point mulie buck. As it happened, I never did kill a sheep on this hunt, because we did not find one that represented a good enough trophy. However, the mule deer gave us some pretty good eating for the last week of the hunt.

Certain parts of any animal you kill will be good for immediate consumption. Even if you don't wish to disturb the carcass by carving any of the body meat, you'll find that the liver is palatable (unless from a scrawny old buck). The heart, the kidneys, and the tongue are also good. The backstraps, or tenderloin, on any game animal also should be removed after the carcass is cooled out. If you wait until the animal has hung for a time, the backstraps will be dried out.

To make a camp livable for any long period, you will need some furniture. As a rule, a hunter is not inclined to bring along folding tables and chairs, particularly if they have to be carried on pack animals. But tables, stools, and whatnot can be made from logs, saplings, and other materials at hand. It must be said that all of this takes time. A hunter looking for the most comfortable camp should figure on spending at least one full day setting it up and getting his gear in good shape before he thinks about hunting.

PICTURE CREDITS

The following sources are repeated frequently in the list below and will, therefore, be referred to by the initials preceding their names.

AG — Arthur Corbin Gould, *Sport; or Fishing and Shooting,* Boston, 1889. Courtesy, University of Michigan.
BB — Photographs by Bill Browning.

CD — Photographs by Charley Dickey.
LC — Library of Congress.
LK — Photographs by Larry Koller.
LR — Photographs by Leonard Lee Rue III.

MC — Montana Chamber of Commerce.
NYPL — New York Public Library.
SI — Currier and Ives lithographs from the Smithsonian Institution.

CHAPTER ONE: 10-11—SI, *American Hunting Scenes,* **A Good Chance,** 1863. 13—Cabinet of Natural History and American Rural Sports, 3 vols., Phila., 1830-34. 14-15 (both)—NYPL; (left)—Theodore De Bry, **America,** 1590-1634; (right)—Alexander Anderson, **A General History of Quadrupeds,** N.Y., 1834. 16-17 (top & middle)—SI, **Woodcock Shooting,** 1852, and **Rail Shooting,** 1852; (bottom)—Robert Mottar. 18-19 (top)—Metropolitan Museum of Art, gift of Wilfred Wood, 1956; (below, left)—Anderson, op. cit.; (below, right)—SI, *Still Hunting on the Susquehanna,* undated. 20—Anderson, op. cit. 21 (top)—Winchester News Bureau; (bottom)—SI, *Life in the Woods,* **Returning to Camp,** 1860. 22—NYPL, **American Shooter's Manual,** Phila., 1827. 23—NYPL, **Sportsman's Portfolio of American Field Sports,** Boston, 1855. 24 (top)—**Cabinet,** op. cit.; (bottom)—SI, *Life of a Hunter,* **A Tight Fix,** 1861. 25-26—Remington Arms Co., Inc. 27 (top)—LC, John James Audubon, **The Birds of America,** 7 vols., Phila., 1840; (bottom)—SI, *Pigeon Shooting,* **Playing the Decoy,** 1852. 28 (all photos)—Winchester News Bureau. 29 (top)—Olin Mathieson Chemical Corp.; (middle)—Smithsonian Institution; (bottom)—Frederic Remington, **Buffalo Hunting,** 1889, Kennedy Galleries, Inc. 30-31—AG. 32-33 (top)—Winchester News Bureau; (lower right)—Aldine Magazine, March, 1876. 34-35 (left)—SI, *American Feathered Game,* **Woodcock and Snipes,** 1854; (middle)—Winchester News Bureau; (right)—SI, *American Feathered Game,* **Mallard and Canvas Back Ducks,** 1854. 36-37 (top)—LC, Arthur Frost, **Sports and Games in the Open,** N.Y., 1899; (bottom)—Browning Arms Co.

CHAPTER TWO: 38-39—BB. 41—LR. 42-43 (left)—CD; (right)—LC, Frost, **Sports and Games in the Open,** N.Y., 1899. 45—LR. 47—BB. 49 (top)—George Laycock; (bottom)—LR. 50—Nebraska Game Commission. 51—Yosemite National Park. 52-53—BB. 54-55—MC. 56-57—AG. 58-59—MC. 61—MC. 62-63—BB. 65—Ontario Dept. of Travel & Publicity. 68-69 (left)—LC, Frost, op. cit.; (right)—Ontario Dept. of Travel & Publicity. 70-71 (top, left & right)—Mac's Foto Service, Anchorage, Alaska; (bottom, left)—James Simon; (bottom, right)—LC, Frost, op. cit. 74-75 (left)—Saskatchewan Photo Services; (right)—Mac's Foto Service.

CHAPTER THREE: 78-79—BB. 81—Canadian National Railways. 82-83 (top, left)—Colo. Dept. of Game, Fish & Parks; (middle, left & right)—BB; (bottom, left)—AG. 84—Frederic Remington, **The First Shot,** Kennedy Galleries, Inc. 86—Mac's Foto Service. 88—Canadian National Railways. 90-91 (left)—MC; (right)—BB. 92—MC. 94-95 (top, left)—Frederic Remington; (top, right; bottom)—BB.

CHAPTER FOUR: 98-99—Mac's Foto Service. 100—**Grizzly Halting the Stage Coach,** Kennedy Galleries, Inc. 102-103 (left)—LC, John James Audubon, **The Viviparous Quadrupeds of North America,** N.Y., 1845. 105—Bob Zwirz. 106-107 (left)—Mac's Foto Service; (top; bottom right)—BB.

CHAPTER FIVE: 110-111—MC. 113—LK. 114 (top)—LR; (bottom)—MC. 115 (top)—LR; (bottom)—Winchester News Bureau. 118-119—MC. 121-122—MC. 123—NYPL, T. B. Thorpe, **The Hive of the Bee Hunter,** N.Y., 1854.

CHAPTER SIX: All photos by Grancel Fitz except p. 128 (lower right)—Alex Rota, Boone and Crockett Club; 130 (top; bottom, left)—MC; (right)—Boone and Crockett Club.

CHAPTER SEVEN: All photos by Leonard Lee Rue except p. 137—LC, Arthur Frost, **Sports and Games in the Open,** N.Y., 1899; 140—Nebraska Game Commission.

CHAPTER EIGHT: 145 (top)—Texas Parks & Wildlife Dept.; (bottom)—Nebraska Game Commission. 146—LR. 147—Texas Park & Wildlife Dept. 148-149 (top, center; bottom, center & right)—BB; (top, right)—LR; (bottom, left)—North Carolina Wildlife Service. 150—U.S. Fish & Wildlife Service. 151—LK. 152-153—Bert Popowski. 155—MC. 156—U.S. Fish & Wildlife Service. 157 (top)—NYPL, Alexander Anderson, **A General History of Quadrupeds,** N.Y., 1834.

CHAPTER NINE: 158-159—LK. 162—Arthur Frost, **Shooting Pictures,** N.Y., 1895, Florida State Univ. 163 (top)—LK; (bottom)—LC, John James Audubon, **The Birds of America,** 7 vols. N.Y., 1840-44. 164—U.S. Fish & Wildlife Service. 165—LR. 166-167—CD. 169 (top, left)—MC; (top, right; bottom)—Pete Czura. 171 (left)—U.S. Dept. of Agriculture; (right)—Florida Game & Fresh Water Fish Commission. 172-173—SI, (bottom, left)—**American Field Sports, On a Point,** 1857; (top, left & right)—CD. 174—LR. 175—Texas Parks & Wildlife Dept. 176—CD. 177 (top)—SI, **Wild Turkey Shooting,** 1871; (bottom, left & right)—CD. 179—Nebraska Game Commission. 180 (top)—James Simon; (bottom, left)—Pete Czura; (bottom, right)—MC. 181 (bottom)—Frost, op. cit. 183—Pete Czura. 184—Colorado Game & Fish Dept. 185 (top, left)—MC; (top, right; bottom)—BB. 186 (top)—Wyoming Game & Fish Dept.; (bottom)—Oregon Fish & Wildlife Service. 188-189 (top, left & right)—CD; (bottom)—Pete Czura. 190—L.R. 192 (top, left)—LC, op. cit.

CHAPTER TEN: 194-195—BB. 197—Nebraska Game Commission. 198 (top)—CD; (bottom)—BB. 199 (top)—CD; (bottom)—BB. 201—North Carolina Wildlife Commission. 202-203—(top, left & right)—CD. 204 (top)—Ontario Dept. of Travel & Publicity; (bottom)—Nebraska Game Commission. 206-207 (top, left & right; bottom, right)—CD; (bottom, left)—Saskatchewan Photo Services; (bottom, center)—SI, **Wild Duck Shooting,** 1852. 208—LR. 209—Florida Game & Fresh Water Fish Commission. 210-211 (left)—CD; (right)—LC, John James Audubon, **The Birds of America,** 7 vols., N.Y., 1840-44. 212—New York State Conservation Dept. 214-215 (top, left)—Pete Czura; (bottom, left)—George Laycock; (all others)—LC, op. cit. 217—Florida Game & Fresh Water Fish Commission. 218—Utah State Dept. of Fish & Game. 219—Karl Maslowski.

CHAPTER ELEVEN: 222-223—LC, Arthur Frost, **Sports and Guns in the Open,** N.Y., 1899. 225 (top two)—Evelyn Shafer; (middle two)—LR; (bottom, left)—Winchester News Bureau; (bottom, right)—Pete Czura. 227 (top; middle, right)—Pete Czura; (middle, left)—Evelyn Shafer; (bottom, left)—CD; (bottom, right)—Saskatchewan Photo Services. 228 (all)—Evelyn Shafer.

CHAPTER TWELVE: 230-231—U.S. Forest Service. 233 (top two)—LK; (bottom)—MC. 234-235—MC. 236 (top, left)—Dept. of Fish & Game; (top, right)—MC; (bottom, left)—Maine Dept. of Inland Fisheries & Game; (bottom, right)—Ontario Dept. of Travel & Publicity.

CHAPTER THIRTEEN: 238-239-241-242—MC. 243—NYPL, T. B. Thorpe, **The Hive of the Bee Hunter,** N.Y., 1854. 244-245 (left)—Mac's Foto Service; (right)—MC.

MASTER GUN LIST

See Page 251 for keyed references

to appropriate calibers and gauges for

all game animals and birds.

SHOTGUNS

TYPE	GAUGE
BROWNING	
Hunting Models	
Standard Grade I	12, 20, 28
Lightning Grade I	12, 20
Pigeon	12, 20
Pointer	12, 20
Diana	12, 20
Midas	12, 20
3″ Magnum Grade I	12
Standard Grade I	28, .410
Automatic-5/Hunting Models	
Plain Barrel	12, 16
Plain Matted Barrel	Light 12, Sweet 16, Light 20
Double Auto./Hunting Models	
Plain Matted Barrel	12
Twelvette	12
COLT	
Standard Pump	12, 16, 20
Standard Ultra Light Auto	12, 20
Custom Ultra Light Auto	12, 20
DALY	
Commander	12, 20, 28
FIREARMS INTERNATIONAL	
Valmet	
E5123H	12
La Salle Pump	
F5733H	12
F5733G	16
F5733F	20
F5142H	12
La Salle Automatic	
F5643H	12
Robust Side-by-Side	
F5313H	12
HARRINGTON & RICHARDSON	
Topper	12, 16, 20, .410
Topper Deluxe	.410

TYPE	GAUGE
Topper, Jr.	20, .410
Pump	12, 16, 20
Pump	.410
Automatic	.410
HIGH STANDARD	
Supermatic Field	12
Supermatic Special	12
Supermatic Trophy	12
Supermatic Duck	12 Magnum
Supermatic Duck-Rib	12 Magnum
Supermatic Deluxe-Rib	12 Magnum
Supermatic Field Model	20
Flite-King Field	12, 16
Flite-King Deluxe-Rib	12, 16
Flite-King Brush Deluxe	12
Flite-King Field	20, .410
Flite-King Slug Gun	12
ITHACA	
Standard	12, 16, 20
Standard, vent. rib	12, 16, 20
Deluxe	12, 16, 20
Deerslayer	12, 16, 20
Deerslayer Super Deluxe	12, 16, 20
MARLIN	
Goose Gun	12, 3″ Magnum, 2¾″ regular
55-Hunter, choke	12, 3″ Magnum, 2¾″ regular
55-Hunter, without choke	12, 3″ Magnum, 2¾″ regular
Swamp Gun	12, 3″ Magnum, 2¾″ regular
60-G	.410
Model 55-G, choke	12, 3″ Magum
Model 55-G, without choke	12, 20, 16, 3″ Magnum
MOSSBERG	
173	.410
173Y	.410
183D	.410
185K	20
190K	16
500A	12
500AK	12
500AS	12
REMINGTON	
Model 1100 TB	12
Model 1100 SA	12, 20
Model 1100 Magnum, plain barrel	12, 20
Model 1100 Magnum, vent. rib	12, 20
Brushmaster Model 870	12
Wingmaster Model 870 Mag./plain	12, 20
Wingmaster Model 870, vent. rib	12, 20

TYPE	GAUGE
Model 11-48, plain	12, 16, 20, 28, .410
Model 11-48, vent. rib	12, 16, 20, 28, .410

SAVAGE/STEVENS

Model 220	12, 16, 20, .410
24DL	.22 LR, 20, .410
24MDL	.22 Mag., 20, .410
24	.22 LR/.410, .22 WMR/20-gauge Magnum
24M	.22 Mag., .410
24S	.22 LR, 20
24MS	.22 Mag., 20
750	12
30	12, 20
30L	12
30-T	12
B DE	12, 20
BST	12, 16, 20, .410
B	12, 16, 20, .410
311	12, 16, 20, .410
940	12, 16, 20, 28, .410
77	12, 16, 20, .410
58	12, 16, 20
59	.410

WINCHESTER

Model 1400	12, 16
Model 1200	12, 16
101 O/U	12, 20
Model 59	12

RIFLES

BROWNING	CALIBER
Safari Grade:	
Lightweight	.222, .222 Mag., 243
Standard	.270, .284, .30/06, .308, .264 Mag.
Magnum	7mm, .300 H&H, .300W, .308 Norma, .338W, .375 H&H, .458W
Automatic Grade I, LR	.22

COLT

Colteer	.22 RF
Colteer-Autoloader Carbine	.22 RF
Coltsman Standard Hi-Power	.222 thru .375
Coltsman Custom Hi-Power	.222 thru .375

FIREARMS INTERNATIONAL

Sako Forester:	
Sporter	.243, .308, .270, 7mm, .30/06, .300W Mag., .264 Mag., 7mm Mag.
Heavy Barrel	
Mannlicher	

TYPE	CALIBER
Sako Vixen-Sporter	.222, .222 Mag., .223
Mannlicher	.222, .222 Mag., .223
Heavy Barrel	.222, .222 Mag., .223
Sako Finnbear-Sporter	All standard calibers
Deluxe Sporter	All standard calibers
Supreme	.243, .270, 7mm, .30/06, .308, .300W Mag., .264 Mag., 7mm Mag.

HARRINGTON & RICHARDSON

Pioneer	.22 RF
Sahara	.22 RF
Plainsman	.22 RF

HIGH STANDARD

Sport-King Carbine	.22 RF
Sport-King Special	.22 RF
Sport-King Field	.22 RF
Sport-King Pump	.22 RF
Hi-Power Deluxe	.30/06, .270
Hi-Power Field	.30/06, .270

ITHACA

Saddlegun	.22 RF

MARLIN

336-C Carbine	.30/30, .35
336-T Texan Carbine	.30/30, .35
336 Marauder	.30/30, .35
336 Magnum	.44 Magnum, .444 Marlin
39-A	.22 S, L, LR
39-A Mountie	.22 S, L, LR
39 Carbine	.22 S, L, LR
57-M	.22 Magnum
57	.22 RF
62	.22 Jet, .256 Magnum
56	.22 RF
99-C	.22 LR
99-DL	.22 LR
989	.22 LR
99 M1 Carbine	.22 LR
980	.22 Mag. RF
81-C	.22 S, L, LR
81-DL	.22 S, L, LR

MOSSBERG

144LS	.22 RF
320K	.22 RF
340K	.22 RF
342K	.22 RF
346B	.22 RF
350K	.22 RF
402	.22 RF

REMINGTON

66 MB Mohawk Brown	.22 LR RF
550	.22 RF

TYPE	CALIBER
552 Speedmaster	.22 RF
Nylon 10	.22 S, L, LR
514 A	.22 S, L, LR
Nylon 11	.22 S, L, LR
511-X	.22 S, L, LR
512-X	.22 S, L, LR
Nylon 76 Trail Rider	.22 LR RF
572 Fieldmaster	.22 RF
600	.222R, .22/250, 6mm, .35R, .308W
600 Magnum Carbine	.350 Magnum
700 ADL	.222R, .222R Mag., 6mmR, .243W, .264W Mag., 7mmR Mag., .270W, .280R, .30/06, .308W
700 BDL	.222R, .222R Mag., 6mmR, .243W, .264W Mag., 7mmR Mag., .270W, .280R, .30/06, .308W, .300W Mag., .375 H&H Mag., .458W Mag.
700 Custom Deluxe	.270W, .280R, .308W, .30/06, 7mm Magnum
742	6mmR, .280R, .30/06, .308W
760	.223R, .270W, .280R, .30/06, .308W, .35R
760 Carbine	.30/06, .308W, .35R
700 BDL Special	.375 H&H Mag., .458W Mag.

RUGER

TYPE	CALIBER
44	.44 Magnum
44RS	.44 Magnum
10/22	.22 LR

SAVAGE
SAVAGE/ANSCHUTZ

TYPE	CALIBER
1413	.22 LR
1411	.22 LR
64	.22 LR
153	.222R
141	.22
110 Premier Grade	.22/250, .30/06 Spfld., 7mmR Mag.
110 Presentation Grade	7mmR Mag., .264, .300, .338W Mag.
110 Magnum	7mmR Mag., .264, .300, .338W Mag.
110 MC	.22/250, .30/06 Spfld., .243, .270, .308W
110 E	.30/06, .243, 7mmR Mag.
340	.222R, .225W, .30/30 W
99 Citation Grade	.243, .284, .300 Savage, .308, .358W
99 Presentation Grade	.243, .284, .300 Savage, .308, .358W

TYPE	CALIBER
99C	.243, .284, .308W
99DL	.300 Savage, .243, .284, .308, .358W
99F	.300 Savage, .243, .284, .308, .358W
99E	.300 Savage, .243, .308W
6 Deluxe	.22 LR, L, high-speed S
63M	.22 Magnum
4M	.22 Magnum
29	.22
24 Combination	.22/410, .22 WMR/20-gauge Magnum

SAVAGE/STEVENS

TYPE	CALIBER
87	.22 LR, L, high-speed S
84	.22
86	.22
15	.22
15Y Youth's Model	.22

TRADEWINDS
HUSQVARNA

TYPE	CALIBER
Lightweight Sporter	.270, 6mm, .30/06, .308, .243
Full Stock Sporter	.308, .270, .30/06, .243
Crown Sporter	7mmR Mag., .270, 6mm, .30/06, .308, .243
Tradewinds Husky	7mmR Mag., .270, .30/06, .243W

WALTHER

TYPE	CALIBER
KKJ	.22 LR, .22 Mag.
A	7mm, 7X64, .270, .30/06
B	7mm, 7X64, .270, .30/06

WEATHERBY

TYPE	CALIBER
Mark XXII	.22 RF
Weatherby Rifles	All Magnum calibers: .224, .257, 7mm, .270, .300, .340, .378, .460

WINCHESTER

TYPE	CALIBER
Alaskan	.338W Mag., .375 H&H Mag.
African	.458W Mag.
70	.300W Magnum
70 Standard	.225W, .243W, .264W Magnum, .270W, .30/06 Spfld., .308W
70 Varmint	.225W, .243W
100	.243W, .284W, .308W
88	.243W, .284W, .308W
94	.30/30W, .32W Special
250	.22 RF
255	.22W Mag. RF
270	.22W Mag. RF
275	.22W Mag. RF
290	.22 S, L, LR
52D	.22 LR

250

CALIBERS, GAUGES & LOADS

A selection designed to match

effective ballistic performance with

the game being hunted.

ANTLERED GAME (PAGES 38-77)

Whitetail & Mule Deer
In timber: .270 Winchester (150 grains), .280 Remington (165 gr), .30 Win (170 gr), .300 Savage, .308 Win, and .30-06 (all 150 or 180 gr), .35 Rem (200 gr), .44 Magnum (240 gr).
In prairie & high-mountain country (to 400 yds): 6mm Remington, .243 Winchester, and .257 Weatherby Magnum (all 100 gr), .264 Win Magnum (140 gr), .270 Win (130 gr), .280 Rem (150 gr), 7mm Rem Magnum (150 gr), 7mm Weath Magnum, .270 Weath Magnum; .308 Win and .30-06 (both 150 gr), .300 Win and .300 Weath Magnums (both 150 or 180 gr).

Whitetail
16 gauge; 12 gauge rifled slug (7/8 or 1 oz); 12 gauge, #0 or #00 Buckshot.

Elk
Moose
Caribou
In timber: .300 Winchester and .300 Weatherby Magnums (both 180 or 220 grains), .308 Win (200 gr), and .30-06 (220 gr), .35 Remington (200 gr), .350 Rem Magnum (200 or 250 gr), .358 Win (200 or 250 gr), .444 Marlin.
In high-mountain country: 7mm Remington Magnum (175 gr), .300 Winchester and .300 Weatherby Magnums (180 or 220 gr), .338 Win (200 gr), .340 Weath Magnum (210 gr).

HORNED GAME (PAGES 78-97)

Bighorn Sheep
Stone & Dall Sheep
Rocky Mountain Goat
Same as for Deer in high-mountain country.

Pronghorn Antelope
6mm Remington, .243 Winchester, and .257 Weatherby Magnum (all 100 grains), .264 Win Magnum (140 gr), .270 Win (130 gr), .280 Rem (125 gr), 7mm Rem Magnum (150 gr).

BEARS (PAGES 98-109)

Grizzly
Same as for Elk, etc.

Alaskan Brown
.300 Weatherby Magnum (220 grains), .338 Winchester Magnum (250 or 300 gr), .340 Weath Magnum (250 gr), .350 Remington Magnum (250 gr), .378 Weath Magnum (270 or 300 gr), .458 Win.

Black
Same as for Deer in timber.

SMALL FURRED GAME (PAGES 134-141)

Cottontail &
Snowshoe Rabbits
Fox & Gray Squirrels
.22 Long Rifle H.P., .22 WRF, .22 WMR MC.

Cottontail
28 gauge (3/4 oz), 20 gauge (7/8 or 1 oz), #6 or #71/2 shot.

Snowshoe
16 gauge, 12 gauge (11/8 oz), #4 or #6 shot.

VARMINTS (PAGES 142-157)

Cougar
When treed, any short-range gun. Otherwise, same as for Coyote.

Coyote
6mm Remington, .243 Winchester (both 100 grains), .270 Win (130 gr), .257 Weatherby Magnum (100 gr), .264 Win Magnum (140 gr), 7mm Rem Magnum (150 gr).

Bobcat
Fox
Prairie Dog
Woodchuck
Jack Rabbit
Short range (to 75 yards): .22 Long Rifle H.P.
Medium range (to 125 yards): .22 WMR H.P., .256 Winchester Magnum, .22 Jet.
Medium to long range (to 250 yards): .222 Remington, .222 Rem Magnum.
Long range (to 400 yds) .225 Winchester, .224 Weatherby Magnum, .22-250, .243 Win, 6mm Remington, .270 Win (100 gr), .257 Weath Magnum (100 gr), .264 Win Magnum (100 gr), 7mm Rem Magnum (150 gr).

Jack Rabbits
16 gauge, 12 gauge (11/8 oz), #4 or #6 shot.

Crows
Magpies
12 gauge (11/8 or 11/4 oz), #71/2 or #8 shot.

UPLAND GAME BIRDS (PAGES 158-193)

Ruffed Grouse
28 gauge Magnum (1 oz), 20 gauge, #71/2 shot.

Woodcock
Quail
Dove
28 gauge (3/4 oz), 20 gauge (1 oz), #8 or #9 shot.

Pheasant
Sage, Blue & Franklin Grouse
Prairie Chicken
Hungarian & Chukar Partridge
20 gauge Magnum, 16 gauge (11/8 oz), #6 or #71/2 shot.

Wild Turkey
12 gauge Magnum (15/8 or 17/8 oz), #2 or BB shot.

WILD FOWL (PAGES 194-219)

Geese
12 gauge, 12 gauge Magnum (11/2, 15/8 or 17/8 oz), #2 or #4 shot.

Ducks
20 gauge Magnum, 12 gauge, 12 gauge Magnum (11/4 or 17/8 oz), #4 or #6 shot.